Writing and Developing Your College Textbook

Mary Ellen Lepionka

ATLANTIC PATH
PUBLISHING

www.atlanticpathpublishing.com

The information and advice in this book are accurate and effective to the best of
our knowledge but are offered without guarantee. The author and Atlantic Path
Publishing disclaim all liability in connection with the use of this book.

Cover and Book Design by Stevens Brosnihan

ISBN 0-9728164-0-2

Library of Congress Control Number: 2003091857

Printed in USA

10 9 8 7 6 5 4 3 2 1

Writing and Developing Your College Textbook

CONTENTS

Preface   **viii**

Chapter 1 How College Textbooks Get Published   **1**
The College Textbook Industry 2
Finding the Right Publisher for Your Book 2
Manuscript Acquisition 4
Editorial Development 6
Book Production 7
Book Manufacturing 9
Book Fulfillment 10
The Publishing Cycle 11
Appendix: A Sampling of Publishers of College Textbooks,
    by List Subjects 15

Chapter 2 Interest a Publisher in Your Manuscript   **19**
Meet Prerequisites 19
   A Market for Your Book 19
   Institutional Affiliation or Recognition 20
   Joining an Author Team 20
Reviewing and Contributing 21
   Good Reviewing 22
   Why You Should Submit a Careful Review 23
Do Your Homework: Know the Market 23
Making Contact 25
   When to Call and What to Say 26
   What to Submit 27
Your Prospectus 28
Your Preliminary Book Outline 30
Your Sample Chapters and Cover Letter 31
Appendix A: Selected Online Resources for Doing Your Own
    Market Research 33
Appendix B: A Simple Sample Prospectus 34

Chapter 3 Use the Signing Process to Your Advantage   **37**
Steps to Getting an Offer 37
Establish a Positive Relationship 39
Know How to Negotiate Your Agreement 41
   Royalties and Advances 41

Contractual Rights and Responsibilities 42
Understand the Company's Investment 45
Trends in the Textbook Publishing Industry 47
Appendix A: Selected Resources for Custom Publishing and
    Self-Publishing 49
Appendix B: Selected Resources for Legal and Business Advice
    for Authors 51

Chapter 4 Development and Why Your Textbook Needs It 53

Development Decisions 53
Negotiating for Development Help 55
Working with a Development Editor 55
    Understand the DE's Role 56
    Establish a Good Working Relationship .56
Doing Your Own Development 58
    Get the Input You Need 59
    Chart Your Comparative Survey of the Competition 59
    Network 60
Getting and Using Helpful Reviews 61
Appendix A: Online Resources for Textbook Authors 65
Appendix B: Guidelines and Questions for Peer Reviews 67

Chapter 5 Write to Reach Your True Audience 69

Reflecting on Your Mission 69
Identifying Your Real Reader 70
Avoiding Undeclared Bias 71
    Political Correctness and the Mainstream Text 71
    Pitfalls of Unintended Bias and Unwarranted Assumptions 72
    The Place of Ideology 73
Writing to Reading Level 74
    Principles of Reading Comprehension 75
    What Is Clarity? 78
Writing Well 79
    What Is Wordiness? 79
    What Are Unity, Coherence, and Emphasis? 80
    What Is Style? 81
Appendix: Academic Style Manuals, by Discipline 83

Chapter 6 Establish an Effective Authorial Voice 87

Reflecting on Your Voice 87
Your Attitudes Toward Your Subject 87
Your Philosophical and Political Orientations 89
What Is Tone? 91

Your Attitudes Toward the Reader 91
Your Personality or Persona 92
Achieving a Voice Through Style 93
Integrating Coauthors' Voices and Styles 95
Appendix: Some "Bad-Voice" Archetypes 97

Chapter 7 Heading Structure and Why It Matters　　99

The Organization of Your Book 99
Writing Outlines vs. Tables of Contents 101
Levels of Heading 102
Wording Headings and Developing Text Sections 103
　　What Headings Really Mean 105
　　Role of Headings in Topical Development 107
Role of Concrete Examples in Supporting Topical Development 109
Role of Headings in Marketing and Sales 111

Chapter 8　Pedagogy and What It Does for Your Textbook　113

The Functions of Pedagogy 113
　　Principles of Direct Instruction 113
　　Principles of Nondirect Instruction 114
　　Students as Active Learners 115
Role of Pedagogy in Marketing and Sales .117
Forms of Apparatus and Pedagogy 117
　　Openers and Closers 117
　　Integrated Pedagogical Devices 118
　　Interior Feature Strands 118
Pedagogy Pitfalls 119
Appendix: Developing Your Pedagogy Plan 123

Chapter 9　Create Truly Useful Chapter Apparatus　　125

The Chapter Opener 125
　　The Overview and Introduction 125
　　The Outline and Focus Questions 127
　　Learning Objectives or Outcomes 128
　　Scenarios and Vignettes 131
　　Epigrams 136
Internal Apparatus 138
Chapter Closers 138
　　The Conclusion 138
　　The Summary 140
　　Other Chapter Endmatter 141
Appendix: Planning Your Apparatus 143

Chapter 10 Develop Successful Feature Strands   **145**

Types of Internal Text Features 145
    Case Studies 146
    Profiles 149
    Debates 149
    Primary Sources 150
    Models 152
    Reflection and Critical Thinking Questions 152
Thematic Boxes 154
Supplement Tie-Ins 155
Your Pedagogy Plan 156
Appendix: Planning Your Feature Strands 159

Chapter 11 Make Drafting and Revising Easier on You   **161**

Preparing Manuscript 161
Submitting Complete Manuscript 163
Preparing a Draft 163
    Make a Commitment to Consistency 165
    Develop Drafting Checklists .165
    Manage Resources 168
Monitoring Balance in Topical Development 168
Managing Source Citations 169
Completing Notes and References 170
Appendix: Selected Resources on Expository Writing 173

Chapter 12 Control Length and Manage Schedule   **175**

Why Length Is Important 175
Calculating Length 176
Disaster Control Guidelines for Length 178
Avoiding Length Creep in Revisions .181
Why Schedule Is Important 181
Types of Schedules in Publishing and Key Dates 181
Developing Your Own Drafting Schedule 183

Chapter 13 Do Permissions Right   **187**

Copyright Law 187
    Public Domain and Paraphrases 188
    Fair Use and Other Restrictions 188
Permissioning Internet Sources 189
Permissioning Photos and Art 190
Cost of Permissions 190
Developing a Permissions Log and Tracking Requests 191
Requesting and Handling Grants of Permission 192

Disaster Control Solutions for Permissions 193

Chapter 14 Enhance Your Textbook's Value Visually   195
The Importance of Presentation 195
Using Graphic Organizers 195
Presenting Figures and Tables 196
    Use Figures and Tables Appropriately 197
    Provide Narrative Context for Figures and Tables 197
Preparing Art and Map Specs 198
Visualizing Information and Creating Original Figures 201
Planning a Photo Program 203
    Evaluating and Choosing Images 204
    Writing Photo Specs 205
The Art of Writing Captions 206
Putting It All Together 208
Appendix: Ways of Visualizing Information .209

Glossary   211

References and Bibliography   222

Index   227

PREFACE

This book is an outgrowth of my long and diverse experience as a classroom instructor, curriculum developer, and professional development editor in educational publishing. For more than 18 years I have helped editors and authors achieve commercially successful first editions as well as successful revisions of their high school and college textbooks. As of this printing I have developed or contributed to the development of 70 editions in history, political science, English composition, literature, business, education, sociology, anthropology, psychology, child development, archaeology, criminal justice, and communication. Most of the first editions I worked on warranted revision, and most of the revisions increased their market share. I have learned something about making good textbooks that succeed.

In commercial textbook publishing, as in other businesses, success is measured in revenues from sales over the costs of being in business. Sales figures are based on the number of instructors who adopt your textbook and the number of students who use it in the course of study for which you wrote it. Factors that contribute to these figures include the publisher's level of investment; channels for marketing, distribution, and sales; and corporate systems for productivity and efficiency. I believe that the greatest source of success, however, is a truly good textbook.

What makes a truly good textbook? Minimally, a good textbook teaches, using good content and organization expressed in a good voice and style. This guide aims to explain in each case what I think "good" means. What makes a textbook truly both good and successful? Development and authorship, and that's what this guide is about. I have seen good textbooks fail because they missed their market or were somehow mismanaged, and I have seen mediocre books succeed initially because of publisher hype and aggressive sales campaigns. Textbooks that are both good and successful, however, become classics in their field, indispensable. They last into their 10th editions and beyond, even outlive their original authors. And they consistently make good money.

My principal goal in writing this book is to empower authors to undertake textbook development on their own to enhance their chances of success. Writing and crafting a textbook and attending to other authoring tasks is a time-consuming, complex—some would say monumental—project, even harrowing at times. Publishers may contribute little to this process beyond assigning advances. Even large houses seldom employ more than a dozen staff development editors, who tend to be reserved for signings with the highest projections of sales. At the same time, outsourced development projects may lack commitment or quality control. As the textbook author, therefore, you are your best bet.

You are an expert in your field, but you are not an expert in textbook publishing, which is equally multifaceted, layered, and nuanced. Thus, you need the publisher and the publisher's agents, or else the publishing agents' knowledge and skills. This book aims to share with you the knowledge and skills of the higher education development editor that you can use to your advantage as an academic author and textbook writer. Welcome to my world.

—Mary Ellen Lepionka, 2003

How College Textbooks Get Published

Demand for college textbooks is based on course enrollments on campuses worldwide, and the authors of college textbooks often are instructors dissatisfied with existing course offerings. Perhaps you are one of these and have picked up this book to learn more about higher education publishing. Being the author of a college textbook can be immensely satisfying—personally, professionally, and financially—but it is a lot of work.

The publishing process has five basic, equally important phases. The first is the acquisition phase, in which you submit a portion of your manuscript and sign a contract, while your editor prepares a publishing plan for your proposed textbook. The next phase is development, in which you draft and revise your manuscript in response to editorial input and peer reviews, while your publisher prepares a marketing strategy. Your complete and final manuscript with all its components then enters the production phase, which ends when your edited, typeset manuscript is sent to the printer for manufacture. The manufacturing phase ends when your bound books are shipped to the warehouse. Finally, your publisher arranges for the advertising, stocking, sampling, sales, and delivery of your book and its supplements to customers through college bookstores.

Five Phases of the Publishing Process

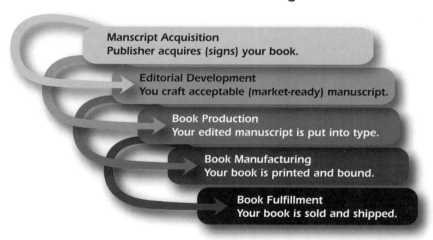

Manscript Acquisition
Publisher acquires (signs) your book.

Editorial Development
You craft acceptable (market-ready) manuscript.

Book Production
Your edited manuscript is put into type.

Book Manufacturing
Your book is printed and bound.

Book Fulfillment
Your book is sold and shipped.

This book is chiefly about development, but this first chapter is to acquaint you briefly with the publishing process, the publishing cycle, and the college textbook industry.

The College Textbook Industry

Four main kinds of higher education publishing houses are university presses, scholarly or academic small presses, professional association publishing groups, and college textbook divisions of large commercial publishers. Companies within each category vary widely in the number and size of lists they serve, in the number of titles they publish annually—between a handful and thousands—and in the amount of revenue they generate in total annual sales.

As an illustration of this diversity, consider that the 1997 sales figures among the top ten commercial college houses alone ranged from $32 to $565 million dollars in an industry that totaled nearly two and a half billion dollars that year (ESN, 1998). In 2000, total higher education sales increased by 3.5 percent to $3.24 billion, while sales of scholarly and professional books rose 8.7 percent to $5.13 billion (AAP, 2001). In the 2000-2001 academic year, the total college textbook and course materials market in the U.S. and Canada was estimated at $7.1 billion, and at $10.7 billion if used textbooks are included (NACS, 2002). The term "big business" definitely applies to college textbook publishing.

Each type of college house has advantages and disadvantages for you as an author. The 200 or so universities and professional associations that publish textbooks may offer special consideration to members, greater prestige in the academic or professional community, and greater authorial control over the product. These publishing houses, along with many smaller academic presses, sometimes offer high quality; however, they typically invest less in marketing, sales, and distribution. For example, they often lack sales forces in the field, and their products tend to be professional books, supplemental texts, and adult nonfiction trade books for postgraduate readers. Authors seldom make much money with smaller association-dependent or university-affiliated commercial presses.

In contrast, larger independent commercial houses offer greater investment in your book and potentially more sales with larger royalty checks. Because of their expense, textbooks, especially those for introductory survey courses, mainly are the preserve of big publishers who are in business to make big money. Thus, these publishers focus on serving faculties who teach specific undergraduate courses listed in the course catalogues of colleges and universities.

The chapter appendix presents a sampling of selected college houses by subject area specialties, including the top 6 in the nation. The sample includes some small highly specialized companies that publish in only one subject, as well as giant companies with many imprints that publish in all subjects taught at the college level. Be aware, however, that the number and diversity of textbook publishers have continued to shrink in this highly competitive merger-driven industry.

Finding the Right Publisher for Your Book

A key to finding the right type of publisher is determining what kind of a book you wish to publish, why, and for whom. Prospective authors can misidentify their work, thinking they have produced a textbook, for example, when actually they have created a professional book for practitioners, a scholarly trade book for colleagues, a contributed volume, a reference work, or a course supplement. The list below offers some rules of thumb for identifying the right type of publisher for what you have in mind.

Identifying Your Publisher

University, Scholarly, and Academic Presses: Publish theoretical discourses, research findings, intellectual syntheses, dissertation conversions, original contributions to a field of study, critical reviews of the literature of a field, translations, and symposium papers. Acquisitions are based on institutional affiliation, subject and discipline, and author reputation.

Professional Associations: Publish books by members and others for practitioners in the specific field or profession for which the association or society exists. Acquisitions are based on membership or author reputation and the relevance or currency of the work for the advancement of the field of study.

Publishers of Library and Reference Works: Publish annotated bibliographies, topical dictionaries and encyclopedias, anthologies, guides, data, atlases, and handbooks. Acquisitions are both general and by subject.

Publishers of Professional Books: Publish how-to books, manuals, and guides to practice; desk references; readers or contributed volumes; surveys of literature and research on practice; point-of-view books for colleagues and practitioners; and books on theory and research for graduate and postgraduate students. Acquisitions are by affiliation and field.

Trade Book Publishers: Publish adult nonfiction, professional memoirs, and popularizations of academic subjects for the general public for both entertainment and enlightenment (and sometimes television or film rights). Acquisitions are based on author reputation and mass market appeal of subject.

Commercial Publishers of College Textbooks: Publish introductory and intermediate textbooks and supplements for undergraduate students and graduate students enrolled in titled college courses, including surveys and introductions to fields of study and their history and philosophy, theory and methods, and applications. Acquisitions are based on academic department or course and author reputation.

As you will see, finding the right publisher, making contact with the right editor, and signing the right contract are half the battle in publishing your textbook.

Your research in the chapter appendix, your college bookstore, online bookstores, and the LMP (*Literary Market Place*) in the library or online will help you identify the specific companies that publish textbooks in your subject. In addition, your published colleagues can be a valuable resource for identifying companies that publish in your field. Following are some recommended web sites for exploring the world of college textbook publishing.

Online Publisher Directories

American Association of Publishers (AAP) 2002-2003 Greenbook (of College Textbook Publishers): **www.aap.org/**
American Library Association (ALA): **www.ala.org/**
Association of American University Presses (AAUP): **www.aaup.org/**
Library of Congress (LOC): **www.loc.gov/**
Literary Market Place (LMP): **www.literarymarketplace.com**
BookWire: **www.bookwire.com**
Book Publishing Report:
   www.simbanet.com/sources/bookpub1.html
Pubnet: **www.pubnet.org/publishers/index.html**

This book assumes that you wish to publish a major market college textbook for undergraduates and that you will most likely be dealing with a comparatively large commercial publisher. On this basis, Chapters 2 and 3 offer basic advice on how to interest a publisher in your book idea or manuscript and how to negotiate your contract.

Manuscript Acquisition

College publishing houses have editors whose job is to acquire manuscripts. Depending on company mission and size, this job is usually termed acquisitions editor, alternatively sponsoring editor, series editor, managing editor, associate editor, executive editor, or publisher. Acquisitions editors choose book projects and acquire manuscripts mainly through networking and recommendations from sales representatives in the field. They also attend professional meetings, survey professional literature, cultivate the colleagues of their current authors, and work at conventions, where product displays and company-sponsored events are staged to attract prospective authors as well as new customers.

Acquisitions editors manage the publishers' book lists. A list covers a particular subject area and includes formerly published titles (backlist), the current year's titles (frontlist), and forthcoming signed books. Lists may be organized by field of study or academic department. Large lists might be divided among different editors according to finer distinctions within a subject area. For example, a history list might have different editors for American history and world history. In addition, books for graduate students and professional colleagues or practitioners in your field might be managed by one editor and books for undergraduates by another.

Publishers specialize in particular fields; therefore, their lists pertain only to certain subject areas. Even very large houses specialize, usually according to the books they have sold most successfully and their areas of strength as a result of list acquisitions, trades, or sales negotiated with other publishers as part of a larger corporate plan. The right publisher for your textbook may turn out to be a subsidiary (a publishing unit) or an imprint (a publishing name or brand) within a much larger parent company.

During the acquisition phase, publishing executives plan the level of investment in your project. Levels of investment are expressed in a ranking system that reflects the book's market and projected sales. Ranking systems vary from publisher to publisher. Typically an "A-book" (or a double-A or triple-A) is a 4-color (full-color) product with an art and photo program, a "package" of print and electronic supplements for students and faculty, and an instructor's edition. In the trade, an A-book is referred to as a "major market book." A "B-book" usually is a two-color product with black and white photos, an instructor's manual, and a test bank and study guide; and a "C-book" is a one-color product, often without photos or supplements.

Rankings are not intended to reflect the quality or worth of a textbook, only the cost of investing in it, insofar as that cost is justified by the size of the market, the projected sales, and the competition. For example, your book probably will be designated as a C-book if the publisher expects to sell only 4,000 copies of your first edition textbook because only 8,000 people currently enroll in that course annually nationwide and competitors are already in this market with C-book offerings.

Publisher investment also includes print and nonprint supplements, most of which the publisher must provide for free in order to remain in competition. As the following list suggests, textbook packages often are far more complex than anyone might realize. Your role in any of the package components is determined during the acquisition and development phases of publishing.

Possible Textbook Package Components

Main Text
- parts and chapters with pedagogical features
- figures and tables with source notes and captions
- chapter appendices, notes, references
- photo and art specifications and captions
- permissions logs and grants
- half-title, title, copyright, and dedication pages
- brief and full tables of contents
- instructor's preface with acknowledgments
- student preface or advertisement

- text appendices, notes, references, bibliography
- glossary
- name index and subject index

Special Texts
- instructor's annotated edition
- interactive edition with CD-ROM
- web edition or E-book

Print Supplements
- instructor's manual
- transparency masters or acetate transparencies
- test bank or alternate test banks
- student practice tests, workbook, or lab manual
- student study guide
- companion reader or magazine
- user's guides to supplements
- other value-adding student supplements or promotional materials

Nonprint Supplements
- computerized test bank and study guide
- tutorial, application, or simulation software
- videotape or audiotape
- PowerPoint course presentation software
- course management software
- digital image or digital media archives
- models or manipulatives
- companion web site

Typically, only larger commercial publishing houses are in a position to publish this range of print and nonprint supplements.

Editorial Development

Depending on your publisher, the development phase of the textbook publishing process is the most variable. At one extreme, this phase might consist simply of you revising your manuscript without outside input from reviewers or market analysts, without editorial assistance, and without any special fulfillment planning on the part of your publisher. Your book sinks or swims with little investment and no guarantees. At the other extreme, your publisher calls and manages your book and everything connected with it for maximum commercial success.

Development is a complex recursive process. Editors and authors collaborate to bring a manuscript and its ancillaries and supplements to market level and prepare them for production. Major college houses have development editors on staff, or they hire the services of development editors or consultants, either directly on a freelance basis or indirectly through development houses or packaging firms that exist to serve publishers. Small academic publishing houses, universities, and special presses rarely use development editors and may not even provide the services of a copyeditor.

Chapter 4 of this book explains what is involved in textbook development, describes the roles of development editors, and offers advice on how to do your own planning and development. Chapters 5 through 10 elaborate on the critical authoring tasks involved in textbook development. Chapters 11 through 13 offer guidelines and strategies for pain-free achievement of a final draft, and Chapter 14 guides you in preparing figures and tables and thinking about the visual presentation of your book.

Book Production

Assuming you bring your manuscript to completion successfully and on time—and that your publisher deems it acceptable—book production, the process by which an edited and developed manuscript becomes a book, can take up to another whole year. You and your editor usually remain involved during this time. Work also begins on any supplements intended to accompany your text.

Each publishing house has its own unique systems for assigning bookmaking responsibilities and producing a book. After editors turn over a final manuscript to the production department, typical stages of book production might include the tasks shown in the figure on page 8.

In many larger commercial houses, the book production process typically goes something like this: Your manuscript in hard copy and on disk is turned over from editorial (acquisition and development editors) to production, and another whole group of people comes into play. A production administrator or coordinator might assign your book to an inhouse production editor but more likely to a packager. A packager is an outside firm that secures talent and production services depending on what your book needs. These are services that you have not provided yourself or are not contractually obligated to provide. For example, your book might or might not need an artist, a permissions researcher, photo researcher, copyeditor, indexer, proofreader, book designer, page formatter, or others.

Editors might release sample chapters of your manuscript to the production department in advance of your manuscript so that your book can be designed. While the production administrator or packager is having a book design, art samples, and sample pages prepared, the company's composition or manufacturing buyer might be sending out for bids on the paper, printing, and binding for your book.

In commercial publishing, if all is well, your book is officially launched in a series of meetings and paperwork distributions involving people in corporate management, editorial, marketing, production, and manufacturing. The budget is

General Stages of Book Production

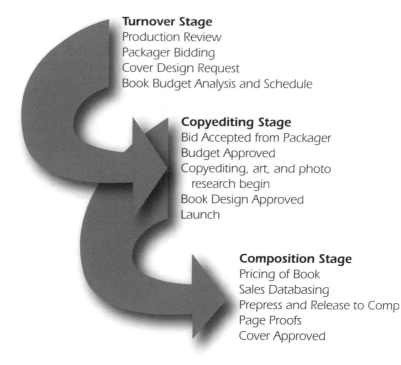

Turnover Stage
Production Review
Packager Bidding
Cover Design Request
Book Budget Analysis and Schedule

Copyediting Stage
Bid Accepted from Packager
Budget Approved
Copyediting, art, and photo
  research begin
Book Design Approved
Launch

Composition Stage
Pricing of Book
Sales Databasing
Prepress and Release to Comp
Page Proofs
Cover Approved

approved. The marketing strategy is approved. The design is approved. The schedule is approved. Composition is assigned to a vendor, and initial pricing (what it will cost to produce and manufacture the book and what college bookstores will have to pay for it) is approved.

During production, a copyeditor marks your manuscript and sends it back to you for corrections. You respond to the copyeditor's queries and turn manuscript around, while the packager reviews what the copyeditor says about the state and status of your manuscript.

It is possible that your manuscript may go over budget or be delayed during production—or even be pulled from production—if things are not working out. Disasters sometimes happen if authors have not followed the agreed plan, have omitted components, have gone over length, or have not attended to permissions (the subjects of chapters 12 and 13 of this book).

However, the more time and money that go into your book, the greater the publisher's desire to see it into print. Your book has already become part of a larger publishing plan that aims to cover all bases in the publisher's chosen market with an array of new titles and revisions for each copyright year.

Your copyedited manuscript with all its components is then released to composition (comp)—an old-fashioned term from the days when book pages were set from trays of inked lead type. Today, "composition" refers to electronic page make-up and printing from disk.

The compositor may estimate the length of your work in book pages (known as a "cast-off"), based on word count in relation to the fonts, type sizes, and design elements chosen for your book. Assuming that your manuscript is not discovered to be too long at this late date, it is "poured" into its coded design (or, in the old days, it is "typeset").

Today, electronically produced manuscripts first appear in page proof rather than galleys, which is proofread in production and sent to you for your review. The compositor checks all your changes and generates a set of corrected, usually final, page proof. Final page proof shows numbered pages and the placement of art and photos and captions.

Usually, two or more rounds of page proof are needed before your book is right. However, changes during page proof require costly extra outlays of money for page formatters and proofreaders. Your role and responsibility as author is to make as few changes as possible during the production phase. Because page proof indicates the specific page numbers on which your index, table of contents, text cross-references, and supplements correlations are based, any changes you make have a ripple effect.

For the people whose job it is to make your book come out right in time, the ripple effect can achieve nightmarish proportions. If you have ever felt disgusted by "sloppy" books in which page references did not lead you to the information you were seeking, for instance, now you know why this happens: the author's late changes required extra stages of page proof. The page layout affected the imposition (sequence) of pages, and thus the page numbers changed as a result. The author, production editor, and indexer could not reconcile the page references or afford to fix them in time. When it comes to time, the publishing process is unforgiving, such that your publisher will draw the line on changes, even if an imperfect product is the result.

While your book is going back and forth among you, the editors and other company agents, and the compositor, your art and art caption manuscript might be with an artist or computer graphics specialist and your photo specifications and photo caption manuscript might be with a photo researcher. On the other hand, depending on the market and level of investment, you may be responsible for supplying photos (and photo releases), which the publisher then has scanned into the book. Today, electronic art and digitized photos are the norm in textbook publishing.

Book Manufacturing

Final page proof includes all frontmatter, endmatter, art, and photos in addition to the body of the manuscript. The processes by which all the elements are successfully put together in bookmaking are very complex and well beyond the scope of this book. Basically, your book goes to the printer, who puts it on press and runs proofs. After printer's proofs are okayed, your first printing commences, consisting perhaps of 5,000 or 10,000 copies.

If your book is being produced from film, the publisher's agents check the quality of each piece of film and mark for correction any instances of poor registration or alignment, or broken type, for example. The publisher's production administrators and manufacturing managers might travel with your book to the printing plant and to the bindery, overseeing the press run and checking that the cover is put on right side up (and that your name on it is spelled right).

Innovations in printing and allied industries have caused sweeping changes in book manufacture. Your entire manuscript is likely to be scanned onto disk and go directly from disk to printing plate, never at all existing as film. Highly paid computer experts enter corrections on screen. The new technology has major implications for authoring. For one thing, your released manuscript has to be complete and final. Only minor corrections can be entertained in page proof, and books go from final proof directly into their print runs.

The whole process of book publishing is so complex that a perfect book does not exist. In addition to having inevitably less than perfect content, every book contains typographic or formatting errors, something missing or something that shouldn't be in there, and visible and "invisible" (to nonexperts) physical flaws. Egregious, correctable, found flaws usually are fixed in second printings. Although everyone feels indignant about technical errors in textbooks, we should appreciate that publishing professionals do strive for beauty and perfection. In recognition of bookmaking as both art and science, the industry hosts various annual awards for excellence.

Book Fulfillment

"Fulfillment" is sales talk for getting the product to the customer. Your bound book is shipped to the company's warehouse or distributor where it is inventoried. Advance copies go to you and to the publisher's marketers and sales representatives for sampling among potential customers. The company already has sent out promotional material, bought advertising, and/or begun direct mail marketing campaigns. The road to fulfillment actually begins well before your book even exists as a product. Your role in fulfillment might include attending the company's sales meetings in person to help get the word across to the sales force about why they should make every effort to sell your textbook out of the dozens or hundreds of books they must field each year.

On campuses across the country, faculty members place orders for your book. The company's field reps and a home office sales support staff take those orders, and the warehouse ships your book to college bookstores in time for students to buy them before the start of the term.

The Publishing Cycle

The publishing cycle places the phases of the publishing process into a time frame. This time frame is similar for all college houses, and it is much longer than you might think, typically two to four years from start (concept) to finish (customer), plus two to four years between revised editions. Timing is crucial in the textbook publishing industry. At the same time, the publishing cycle is continuous.

Phases of the Publishing Cycle

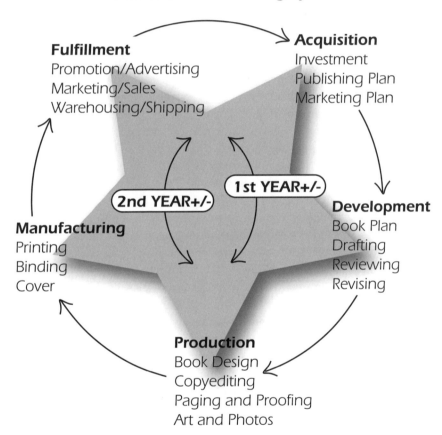

Acquisitions editors sign authors at all times during the year, but the peak signing periods are in the mid-fall and mid-spring. Books are signed one to three years prior to publication, depending on the state of existence of your manuscript, your availability, the publisher's list needs and projected investment, and perceived market forces.

Manuscript development and drafting optimally take place during the six months to a year following signing. This time period includes summer, when you might have more time to devote to writing projects. Reviewing, additional development, and revising continue into the fall. First, second, and final drafts are not unusual for a first edition. If you are the author of a first edition, unless you can devote full time to the project, you would be wise to insist on a two-year drafting and revising schedule.

Your final manuscript is released from "editorial" (manuscript acquisition and development) to "production" by the end of a calendar year, preferably in mid-fall. Production and manufacturing take up all the remaining time—another six months to a year depending on the type of product, the level of investment, the technology in use, and other factors—before your book is ready for warehousing. Books inevitably are out of date by the time they reach customers, although online supplements now make it possible to update books on company web sites during the life of the edition.

New authors often do not understand why they must submit their manuscripts so early—often more than a year in advance of their copyright year. The reason is that books must be in stock in time for instructors (1) to sample them well *before* the copyright year and (2) to order and receive them through campus bookstores in time for students to buy them *before* the start of the copyright year.

In "sampling," your publisher sends out hundreds of free desk copies of your textbook in advance to your potential customers: individual instructors and departmental textbook adoption committees. These special examination copies typically are bound in covers marked "Not For Sale." The hope is that after looking at your book, the people who have been sampled will order it for their students. However, if there is no time for this sampling process to happen—because your book did not come out in time—then your book will lose at least one semester's worth of potential sales nationwide, which is very discouraging for both publisher and author. A consequence may be that your sales numbers are not good enough for the publisher to risk investing in a revision.

The publishing cycle for textbooks explains why editors become so obsessive about due dates. Academic and scholarly presses are less concerned about market timing, because they invest less, are not committed to matching course offerings in college catalogues, and do not depend on specific brokers such as the college bookstores. If you are signed with a large commercial textbook publisher, however, you will be under some pressure to attend to the realities of timing in the publishing cycle.

Ideally, your manuscript goes into production in time to succeed, and your book hits its market. All the time and effort you spent on development begin to pay off as your book does well. Most of the cost of producing and manufacturing your book is recovered in the first year of sales, and you begin receiving royalty checks. Perhaps you begin to see results for sales of subsidiary rights also, and you learn that your book is being adapted for foreign markets.

In no time at all, it seems, your editor calls to discuss starting a revised edition and has some ideas for increasing your market share. And, thus, the publishing cycle begins again. Your textbook may see as many as twenty editions and in the course of a lifetime never go out of print. And you may be able to retire comfortably on your earnings.

Appendix: A Sampling of Publishers of College Textbooks, by List Subjects

This list, taken from the 2002 LMP, is incomplete and is not intended to imply specific recommendations. It emphasizes textbook publishers over scholarly and academic publishers. The five largest college textbook publishers in 2002 were Thomson, Pearson, McGraw-Hill, Houghton Mifflin, and Wiley (HED 2002). This list also may no longer be accurate, as mergers, consolidations, and divestitures are common in the publishing industry, with the effect of moving lists and imprints around and reducing the number of publishers worldwide. As cases in point, in 2002 Vivendi sold Houghton Mifflin to a consortium of investors and in 2003 Bertelsman sought to sell off its Bertelsman Springer company for over a billion dollars.

Aldine de Gruyter (New York City, division of **Walter de Gruyter**): social and behavioral sciences; sociology, anthropology, social welfare.

Avery (Wayne, NJ): history; science and math; military science, history, and technology; social sciences.

Bedford, Freeman, and Worth Publishing Group: corporate training, career education, trade/vocational training, business, government, military, distance learning; Imprints: **Bedford/St. Martins** (Boston, MA): English, history, communications, philosophy, religion, humanities; **W.H. Freeman & Co.** (New York City): science and math; **Worth Publishers Inc.** (New York City): psychology, political science, economics, sociology, anthropology, biochemistry.

Birkhauser Boston (Cambridge, MA, division of **Springer-Verlag**): physics, math, geology, biology, neuroscience, history of science, scientists' biographies, architecture and design. **Springer Publishing** (NYC): psychology, psychiatry, nursing, medical education, public health, rehabilitation, social work.

Blackwell Publishers and **Blackwell Science** (Malden, MA, and the U.K.): humanities, social sciences, business, medical, allied health, earth and life sciences, environment, engineering.

Butterworth/Heinemann (Woburn, MA, subsidiary of **Reed Elsevier Inc.**): medical, technical, security, business. Imprints include **Heinemann-Boynton/Cook**, and **Harcourt Publishers** (medical and health).

F. A. Davis Publishing Co. (Philadelphia, PA): medical, nursing, allied health.

Lawrence Erlbaum Associates (Mahwah, NJ): behavioral sciences, communications, education (mostly scholarly and academic).

Franklin, Beedle and Associates (Wilsonville, OR): computer science, computers in education, computer engineering.

Greenwood Publishing Group Inc. (Westport, CT): education, humanities, social and behavioral sciences, business, law; imprints include **Praeger** (mostly academic and scholarly).

Harcourt Brace (Orlando, FL: all subjects; education, a division of **Thomson**). College imprints: **Elsevier Science** and **Academic Press** (San Diego, CA): social and behavioral sciences, biomedical sciences, physical sciences, engineering and computer science); **Morgan Kaufman Publishers Inc.** (San Francisco, CA): computer science; **Saunders** (Ft. Worth, TX): medicine, dentistry, nursing, allied health, veterinary medicine.

Houghton Mifflin Company (Boston, MA): education, sociology, anthropology, English, humanities, psychology, media and communication, and other subjects.

Jones & Bartlett Publishing Inc. (Sudbury, MA): life sciences, health, nursing, math, computer science, earth science, philosophy, emergency care. Imprint: **Aspen**.

Lyceum Books Inc. (Chicago, IL): social work, history.

McCutchan Publishing Corp. (Berkeley, CA): education, hotel & restaurant management, law enforcement education.

McGraw-Hill Higher Education (Boston, MA): art, music, humanities, communication, foreign languages, ESOL, history, philosophy, psychology, social sciences, political science. Imprints: **Dushkin** (Guilford, CT): social sciences; **WCB** (William C. Brown, Burr Ridge, IL): biology, applied biology, astronomy, chemistry, computer science, engineering, geology, geography, life sciences, nutrition, physics, math, statistics; **McGraw-Hill Educational & Professional Group** (New York City): business, economics, advertising, accounting, finance, business law, management, organizational behavior, marketing, business math, statistics, computer information technology, management information systems; **Mayfield** (Mountain View, CA): education, dance, physical education, anthropology, theater, psychology, sociology, humanities, journalism, English, speech & communication.

W.W. Norton and Co. Inc. (New York City): English, literature, humanities, history, social sciences, and other subjects.

Paragon House (St. Paul, MN): history, religion, philosophy, social science.

Pearson Publishing (Upper Saddle River, NJ). Acquired **Addison Wesley Longman** (business, finance, management, economics, political science) and **Simon & Schuster** in 1998. Higher education imprints: **Allyn and Bacon** (Boston, MA): English, humanities, communication, health, physical education, sociology, anthropology, criminal justice, psychology, education; **Appleton & Lang** (New York City): business and professional; **Macmillan** (Indianapolis, IN): computer science, technical publishing; **Merrill** (Columbus, OH): education, social sciences, and physical sciences; **Prentice Hall** (Needham, MA, & Upper Saddle River, NJ): business, career, technology, engineering, science, math, humanities, social sciences.

Sage Publishers Inc. (Newbury Park, CA): texts in social and behavioral sciences. Imprints: **Pine Forge Press** (Thousand Oaks, CA, a division of Sage): social and behavioral sciences; **Corwin Press; Paul Chapman Publishing**.

M E Sharpe Inc. (Armonk, NY): social science, international relations, area studies, political science, history, economics, environment, literature.

Sinauer Associates Inc. (Sunderland, MA): biological and behavioral sciences; biology, psychology, neuroscience.

Taylor & Francis (Philadelphia, PA): engineering, physical sciences, medicine, nursing, psychology, sociology, toxicology, physics. Acquired **Garland Publishing Inc.** (New York City): humanities, social sciences, science, architecture, and music. Other imprints: **Routledge** and **Curzon**.

Thomson Information/Publishing Group (Stamford, CT): educational, professional, business, medical, and legal. College imprints: **Brooks/Cole** (Pacific Grove, CA): counseling, social work, psychology, health, helping professions, math, physical sciences, chemistry, physics, statistics, career development; **Delmar** (Albany, NY): business, industry, government, education, retail/fashion, electronics, technology, nursing, allied health, child care, agriculture, math, vocational studies, automotive, travel and tourism, engineering, paralegal, building trades, multimedia, graphic arts, distance learning; **Heinle & Heinle** (Boston, MA): foreign and second language textbooks; **South-Western** (Cincinnati, OH): accounting, business, education, social sciences, math, science, career education; **WestLaw**: law; **Wadsworth** (Belmont, CA): sociology, psychology, education. Recently acquired **Harcourt General**.

John Wiley & Sons Inc. (New York City): accounting, business, economics, foreign languages, engineering, math, computer sciences. College imprints include **Van Nostrand Reinhold:** architecture/design, environmental/industrial science, business technology. In 1999 acquired **Jossey-Bass** (New York City) from Pearson: business, psychology, health management, education, biology/anatomy, engineering, math, economics and finance, teacher education.

Interest a Publisher in Your Manuscript

Fiction or trade book publishing houses are notorious for rejecting manuscripts that later become bestsellers or posthumous classics. Textbook publishing, however, is not like that. Acquisitions editors in college houses are always looking for books to sign. In larger companies, editors' performance evaluations and bonuses are based in part on their number of signings each year. In addition, college textbook markets are constantly expanding as enrollments increase and new courses routinely are added to the curriculum. And as educational publishing moves toward electronic archiving and delivery systems, industry demand for books to pour into multimedia platforms is growing exponentially. So, if you and your textbook meet certain basic criteria, you should have no difficulty finding a publisher. What are these basic criteria?

Meet Prerequisites

Basic criteria for publishing a college textbook include (1) having a market for your book, (2) having institutional affiliation or a professional track record, (3) knowing publishers' existing products, and (4) intending to provide an intellectually and pedagogically sound work in an acceptable form.

A Market for Your Book

Your manuscript is on a subject or area in your field that is or will be in demand in courses on campuses nationwide. It corresponds to known departmental course offerings listed in college catalogues and contains at least the basics of what is generally expected or taught in those courses. Publishers refer to this as a "mainstream" text.

A mainstream text addresses a clearly identifiable audience, such as all undergraduates taking organic chemistry. The larger the audience the better. A large market has many potential customers among faculty members whose course assignments give them control over a large number of textbook adoptions. Thus, large markets are the most competitive and the most lucrative for publishers and authors. Small, or niche, markets are served, especially in technical fields and at the graduate level, but they attract less investment on the part of the publisher and usually (but not always) less earnings.

The largest markets are for introductory textbooks, and despite rumors of market saturation there usually is room for a new introductory text in any field. The reason is that a good intro—one that your students can read and like and learn from, that covers adequately material you regard as important, and that is revised often enough to remain current—is hard to find. Many instructors switch texts from semester to semester in search of the right one or resort to photocopied customized tomes. Your motivation for writing a textbook possibly stems from dissatisfaction with existing offerings for a course you teach. In addition, college textbook marketing practices encourage frequent changes in adoptions, such that new intros are marketed successfully each year. The intro market, often with four-color books and large supplement packages, is big business.

Institutional Affiliation or Recognition

In college textbook publishing in most fields authors are recruited on the basis of rank and reputation, and books are sold on the basis of market impact and name recognition. Optimally you are a full or associate professor in a four-year college or university and have published articles, conducted research, reviewed works in your field, and presented at conferences or symposia. In some practice-oriented subject areas, however, administrative responsibilities, classroom experience, commercial success, and specialized knowledge or technical expertise matter more than academic credentials. The main concern of publishers is that a textbook will have credibility with its users.

Joining an Author Team

In lieu of a desirable "track record," you nevertheless can achieve credibility by being part of an author team. If you are a junior faculty member with a good book idea and are seeking to publish for the first time, consider putting together an author team. You might begin by presenting your book ideas to one or two carefully selected colleagues, discussing the mutual potential benefits of a collaboration, and building trust. Publishers like author teams that include individuals who have solid reputations in their field or specialty and who offer balance or perspective in authorship, including women and members of culturally diverse groups. Author teams whose ranks swell to four or more members, however, may be more prone to contractual complications, author collaboration problems, and inconsistencies in style. Key decisions in forging an author team revolve around answers to the following questions, to which everyone on the team equally must be able to make a commitment.

Key Decisions in Forging an Author Team

- What will be the rationale, assumptions or principles, and goals or mission of the book?
- What will be the working scope and sequence or content and organization?
- Who will be the audience?
- What will be the writing style and tone?
- What will be the long-term availability of each member of the author team?
- How will authoring tasks be divided?

- By what dates will each phase of the work be completed?
- Who will be responsible for ensuring that the book has a consistent overall voice and style?
- By what means, how often, and how extensively will the authors communicate with each other to collaborate?
- Who will be listed as the principal author?
- In what order will author names appear on the title page?
- How will advances and royalties be divided?

Reviewing and Contributing

Other routes to establishing credibility and becoming a royaltied author include reviewing manuscripts for publishers and authoring work-for-hire supplements, such as study guides, test banks, and instructor's manuals. Other work-for-hire contributions include original writing for a book, such as a chapter, scenarios, case studies, research briefs, content applications, first-person accounts, or topical features, described in Chapters 8-10.

A publisher may contact you to review a manuscript, especially if you respond to their market survey. To become a reviewer, simply send publishers in your field your curriculum vitae and a letter of interest in reviewing. In the letter to the editor, refer to titles of theirs that you use or have used in the past, and state your areas of expertise. Report the number of adoptions you control by noting the number of courses or sections you teach annually and the size of enrollments in those courses. Editors tend to give priority to reviewers through whom they feel they can seed future adoptions.

College textbook publishers are always looking for reviewers to provide the following kinds of assistance with first and revised editions:

> **User Review:** You use their textbook in your course and know its strengths and weaknesses through direct experience.

> **Comparative Review:** You use their textbook and have an interest in how it is revised. You would like to compare the revised draft with the edition in use, report on improvements, and suggest ways to further strengthen the revision.

> **Nonuser Review:** You looked at their book but chose a competitor's offering instead. You know why their book failed to persuade you to order it and why the other company's book was better for you and your students.

> **Competitive Review:** You have looked at several leading textbooks

for your course and have an interest in comparing them in whole or in part in terms of their strengths and weaknesses.

Expert Review: You are an acknowledged expert in your field but not necessarily an instructor. You have published professional articles or books on your specialty or have served on panels or as a consultant. You are interested in reviewing selected chapters on your area of expertise to check mainly for soundness, currency, completeness, and accuracy.

Developmental Review: You are familiar with the strengths and weaknesses of all the leading textbooks for your course. You would like to review manuscript with a view to seeing how well it fulfills the publisher's stated market needs. You would also like to contribute your ideas to the book plan.

Supplements Review: You have used the supplements package with their book, such as the test item file or the web site, and have found it wanting. You are interested in providing a critical content review with specific suggestions for improvement.

Unsolicited reviews are welcome and often lead to agreements for further reviewing or other contributions. College houses sometimes offer good reviewers assignments as supplements authors, and sometimes offer book contracts to proven supplements authors, a route to publishing that benefits junior faculty.

Good Reviewing

Here are the characteristics of good reviewing that editors prize.

Characteristics of Good Reviewing

- **Reliability:** The reviewer is available for assignments, readily accepts them, and turns them around on time.
- **Legibility:** The review is keyboarded or typed.
- **Efficiency:** The review is neither too long nor too short. Four or five pages is standard for chapter reviews, ten or more pages for whole book reviews; but each publisher has its own criteria.
- **Completeness:** The reviewer answers all the general and specific reviewing questions that the publisher has asked and fills out the reviewer profile sheet, including social security number, which is needed to cut checks, and gives permission to acknowledge the reviewer in the Preface.
- **Conceptual Balance:** The reviewer avoids too broad or too narrow a focus, neither giving blanket approval or condemnation nor

merely correcting typographical errors and errors of spelling and grammar—the job of a paid professional copyeditor.

- **Soundness:** Comments are logical and coherent. They reflect valid concerns and accepted interpretations or trends in the field, not solely the reviewer's personal preferences or idiosyncratic views.
- **Substantiveness or specificity:** The review is detailed and includes specific suggestions with some documentation. For example, the reviewer cites manuscript page references in support of evaluative statements and explains the basis for his or her professional judgments.
- **Fairness:** Comments respect the authors and their effort. The reviewer objectively notes both the strengths and the weaknesses of their draft and uses appropriate language.
- **Reasonableness:** The review realistically guides revision in relation to the book's aims; that is, the reviewer resists wholesale restructuring and radical reconceptualizing of the content.

Why You Should Submit a Careful Review

Some faculty members see reviewing as an unpleasant, unrewarding chore. Honoraria often are pitifully, insultingly, low—as little as $25 per chapter, though an expert review in some subject areas can command as much as $200 per chapter. Companies and editors vary considerably in what they will pay. In addition, reviewing schedules may be inconvenient. Editors might send chapters later than promised and then ask for your response within the week.

Some faculty members feel exploited by the reviewing system and reject assignments when asked. Others feel justified in doing a hasty or mediocre job. In addition to the latter, among the least helpful reviewers are those who lavishly praise a manuscript in the most general terms, thinking this is what the publisher wants to hear. Savvy editors do not call on unhelpful reviewers again, however, and a record of their undesirable performance might go into the files or database to warn off other editors.

From the publisher's standpoint, the purpose of reviews is to determine market fit, to vet the manuscript, and especially to attract potential customers. Asking faculty members with high enrollments to serve as reviewers is known as "seeding adoptions," because reviewers who become invested in improving a manuscript often tend to adopt the textbook. Reviewers' contributions also play a significant role in marketing. With the authors' thanks, reviewers' names appear in print in the acknowledgments section of a textbook. With permission, laudatory quotes from reviews are used extensively in materials for promotion and sales.

Doing Your Homework: Know the Market

"The market" consists of customers' wants and needs as reflected in companies' competing products. Make it your business to know the companies' products. Before making contact with a publisher about your manuscript, acquire and study the publisher's catalogue of books in your field, and order examination copies of any books that seem like the one you want to write or are in the same market. Do not be concerned if the publisher already has a similar book or one that is pitched to the same audience. Large houses, especially in this era of corporate mergers, often have several directly competing titles that are marketed successfully in successive copyright years. The sales base for each book is protected by (1) clearly differentiating it as a product and (2) by putting it on a two-, three-, or four-year revision cycle. Whichever title comes out as a new or revised edition for any given year is supposed to be the one that is emphasized in sales efforts, or "gets sold."

Therefore, when you sign with a publisher, ask about the planned revision cycle if your book is successful. It would be in your interest to request or agree to the shortest revision cycle for which you have the time. It would also be in your interest to avoid having your book come out in the same copyright year as the publisher's other directly competing titles.

Ask the editor about the impacts of recent mergers on his or her list, especially on titles that would compete with yours. An unpleasant outcome of grand-scale mergering is the killing of books, in which leading books from different acquired imprints are pitted against each other, and all but the top sellers are dropped. Although companies vary in the number of directly competing titles they will carry and sell successfully, many perfectly respectable textbooks go out of print in a merger, along with "heirloom" titles that are no longer profitable despite their status as classics in the field. That a textbook was written by the founder of a key paradigm in the history of your field is no guarantee of immortality. In scholarly and trade book publishing, paperback and reprint rights might give classic books new leases on life. However, these rights normally are not sought for textbooks. (Scholars interested in the history of ideas, as well as critics concerned with freedom of information, despise the loss of diversity that corporate libracide implies.) In any event, knowing your publisher's stance on internal competition is part of doing your homework. If you were to become a victim of libracide at some time, the publisher should promptly release you from all further contractual obligations and return rights in your book to you so that you can seek another publisher.

It is also important to study other companies' textbooks intended for your book's course. Those books are your real competition, and your publisher will want to know how you think your textbook will attract market share away from competitors' titles. The best sources of information are publishers' web sites. Chapter Appendix A suggests some online resources for doing your own market research on behalf of your textbook manuscript. Another excellent resource is Monument Information Resource (MIR), which provides detailed market information on leading college textbooks. For more information see "FacultyOnline" at **www.mirdata.com**.

Studying the market also helps you determine if your textbook will be appropriate for it. To borrow from Buddhist expression, appropriateness includes "right form" and "right function." For example, because textbooks are by nature expository, they should present facts, theories, research, analyses, comparisons, contrasts, examples, nonexamples, applications, extensions, and interpretations in an objective, balanced way. Above all, textbooks should teach. Personal syntheses (everything you have learned so far), critical analyses of your field, and crusades (reforming the field or changing the way your subject is taught) unfortunately tend to be too idiosyncratic and difficult (hence inappropriate) for introductory undergraduate textbooks. In this sense, the concept of a "mainstream" text extends to the content as well as to the course or market. Appropriateness sometimes is difficult to judge, however. The chapters in this book on principles of effective instruction (Chapter 8) and on authorial voice and style (Chapters 5 and 6) return to this important theme.

Making Contact

After you have attended to the prerequisites (ascertained the existence of a market for your book and established your credibility or reputation as a prospective author) and have done your homework (gained familiarity with competing books and the courses in which they are used), you are ready to locate the right publisher and make contact, assuming you are ready to write a manuscript proposal.

The right publisher is on your short list of houses that publish textbooks in your field (see the Chapter 1 Appendix). The standard reference work for information on publishers is the *Literary Market Place* (LMP), which is updated annually and can be found in your public or campus library as well as online via links at **www.bookwire.com.** Limited direct access to the LMP as a "Free User" is available at **www.literarymarketplace.com.**

As explained in Chapter 1, the person to contact is the acquisitions or sponsoring editor or the publisher. Often, the quickest way to gain the attention of an acquisitions or sponsoring editor is through the sales representative who comes to your campus to interest you in new books in your field. Tell the sales rep that you have written or are writing a textbook and are looking for a publisher. Identify the subject of your book and the academic level or course for which it is intended (introductory, undergraduate, graduate, professional). Then ask the sales rep for the name and phone number, voicemail, or email address of the appropriate contact editor, or ask to be contacted. As an alternative, try publishers' contact phone numbers and web site addresses printed on the back covers of the textbooks they publish.

Reaching the right editor is important. As mentioned in Chapter 1, depending on company size and the size of its list in a subject area, a publisher might divide the list among different editors. For example, signings of introductory economics or introductory psychology textbooks might be controlled by individuals other than those who sign textbooks on macroeconomics or abnormal psychology. Additionally, books for professional colleagues rather than for students usually are managed separately, in large houses editors may be too busy or too competitive among themselves to share prospects or even to rerefer, and at times staff turnover may be high. Nothing will happen, therefore, if you do not make the right connection.

Published colleagues also are good sources for leads for contacts. Another way to make contact is at professional meetings where publishers have booths displaying their products and where sponsoring editors network among convention participants. Simply point out the books you use, have used, or are considering for adoption, and announce the existence of your manuscript or your intention to draft one. Ask to be contacted or whom to call.

Note that, unlike unsolicited reviews, unsolicited manuscripts are not welcome. With commercial publishers especially, it is best not to attempt a "cold call" or submit an unsolicited manuscript. Nobody has the time for these.

When to Call and What to Say

Because of the general publishing cycle calendar, outlined in Chapter 1, the best time to make contact is in the fall or spring. At those times of the year, sales forces are canvassing campuses, and editors and marketing managers are presenting products at professional meetings and looking for prospective authors. In large houses other times of the year are busy with meetings. Companies' national sales meetings typically are conducted in mid-winter and in late summer when schools are in intersession. Thus, attempts to make contact during these times may fail.

When you call the acquisitions editor, expect to leave a voicemail message. When the editor gets back to you, which may take some time if the editor is on the road or preparing for sales meetings, you might find the following communication sequence helpful.

1. Give your name and institutional affiliation and the name of the referring sales representative or colleague or other contact. Identify any of the company's titles you order or have used (by name of author) and the size of the enrollments you cover—the number of students you teach and thus the number of copies of a textbook (number of units) that you control by ordering a particular title for your course. The editor might ask you about your degree of satisfaction with the titles and service or about competitors' titles you have used. The editor also might ask you on the spot if you are interested in being a reviewer or contributor.

2. Express an interest in reviewing, noting, however, that you are busy writing a textbook. Then identify the subject, grade level, and course, audience, or customer base that you are writing for. Briefly

explain why you are writing this book. For example, perhaps you have identified a segment of the market that is not being served (such as a new course), or perhaps you are addressing important new concerns, discoveries, trends, or developments in your field. List the names of all the courses in which your book might be used.

3. Briefly identify any potentially or partially competing book that the company already publishes, and describe in general terms how yours will be different (based on your review of the book). For example, perhaps your book is aimed at a different segment of the market, such as anatomy and physiology for nursing school students, educational psychology for education majors, or finite mathematics for nonmajors in mathematics. Your book might have a different approach (e.g., constructivist, micro, macro, multicultural, research-based, applied, theoretical, historical, analytical, case-based, interdisciplinary, etc.) or compelling features and a value-adding supplement (e.g., primary source material, models, application activities, casebook, manual, Internet activities, software, video, etc.).

This is not the time to ask editors if they are interested in publishing your book, nor to open any discussion about policies concerning advances or royalties. Decisions to publish are complex, involve a lot of money, involve other people in the company, and take considerable time. Instead, offer to send your curriculum vitae, a prospectus of your textbook, a preliminary book outline, and one or two sample chapters. Editors will say no only if they feel the book you describe is a complete mismatch with the lists they have been assigned to manage. As explained in Chapter 1, publishers specialize. The worthiness and excellence of your book is irrelevant if the company's sales force does not happen to visit the academic departments in which your book might be sold.

What to Submit

The most important part of your quest after making contact is submitting a curriculum vitae, book plan (prospectus and outline), and writing sample (sample chapters). Assuming that you meet the four basic pre-qualifying criteria described in the previous section and that your book idea fits the publisher's needs, the decision to sign you on as an author will be based on these artifacts.

What to Send to the Editor, at-a-Glance

- Full curriculum vitae
- Prospectus
- The story, rationale, goal
- Topic, scope, theme

- Audience, level
- Planned apparatus, pedagogy, art, and presentation
- Analysis of primary and secondary markets
- Competition analysis and unique features
- Preliminary, working, whole-book drafting outline
- Complete sample chapters
- Cover letter
- Present status of the manuscript
- Planned length and drafting schedule
- Contact information

Your Prospectus

Each company has its own requirements for a prospectus and might send you guidelines or a preprinted form. Typically the prospectus is a two- or three-page explanation of what you are doing, for whom you are doing it, and why. That is, the prospectus states your topic, scope and sequence, and theme; identifies your market and audience; and sets forth your rationale or main goal. This is the "story" of your book.

In commercial publishing a book's story is critically important. Editors usually are teamed with marketing and advertising managers, who use the story (1) to determine if the company thinks it can sell your book profitably, (2) to identify specific potential customers, (3) to launch marketing and advertising campaigns, and (4) to educate and win the commitment of the sales force. The story also guides the book designer and others whose job it is to make sure your book looks right for what it is trying to do.

Telling the Story. Because your book is one of dozens or even hundreds presented by editorial teams to the publisher and ultimately to the sales force, its story should be stated briefly. The brief statement is like an abstract containing a working title and the key words that define and sell the book idea. The prospectus should start with this story abstract and then go on to elaborate. Examples of book stories follow:

> SOCIAL WORK will be an introductory text for entry-level courses in programs leading to licensure in social work and will integrate theory and practice using a problem-solving casebook approach.

> TECHNOLOGY AND THE ENVIRONMENT is a thematic, multidisciplinary treatment of the global impacts of technology on human environments from prehistoric times to the present and supports courses in earth science and cultural ecology.

> PRINCIPLES OF SCIENTIFIC RESEARCH will be a comprehensive gener-

al-purpose handbook with guidelines for observing, measuring, describing, and reporting research in the physical and social sciences.

HISTORY THEN AND NOW is a topical survey of the history of history for graduate students taking Historiography I and Historiography II, with an emphasis on the role of culture in the selection and interpretation of evidence.

IN THE FIRST INSTANCE will reexamine theories of the origins of the universe in light of new discoveries from radiotelemetry and particle physics, and will complement general introductory textbooks in physics.

INTRODUCTION TO TECHNICAL WRITING surveys all aspects of professional practice in the field and features authentic models of excellent writing for future technical writers in both technological and nontechnological fields.

BIOLOGY AND THE LIFE SCIENCES: An Introduction is an introductory text for undergraduate survey courses in biology or the life sciences. DNA and the human genome project is the unifying central theme of the book, and a whole chapter is devoted to the implications of recombinant DNA, reproductive technologies, and gene therapies in the treatment of disease.

EDUCATION AND DIVERSITY will focus on the social foundations of education in the U.S. with an emphasis on the social contexts of issues concerning multicultural education, bilingual education, and inclusion.

Planned Contents. The prospectus next walks the editor through the nuts and bolts of the book by describing the organization of it and the elements and features that will be in it—its apparatus and pedagogy, the subjects of later chapters of this book. How will chapters open and close, for example, and what regular features will appear in each chapter? Will there be figures and tables? Photos? How many of each? Will there be a glossary? An instructor's manual? And so on.

Markets. The prospectus should go on to identify the likely primary and secondary markets for the book. Who will buy it? Who will read it? Your primary market is where you expect to sell the most copies, while the secondary market includes others who might be interested in using your textbook. For instance, the primary market for this book is prospective textbook authors, the people for whom I have written it. Secondary markets might include institutions of higher education and college textbook publishers or editors.

Competition. Your prospectus should include your competition analysis. Briefly list and evaluate each competing text you have identified, explaining how your book will be similar to and different from it in goals, structure, and content. This discussion should lead to an explanation of what you believe is outstanding or unique about your book. Also report if your book idea or chapters have been field tested in your own or others' courses. A sample prospectus—the one for this book, which was accepted for signing by a major publisher—is presented in the chapter appendix. While this book is not a college textbook, and the prospectus is brief, the same elements of a good prospectus are there.

Your Preliminary Book Outline

An outline functions as both a writing guide and an organizational scheme. Each part or unit and each chapter is identified by number and title, followed by topics and subtopics in the order you plan to write. Observing the formal rules for outlining rather than merely listing topics will help you establish a structure for the book. Preliminary book outlines typically undergo changes as a result of the publisher's market analyses, analyses of competing books, and feedback from editors and peer reviewers, not to mention needed changes that authors themselves usually discover during drafting. In addition, if your undergraduate textbook involves a large investment, the publisher might propose changes to your outline to ensure any of the following outcomes, based on customer wants and needs:

- Chapters generally have consistent and appropriate lengths.
- The book includes timely topics and topics that customers generally expect. It also foregoes topics that customers insist they do not want or need.
- To a reasonable extent the book organization works according to known ways in which the course is taught.
- The content is appropriate for the intended course level or for the reading or intellectual level of the intended audience.
- The book can compete successfully with market leaders in its field.

The writing outline is the basis for a table of contents (TOC), which is perhaps the most important tool for marketing and selling the book. If you are developing your book in collaboration with editors, you may receive specific informed suggestions for converting your outline into the system of headings and subheadings that will become your table of contents. Otherwise, you will need to do this yourself in an informed way. Chapter 7 of this book is devoted to the art and science of creating a proper heading structure for your book.

Your Sample Chapters and Cover Letter

If possible, include two or three sample chapters with your prospectus and drafting outline, or establish when you will send sample chapters. A sample chapter should be double-spaced with pages numbered consecutively and should have all its components in place, including any apparatus and pedagogical features you have planned, figures and tables, and references. It is assumed that you are working on a computer and saving to hard drive and disk. Aside from giving the editor an example of how far your planning has gone and what you have to say, sample chapters present your voice and show off your ability to maintain a consistent writing style and format (see Chapters 5 and 11).

The cover letter recalls your previous contact, briefly reiterates that you have a manuscript or book idea for the publisher's consideration, and identifies all your enclosures. You also provide detailed information about your availability for your project and where, when, and how the editor can reach you. The editor will need practical information as well, such as the present status of the manuscript, your timetable for submitting sample chapters and for completing the work, the estimated length, and even the word processing program you are using.

In your cover letter also indicate if you are making a multiple submission—submitting a prospectus to more than one publisher simultaneously—although you are not obligated to do so. Publishers naturally discourage simultaneous submissions to multiple publishers, and some will reject a multiple submission outright. Because of the extreme competitiveness of the textbook industry and the amounts of money involved, publishers are sensitive to needs for product secrecy and competitive edge. Authors have used the multiple submission strategy to their advantage, however, as it facilitates an earlier response from the publisher.

Getting an Offer

Waiting is next and often takes longer than one would like. Acquisitions editors may be on the road, traveling to conventions and campuses, and unable to attend to your submission immediately. Editors typically send your prospectus and sample chapters out for professional peer review, which also can take some time. Finally, the sponsoring editor may need to present your book plan to other tiers of corporate management before an offer can be made. Regardless, prospective authors are perfectly justified in recontacting the editor in a month or two if there has been no response.

Sometimes editors will offer you a contract on the basis of your initial submission of your manuscript proposal, but they more typically request more information or more sample chapters or your response to peer reviews. Let us say, for instance, that reviewers unanimously felt that your sample chapter on law enforcement is too long, overemphasizes federal law enforcement over local and state law enforcement, and omits any mention of special law enforcement units such as border patrol, tribal police, and campus police. The editor might ask you to address these concerns by revising and resubmitting the chapter. The decision to make you an offer will rest on your response. Inexperienced or unknown text-book authors who do not respond well or refuse to make changes, perhaps in the belief that their draft is fait accompli, do not get signed.

Let us assume that you offer a thorough, timely, and well thought out response to the editorial suggestions, however, and that, as the next chapter suggests, you get to sign a contract with the publisher of your choice.

Appendix A: Selected Online Resources for Doing Your Own Market Research

To do market research, locate web sites of college textbook publishers via keyword searches. The following list includes URLs for selected parent companies and individual imprints that publish college textbooks.

Addison Wesley and Benjamin Cummings (Pearson): **www.aw.com**
Allyn and Bacon (Pearson): **www.ablongman.com**
Bedford/St. Martin's: **www.bfwpub.com**
Brooks/Cole (Thomson): **www.thomson.com/brookscole/**
Course Technology (Thomson): **www.course.com**
Elsevier Science (Saunders; Mosby; Butterworth-Heinemann):
    www.us.elsevierhealth.com; **www.hbuk.co.uk/wbs**
Focus (R. Pullins): **www.pullins.com**
Franklin, Beedle: **www.fbeedle.com**
W.H. Freeman: **www.whfreeman.com/**
Greenwood Publishing Group (Praeger): **www.greenwood.com**
Harcourt Brace (includes Saunders; Holt, Rinehart, Winston):
    www.thomsonlearning.com
Houghton Mifflin College Division: **www.hmco.com/flash.html**
Jones & Bartlett: **www.jbpub.com**
Jossey-Bass (Wiley): **www.josseybass.com**
Laurence King: **www.laurence-king.com;**
    www.laurenceking.co.uk
McGraw-Hill (includes Irwin; Mayfield): **www.mhhe.com/catalogs**
Norton: **www.wwnorton.com/college.htm**
Pearson: **www.pearsoned.com**
Prentice Hall (Pearson): **vig.prenhall.com/**
Rowan & Littlefield: **www.rowanlittlefield.com/**
Sage: **www.sagepub.co.uk**
Sinauer: **www.sinauer.com**
South-Western Publishing (Thomson): **www.swcollege.com/**
St. Martin's: **www.smpcollege.com/**
Wadsworth (Thomson, includes Peacock):
    www.thomson.com/wadsworth/
Waveland: **www.waveland.com**
Westview: **www.perseusbooksgroup.com/westview**
Wiley: **jws-edcv.wiley.com/college**
Worth: **www.worthpublishers.com/**

Appendix B: A Simple Sample Prospectus

Thank you for sending me your submission guidelines and inviting me to submit my book proposal and sample chapters. I am writing a professional book for authors and editors on WRITING AND DEVELOPING YOUR COLLEGE TEXTBOOK. Enclosed please find my résumé, a working TOC, and three sample chapters of my manuscript.

The work is based on my many years of experience as a development editor in secondary and higher education publishing. As you will see from my résumé, I have developed textbooks and textbook packages, including many first editions, for Allyn and Bacon; Houghton Mifflin; Little, Brown; McGraw-Hill; Macmillan; and several other educational publishers. I also have taught at both the secondary and college levels.

The main audience for my book is current and prospective authors of textbooks for college courses in all academic disciplines, especially introductory textbooks for undergraduates. Direct mail marketing, college bookstores and libraries, professional meetings, and the Internet seem suitable avenues for reaching this target audience. Although writing and editing advice and self-help books for authors and academics abound, I know of no title that addresses textbook development for college markets specifically and in detail, although I have seen articles on the subject by members of the Text and Academic Authors Association. My book seeks to inform on standard practices and best practices in commercial textbook publishing and will be the first of its kind in the marketplace.

A secondary market for my book is editors and publishers of college textbooks, who may wish to use it in whole or in part as instructional material for their authors or as professional development material for their editors. The work is easily adaptable to publishers' unique needs and also is appropriate for site-based professional workshops or campus seminars, which I am interested in conducting. I am presently developing an online course in textbook development for schools that offer certificate programs in publishing. I also have drafts of two companion titles for authors and editors respectively, *Writing and Developing Your College Textbook Supplements* and *Managing Your Authors*.

I think you will agree that there is a clear need for the kind of book I am proposing. In commercial higher education publishing today development tends to be reserved for a small number of high-projection titles and their supplements. I wrote *Writing and Developing Your College Textbook* to help improve the quality and shelf life of instructional materials for college students by teaching authors how to craft a commercially successful textbook on their own through self-managed product development.

I visualize this project as a 14-chapter handbook under 300 pages in length. Style and tone are succinct, no-nonsense, and highly practical. My research- and experience-based insider advice tends to be both encouraging and outspoken, which may serve to entertain as well. The initial draft has approximately 110,000 words, 8 rendered figures, several matrices, and at least 14 chapter appendices.

I chose your company because of similar titles you publish on writing and scholarly publishing. I am working on the book part time and expect to achieve a completed revised draft by June 1, 2002. If my project fits your list needs, I will be glad to send you more manuscript. This query is not part of a multiple submission, however, so I would appreciate it if you would let me know within 30 days of receipt if you are interested in talking with me about publishing and marketing possibilities. My contact information appears below.

Thank you very much for your consideration.

Sincerely,

Use the Signing Process to Your Advantage

When the acquisitions or sponsoring editor receives your prospectus and enclosures, he or she will read it and decide whether to reject it or to send it out for peer review. In some smaller houses, an inhouse editorial board or panel decides. This is what is happening during the weeks or months that you receive no response. A considerate editor will let you know the status of your submission.

Steps to Getting an Offer

On receiving generally positive reviews, the editor will call you to discuss the project further. Before discussing contracts and royalties, however, the editor will want to get to know you a little and feel you out on the following questions. These are questions you should also answer for yourself before you proceed.

Ten Things Your Sponsor Wants to Know about You before Signing

1. Are you and your book a good choice for the company and for the market?
2. How committed are you to the project?
3. Can you put aside enough time for this monumental task?
4. What resources do you have for getting help with your project and completing it on time?
5. How knowledgeable are you about what is involved in textbook publishing?
6. How responsive are you to market issues and company needs?
7. How responsive are you to professional peer review and to editorial input?
8. How willing are you to consider suggested changes?
9. Do you seem to have good interaction and collaboration skills?
10. Do you seem to have positive attitudes toward the editor's and the publisher's roles?

- **How committed are you to the project?** Can you put aside enough time for this monumental task? What resources do you have for getting help with your project and completing it on time? How knowledgeable are you about what is involved in textbook publishing?

The sponsoring editor has compelling reasons to try to gauge your ability to deliver. Publishing a textbook involves a major commitment of time and resources. Ask anyone who has done it. The publishing process, like the writing process, is complex, ongoing, and recursive. Also, in most commercial houses, publishing schedules have decision points, points of no return, and only minor flexibility. Smaller houses and academic presses usually are less concerned with schedule than major market textbook publishers.

If authors cannot fulfill all their authoring tasks in time, it is expected that they will be able to delegate or let the publisher do so. If scheduling does not work out for any reason, a book can miss its intended copyright year, thus upsetting the company's publishing plan. The book could then be bumped one to three years depending on other titles already in the pipeline. Delayed books usually need further revision before they are ready again for production, and some delayed books never see print. The editor has a stake in seeing that this does not happen, which is why he or she must try to develop a relationship with you before deciding to make an offer.

- **How responsive are you to market issues and company needs?**
  How responsive are you to professional peer review and to editorial input? How willing are you to consider suggested changes?

In the company's eyes, your commitment is not only to your book but also to its market—the customers your book serves. It is expected that you will be responsive to reviewer concerns and proven customer needs. Further, author commitment may not end with publication, especially if the company is handling your book as a major-market offering. You might be called upon to contribute material for advertising and promotion, talk to potential customers, provide signed copies of your book, conduct a newsgroup on a companion web site, or help present your book at company sales meetings. The sponsoring editor therefore has strong reasons to gauge your market savvy and sensitivity and interest in helping to make your book a commercial success.

- **Do you seem to have good interaction and collaboration skills?**
  Do you seem to have positive attitudes toward the editor's and the publisher's roles?

A prospective author's attitudes and ability to work well with other professionals are important factors for the success of a project. In addition to teaming with an acquisitions editor and possibly a coauthor or two, you also might be working with a development editor or managing editor, production coordinator, copyeditor, photo researcher, packager, marketing manager, supplements authors, and others. Through interpersonal conflicts and misunderstandings about the roles of all the players, projects can fail to meet their potential or can altogether crash. Legendary cases involve lawsuits. Your sponsoring editor therefore has a stake in establishing friendly rapport with you and gauging your cooperative spirit.

Establish a Positive Relationship

Unproductive author attitudes toward publishers and editors usually relate to issues of trust, power, and control. Mistrust about contracts and the publisher as capitalist is common. It certainly is true that publishers try to cut themselves the best possible deal and are not above misrepresentation. So-called "standard" contracts definitely favor the publisher. You should be aware, however, that there are industry standards regarding ethical practices, and reputable publishers take those standards seriously. Normally, it is not in a reputable publisher's long-term interests to be underhanded with authors. In abnormal situations, however, such as small subsidiaries being squeezed for profits, things can change. Also, in giant mergers large numbers of books on the same subjects change hands, and publishers routinely discontinue less profitable titles by putting them out of print. Discontinued authors justifiably feel abused, although, as mentioned previously, all rights are reassigned to them eventually and they can seek another publisher. In the balance, authors should be wary of potential ruthlessness but should not assume that author-publisher relations are predicated on opportunities for this.

Many power and control issues concern the manuscript. Some authors believe strongly that their words should not be subject to outside forces. They are the experts and no one can tell them what to write. Reviewers have their own axes to grind and thus can be ignored. Customers should have the sense to want what the author is providing. Yet editors, too, are experts. They can save you from yourself and help you craft a successful book—the editor's true purpose. Reviewers and customers also are experts. Authors uninterested in satisfying the people who will order, buy, and read their textbook might consider self-publishing or custom publishing to get a textbook for personal use in their own classrooms. If this is you, see Appendix A at the end of this chapter for a list of resources for self-publishing and custom publishing.

Some academics are insulted or disappointed to discover that textbooks are products and obey the dictates of a market economy. They may treat requests for changes to their manuscripts as Faustian confrontations in which making any amendment is selling out. A common misperception is that marketability requires books to be watered down or dumbed down. Actually, textbooks need to address their true readers—students for whom the book is intended, students whose learning is at stake. For most introductory college textbooks, for example, this reader is an 18- or 19-year-old person in late adolescence with little or no prior exposure to the field. If you do not wish to write for this audience, but prefer to maintain the language and style of discourse you use in your journal articles and monographs, you should not attempt to write an introductory or undergraduate textbook.

Another common misperception is that books must be made into clones of all the other books on the market. On the contrary, publishers know that each textbook needs to be unique or special or innovative in some way to distinguish itself among the competition. At the same time, they know that textbooks that are too different or too far before their time, even great ones, like other great ideas for which the world is not ready, will fail.

Some prospective authors believe that the publishing industry is a threat to academic freedom, not to mention democracy. Critics in the media police and in higher education often portray publishing conglomerates as bastions of thought control. The reasoning seems to be that by determining or censoring what gets published, unscrupulous plutocratic monopolists can amass megawealth and global political power through the control of information. Certainly the control of information is a crucial concern of the twenty-first century, and no doubt there are managers and CEOs who fantasize along these lines daily. In reality, however, for better or for worse, corporations as capitalists tend to be the slaves, not the masters, of the public. As in other media, it is the ratings—hence profits—that count.

This is not to say that publishers in higher education only follow market trends. They innovate to create demand, sometimes making it difficult for customers to stick with tried and true ways. The revolution in electronically delivered instruction is one example. In the 1990s many colleges and universities were "dragged kicking and screaming" into the Internet Age mainly through the new product lines and competitive marketing strategies of big publishers.

If you tend to hold strongly Orwellian views, consider the following list of reasons other than thought control that editors might have for asking authors to revise, add, or delete material.

Some Reasons Editors Ask for Changes to Organization or Content

- The book is too long for its intended market or its budget and has to be cut.
- Undocumented opinion is presented as fact.
- Undocumented facts seem inaccurate or misleading.
- Information seems outdated or lacks currency.
- Topical coverage seems unbalanced or biased.
- Material is judged to be strongly offensive to some or all readers.
- Examples, language, or expression seem inappropriate to the subject, course, or reader.
- Digressions or redundancy compromise meaning or coherence.
- The manuscript departs significantly from the agreed-upon book plan.

In addition, see Chapter 5 for further discussion of that great bugbear of twentieth-century publishing: political correctness.

Know How to Negotiate Your Agreement

Let us assume that on the basis of peer reviews of your prospectus, outline, and sample chapters the sponsoring editor wants to get you under contract to do the book and is satisfied that the company can work with you amicably, productively, and profitably. Now, finally, comes the discussion of mutual contractual obligations and royalties and advances.

In commercial publishing, contracts favor the publisher, read like you are signing your life away (or selling your soul to the devil), and make you wonder if you should retain a famous lawyer. Having the contract reviewed and amended by an attorney who knows publishing certainly is a very good idea. After all, you are signing a legally binding agreement. Intellectual property rights lawyers are expensive but really worth it if you first figure out as much as possible on your own. Pro bono advice for authors also is available. Appendix B at the end of this chapter lists some resources for legal advice for academic and textbook authors.

The formidability of the Agreement as a legal document reflects the fact that publishers—in addition to being under pressure for profits from their parent company and stockholders—routinely take serious losses on a percentage of their titles each year. They are also regularly sued. The larger the company the greater the need for profit protection and legal safeguards. Hence, awesome-looking contracts that favor the publisher.

Royalties and Advances

Today, royalties can range from 2 to 20 percent depending on the following factors:

- across-the-board ceilings decided at the corporate level
- how badly the company wants your book or you as an author
- how high the projected sales are for your book
- how much it will cost to develop, produce, manufacture, and sell your book

Royalties of 8 to 15 percent total are typical for major market textbooks, but smaller houses offer less. Academic and scholarly presses may offer royalty splits as low as 5 percent on the net for the first 1,000 copies sold, 7.5 percent on the next 1,500, and 9.5 percent above that. In large and small houses, royalty amounts commonly are split, with one percentage rate for an initial number of units (say, the first 2,000), a higher rate for the next set of units (say copies 2,001 to 4,000), and so on. Companies cut their losses this way if your book does not sell as many copies as hoped.

Authors typically do not make much money with academic and scholarly presses, however, or with small or niche textbook publishers. These publishers often can get away with outrageously one-sided contracts because of the "publish or perish" syndrome and the naivety of academics who spurn capitalism in connection with their intellectual mission and life's work. Authors who need to publish to win a place in their field or advance their careers may be content simply to get into print. They sign with or without illusions of income and do not make good advocates for publisher responsibility and contractual fairness.

On the other hand, some authors do very well. Those few with routinely revised best-selling introductory textbooks in popular undergraduate courses with large enrollments have been known to earn in excess of $100,000 a year in royalties, and more than one college instructor-author has been able to retire comfortably on royalty earnings.

Your share of the royalty will be affected by the number of authors or the amount of material you contribute to the book. Coauthors agree among themselves on how to further subdivide the pie, and this decision is written into the contact. Royalties are then paid periodically—typically on the net of copies sold. You should request to receive royalty statements at least twice a year, and you should make sure that "net sales" and all similar language is explicitly defined in the contract.

Advances against royalties are standard practice in larger commercial houses, but, like cash grants, are becoming rarer. In smaller houses they are nonexistent. Companies and contracts vary widely in the allocation of assets and responsibilities and the flexibility for negotiating them. Royalties usually kick in after a break-even number has been reached—that is, after the publisher has recovered a percentage of the plant costs, including advances against royalties. Theoretically, if a book does not do well enough, the authors can end up owing the company money, a risk the publisher traditionally underwrites. In twenty-first-century publishing, as publishers continue to absorb losses of profit, authors increasingly are threatened with being billed for their books that fail to break even.

Ethical standards notwithstanding, publishers will pass on as much as possible of their costs, first to authors through the contract. For instance, publishers may try to deduct some of their legitimate costs from royalty schedules, such as insurance and freight. Publishers also pass on the costs to the college bookstores, who buy the books through discount pricing policies and then mark them up. The students pay the bookstores' higher prices, driving the price even higher by selling back their books to used book dealers, which reduces demand for the higher-priced new book. In the twenty-first-century economy, some publishers appear to be at risk of pricing themselves out of the market, and the scramble is on for developing new product models.

Contractual Rights and Responsibilities

Check carefully the services your publisher intends to charge against your royalties, which should be made clear to you at the outset. In particular, ask who does the following, who pays for it (directly or indirectly), and for how much (in rate or percentage):

- permissions research
- permissions fees

- photo research
- photo use fees
- art rendering
- captioning
- copyediting
- proofreading
- indexing
- authors' alterations (the changes you make during production after the book is set into type)
- print and electronic supplements that are free to customers
- print and electronic supplements that are sold to customers

All standard contracts, or "Agreements," identify "the Author," the nature of "the Work," the length of the Work (or the number of words), and the date the Work will be delivered. The Agreement further specifies what rights you are giving to the publisher, for example, all rights exclusively throughout the world in all languages for the life of the copyright including revised editions and derivative works, such as electronic editions. You should carefully consider each right you are granting. Authors with agents typically withhold some rights and assign them themselves. For instance, you might wish to retain first serial rights and recording rights to create and sell other forms of your work yourself, or you may wish to have subsidiary rights (such as publishing rights to British Commonwealth nations) returned to you if the publisher does not assign them within two or three years of publication of your textbook.

After specifying the rights being granted to the publisher, agreements then declare the royalty percentage and the manner in which it will be paid. Codicils to the Agreement present further conditions and iron out details. Details include what happens to your book if you cannot or will not provide a satisfactory revision (the company might want to get someone else to do it at your expense), or if not enough copies of your book get sold (the company might want to put it out of print and destroy all existing forms of it). All companies will seek to bar you from publishing a directly competing work with another company during the term of your contract and will shun all liability for any copyright infringements on your part. Some contracts specify that you will pay court costs for any claims against your book, but you should try to restrict this to only successful claims. Protecting yourself in view of copyright laws is the subject of Chapter 13 of this book.

Other contractual details specify exactly what you will provide in what form, including the authoring tasks you will perform, such as correcting proofs and furnishing various elements—a table of contents, index, illustrations, photos, instructor's manual, etc. The publisher's duties are similarly spelled out. All companies reserve the right to edit your book, so long as your meaning is not changed, and to manufacture and sell your book as they see fit, choosing the design, paper, binding, cover, and price. In addition, publishers usually reserve for themselves all decision-making rights concerning the quality of materials and visual presentation. If you feel strongly about having a say in your book's presentation, therefore, you would be wise to discuss this at the time of signing. Here are ten questions you should ask the publisher before signing a contract.

Ten Things You Want to Know from Your Publisher before Signing

1. Why should you publish with them rather than with another publisher?
2. What will be the publisher's investment in your book and its package?
3. How will your book be marketed, promoted, advertised, and sold?
4. How many copies of your book can the publisher expect to sell and to whom?
5. What will be your royalty percentage and how will royalties be paid?
6. Will you receive a grant or an advance on royalties, how much, and when?
7. What are all your rights and responsibilities regarding your manuscript? What are all the publisher's rights and responsibilities?
8. How many chapters, pages, or words will you be expected to provide, and when will the manuscript be due?
9. By what process and criteria will the publisher determine that your manuscript is "acceptable"? How extensively and by whom will your manuscript be reviewed?
10. Will you have the assistance of a development editor? How will you be rewarded if you undertake development on your own? (See Chapter 4.)

In addition, you would be wise to try to insist that the following points be included in the Agreement, although you will find a lot of resistance:

- Restrictive language defining what is meant by the manuscript's "acceptability" to the publisher.
- Return of all rights to you within a specified period of time if your book is not published within a certain agreed time.
- Return of all rights to you or automatic renegotiation of contract if the company is acquired by or merged with another company.
- Rights that you decide you do not wish to assign, such as electronic rights, which the publisher would then have to renegotiate with you in another Agreement.
- Royalty rates based on payable net sales to bookstores.

- Divisions of income from the licensing of subsidiary rights.
- Terms under which the contract will terminate.

Understand the Company's Investment

Considering all that you give up in a contract, what can you expect a commercial publisher to do for you? If your textbook is a C-book, your publisher probably is investing at least $20k just to get it into print; if it is an A-book, perhaps a half a million dollars or more. If the company is producing a videotape, CD, and web site to license or to give away free to adopters of your book, then its direct investment is even higher.

Depending on company size, besides direct investment the publisher has other resources and networks for bringing your book to market that a small publisher or an author alone cannot easily match:

- wholesale buyers
- processes and vendors for mass production and manufacturing
- nationwide marketing research
- advertising and promotion budgets
- direct-mail and Internet marketing capabilities
- professional sales force in the field and sales support staff
- editors, book designers, photo researchers, artists, and a host of other specialists
- systems for providing print and nonprint supplements, such as acetate transparencies, software, and video
- warehousing and distribution
- access to foreign markets

The combined cost of direct and indirect investment can be quite high. An area of misunderstanding between authors and publishers stems from authors' ignorance about the hidden costs of publishing. Over the past two or three decades, escalating competition within the college textbook industry led to the well-known "freebie" phenomenon, for example. Commercial publishers have tried to outdo each other by giving away products and services free to adopters, although this practice is changing today as the cost of producing freebies becomes increasingly prohibitive. Freebies sometimes include supplements such as transparency sets, videotapes, digital archives, and web sites, along with posters, calendars, engraved pens, and the like.

Other examples of hidden costs of publishing are increases in postage rates, production and printing costs, price of paper, warehouse leasing, salaries of computer experts and other specialists, benefit packages and incentive plans for employees, and other overhead. The following examples of publishing costs may give you an idea of the publisher's investment.

Typical Publishing Costs in 2002: A Sampling

EDITORIAL
Development: $200 - $400 per day

PRODUCTION
Project Coordination: $2 - $15 per book page
Copyediting and Proofreading: $1 - $3 per page
Book Design: $500 - $3800
Art and Photo Coordination: $4 - $6 per piece
Cost of Production: $10 - $26 per page (depending on level
of investment)

MANUFACTURING (PLANT COSTS)
$25 - $250 per page (depending on level of investment)

SUPPLEMENTS
Instructor's Manual: $1,500 - $4,500
Videotape: $5,000 - $15,000
Web Site: $10,000 - $50,000

At the same time as the cost of doing business has increased, publishers have been unable to control the brokers—the college bookstores through which instructors must order their texts. These same bookstores mark up the price of the product for retail sale to students. Bookstores may get deep discounts of as much as 60 percent from the publisher, plus full reimbursement for returns of unsold books. Students, meanwhile, increasingly team up to share their high-priced tomes and then sell them back to the bookstore as soon as the course is over. As mentioned previously, bookstores also buy used texts from used book dealers. Each semester, students buy up the used books first, and orders for new books dry up.

As an instructor you already may have had the experience of being approached by used book dealers asking you to sell your old textbooks to them right off the shelves of the bookcase in your office. If you did so, you unwittingly stole royalty earnings from the authors of those books, and the same thing can happen to you. Your book, so promising, can fail for reasons entirely unrelated to its quality or content. As the used books get sold first and the bookstore returns unsold new copies, the publisher's sales reports start to show sharp declines. Two consequences of this cycle have included ever higher prices on textbooks and ever shorter revision cycles to replace used books with new editions. A new edition, even one with cosmetic changes and little actual revision, automatically puts the previous edition out of print.

Trends in the Texbook Publishing Industry

The turn of the twenty-first century saw a sea change in customers' attitudes toward publishing practices. Customers began to rebel against forced roll-overs and ever higher prices for textbooks cranked out too soon as new editions. When students share books, circulate pirated copies, or try to get through the course without a textbook, sales figures discourage the publisher from investing in a revision. Publishers have responded to this crisis by seeking new product models and cheaper alternative means of delivery, such as e-textbooks, and serialized textbooks delivered on dedicated web sites. Who knows where this will lead? Today customers can get bargain textbooks printed on demand on three-hole-punched paper without covers, and students can download textbooks from the Internet, paying only for the chapters they want. There are even "shadow texts"—products for students who want to get through the course without actually buying or reading a textbook.

Returned copies of unsold new textbooks, meanwhile, must be remaindered or destroyed at publisher expense. Tax laws prevent publishers from writing off unsold inventory. Together with the high cost of personnel, overhead, vendor services, and technology, all the above conditions put a tight squeeze on companies' profit margins at the same time as corporate chiefs continue to demand double-digit growth in profits. Giant mergers are one response, along with dubious economies of scale. Publishing conglomerates' strategies for protecting profit margins, as in other industries in the twenty-first century, sometimes lead to overstandardization; overburdened or downsized inhouse staffs; excessive outsourcing and the exporting of manufactory; products of lesser quality or lesser variety or with "loose bolts" as a result of cost-cutting measures; and profit-squeezing contracts, wholesaling practices, and fulfillment policies.

All these realities underlie publishing contracts, but publishers' problems should not discourage you as a prospective author. As formidable as they are as legal documents, contracts are negotiable. Many contracts have passages added or crossed out and initialed amendments modifying one detail or another. Savvy authors ask a lot of questions and return point-for-point memos requesting changes, clarifications, additions, or deletions in their contract. You would be wise not to sign with a publisher that treats their contract as nonnegotiable.

Savvy authors also find out what is planned for their book. The bigger the plans or possibilities—maybe your work is going to be sold as both a book and a text-web hybrid—the bigger the royalty or advance you might be able to command. In commercial textbook publishing, mutually lucrative author-publisher agreements are more the rule than the exception, and this should be the principal goal of your negotiations during the signing process. Let your acquisitions editor know at the outset that this is what you expect.

Appendix A: Selected Resources for Custom Publishing and Self-Publishing

Custom Publishing

Most large college houses have custom publishing units in which your syllabus, bibliography, and unique course materials can be bound together with chapters you select from publishers' textbooks. For example, Pearson Education has a Custom Publishing unit (**www.pearsoncustom.com/**), McGraw-Hill has Primis Custom Publishing (**www.mhhe.com/primis/**), and Thomson also has a Custom Publishing unit (**www.thomsoncustom.com/**). These are the three largest college publishers today.

Large copy centers, such as Kinko's, and a myriad of desktop publishing enterprises also do custom publishing from camera-ready copy or from disk. Usually, the author-instructor arranges for the college bookstore to sell the custom text to his or her students at cost plus the bookstore's markup. Colleges and universities often have policies prohibiting the direct sale of course materials to students by instructors. Custom publishing cost includes permissions fees, for permissions must be scrupulously compiled. Custom publishers will not produce a book until all permissions are cleared. However, some offer the paid service of querying copyright clearance centers for you.

Custom Electronic Publishing

Branded course management software, such as Blackboard, Web-CT, or Course Compass, offer opportunities to customize by selecting course modules and readings and adding specific, unique course information and instructional materials. Many companies also exist that produce custom electronic textbooks accessible via the Internet or printed on demand, for example:

> Atomic Dog Publishing: **www.atomicdogpublishing.com/**
> Book Publisher (e-books and print on demand):
>   **www.bookpublisher.com/**
> Booktech.com, Inc.: **www.booktech.com**
> ConnecText is a registry for online textbooks. See
>   **www.connectext.com**
> ETEXT Electronic Textbook Publishing: **www.etext.net**
> Virtual Book Publishing Company:
>   **www.virtualbookpublishing.com/**

PowerPoint or other presentation software can be used to customize instruction. The electronic slides can be projected in class or delivered to students via CDs or web sites. Many academic departments and individual instructors have web sites through which they deliver original course content.

Self-Publishing

Self-publishing involves being an independent publisher and getting an ISBN number for your book, which you write, produce, promote, advertise, market, sell, and, often, ship by yourself. You pay the printer for the print run, the freight, the phone, and other costs. To break even or turn a profit, textbook authors who self-publish need more customers than their own students. If you are interested in this idea, the following general resources might give you some information and inspiration.

Beach, Mark, and Eric Kenly. *Getting It Printed: How to Work with Printers and Graphic Imaging*, 3rd ed. North Light Books, 1999.

Bell, Patricia J. *The Prepublishing Handbook: What You Should Know Before You Publish Your First Book.* Cat's paw Press, 1992.

Bodian, Nat G. *Direct Marketing Rules of Thumb.* McGraw-Hill, 1995.

Burgett, Gordon. *Publishing to Niche Markets.* Communications Unlimited, 1995.

Cardoza, Avery. *Complete Guide to Successful Publishing.* Cardoza Pub., 1998.

Cole, David. *Complete Guide to Book Marketing.* Allworth Press, 1999.

Henderson, Bill. *The Publish It Yourself Handbook.* Pushcart Press, 1987.

Kremer, John. *1001 Ways to Market Your Books*, 5th ed. Open Horizons, 2000. (See Chapter 2 at **www.bookmarket.com/2.html**)

Lee, Marshall. *Bookmaking: The Illustrated Guide to Design and Production*, 3rd ed. W.W. Norton & Company, 1997.

Poynter, Dan. *The Self-Publishing Manual: How to Write, Print and Sell Your Own Book*, 8th ed. Para Publishing, 1995.
www.parapublishing.com

Publishers Marketing Association: **www.pma-online.org**

Rose, M. J. and Angela Adair-Hoy. *How to Publish and Promote Online.* Griffin Trade, 2001.

Ross, Tom, and Marilyn H. Ross. *The Complete Guide to Self-Publishing*, 4th ed. Writer's Digest Books, 2001.

Silverman, Franklin H. *Self-Publishing Books and Materials for Students, Academics, and Professionals*, 2nd ed. CODI Publications, 2000.

Small Publishers Association of North America: **www.spannet.org**

Yudkin, Marcia. *Internet Marketing for Less than $500 a Year*, 2nd ed. Independent Publishing Group, 2001.

Appendix B: Selected Resources for Legal and Business Advice for Authors

Acq Web: **www.acqweb.library.vanderbilt.edu/law/**
Association of Authors' Reps: **www.aar-online.org**
Author's Guild: **www.authorsguild.org/**

Balkin, Richard, and Nick Bakalar. *A Writer's Guide to Book Publishing*, 2nd ed. Plume, 1994.

Bunnin, Brad, and Peter Beren. *Writer's Legal Companion*, 3rd ed. Addison Wesley Longman, 1998.

Burgett, Gordon. *The Writer's Guide to Query Letters and Cover Letters*. St. Martin's Press, 1991.

Crawford, Tad. *Business and Legal Forms for Authors and Self-Publishers*. Allworth Press, 2000.

Crawford, Tad, and Tony Lyons. *The Writer's Legal Guide*, 2nd ed. Allworth Press, 1998.

DuBoff, Leonard. *The Law in Plain English for Writers*. Wiley, 1992.

Frohbieter-Meuller, Jo. *Writing: Getting into Print: A Business Guide for Writers*. Glenbridge Pub. LTD, 1994.

Gillen, Stephen E. "Ten Tips for Your Next Book Deal," *Academic Author*. Text and Academic Authors Online, 1997.

Kirsch, Jonathan. *Kirsch's Handbook of Publishing Law*. Acrobat Books, 1994.

Levine, Mark. *Negotiating a Book Contract: A Guide for Authors, Agents, and Lawyers*. Moyer Bell, 1994.

Moxley, Joseph M. *Publish Don't Perish: The Scholar's Guide to Academic Writing and Publishing*. Praeger, 1992.

Parsons, Paul. *Getting Published: The Acquisitions Process in Scholarly Publishing*. University of Tennessee Press, 1990.

Pinkerton, Linda F. *The Writer's Law Primer*. Lyons and Burford, 1990.

Woll, Thomas. *Selling Subsidiary Rights: An Insider's Guide*. Fisher Books, 1999.

Development and Why Your Textbook Needs It

As defined in Chapter 1, *development* is a complex recursive process in which authors and editors collaborate to bring a manuscript and all its ancillary material to market level and prepare it for publication. If you already have a completed manuscript in hand, you might wonder why your book needs development. As one author recalls, anonymously:

> "It was my magnum opus—brilliant, classroom-tested, as near perfect as I could make it, the fruit of long years of painstaking study and splendid revelation and long nights at the computer. It was a labor of love and professional fulfillment in a publish or perish world. I had said exactly what I meant to say in exactly the way I wanted to say it. My colleagues in my department, my students, and my spouse all said that they liked it. As far as I was concerned, it was done. This was it, take it or leave it. Then I met my development editor."

This author learned that every writer needs an editor and that most textbooks need development to succeed in a big way. With development, a textbook can double its sales in its first two editions, as this author's did.

Development Decisions

Development involves the following decisions, among others:

Market and Audience
What is the book's market? Whom will the book be for?
How will it take away business from the competition?
What will be the intellectual level, style, and tone?
On what basis will the book be marketed and sold?

Organization and Content
What topics will the book cover and in what order?
How many parts and chapters of what length will the book need?
How will content be organized in terms of headings and
   subheadings?
What figures and tables will be included and how many?

Apparatus and Pedagogy

How will chapters consistently open and close?

What pedagogical features will be included and how frequently will they appear?

Will there be pedagogical captions? A glossary? Marginalia?

What will be in the frontmatter and endmatter?

Authoring and Managing Tasks

How will each authoring task be accomplished?

Who will review manuscript, how many reviewers will there be, and to what questions will they respond?

What will be the schedules for drafting, reviewing, and revising?

What will be the supplements, who will do them, what will be in them, how will they be done, and when?

Presentation

What photos and illustrations will be included and how many?

What will the book look like? What will be on the cover?

How will the book be promoted and advertised?

These authoring decisions reflect the ten domains of development. Although many of the questions are in the publisher's purview (they typically reserve final say on the book's appearance, for instance), it's a good idea to keep the big picture in mind as you work on answering your authorship questions.

Ten Domains of Development

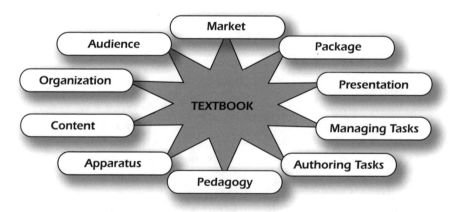

Ideally, development is done up front before manuscript even exists, and certainly before you have polished a presumed final draft. As with technological applications, retrofitting a manuscript to match a later development plan can be a nightmare for all involved. Thus, plan early and well, and, if possible, get development help.

Negotiating for Development Help

Ask your publisher or sponsoring editor if you will have the help of a development editor (DE). It would be in your interests to ask for development help as part of your contract negotiation. If your publisher declines to invest in development, ask what the sales projection will be and negotiate for development on the next edition if expectations are met. If your book is an untried first edition in an uncertain market, is already in its tenth edition with declining sales, or serves a small, specialized readership, investment in development might not be forthcoming. If, however, the sales projection is, say, 5,000 units in a new market or 10,000 units in an established market, some professional development help might be warranted. Note, however, that publishers vary in the cutoff figures used to determine if a book can afford development.

Publishing houses also specify different levels of development consistent with the level of investment. Minor development might involve only a few days of developmental review by an editor who does not establish contact with you, while full development might involve having your project managed in every detail, your manuscript line-edited by the DE, or, rarely, the DE traveling to your campus to work with you. Thus, if your publisher is investing in development, ask what level of development is planned. If help is not forthcoming, however, negotiate for some consideration of your personal investment of time and resources for development and announce your intention to develop the book yourself.

Unless your work is slated as a 4-color introductory textbook, your chances of having development help are small. Development usually is reserved for products with high-volume sales projections and for promising new markets into which the company hopes to expand. In some companies a portion of the staff development editor's annual salary is figured as part of the cost of a book, so only the books with the largest sales projections can afford a DE. The publisher might prorate the services of an inhouse or freelance DE at $200 to $400 per day, charged to the plant costs for your book.

Working with a Development Editor

A development editor has a different role from the acquisitions editor and the copyeditor. As you have seen, the acquisitions editor sponsors your book—signs you on, proposes budget considerations for the project, often is responsible for arranging professional peer reviewing, and decides whether or not to invest in development. The copyeditor checks your writing style, spelling, punctuation, grammar, sentence construction, paragraphing, and other mechanics. The development editor, on the other hand, analyzes your competition and reviewer feedback and collaborates with you to improve your organization and content; to create a heading system, a pedagogy plan, and a program of figures and tables; and to prepare your manuscript for release to production.

In some houses, development editors also are responsible for a variety of other tasks. They may be involved in commissioning reviewers, developing an art and photo program, assisting with permissions research, presenting your book to a book designer, checking stages of proof, developing the supplements and working with supplements authors, and tracking and routing all the paperwork for your project. In some instances, DEs might help you revise or rewrite or as content experts might even contribute original material for your book. Every house defines the role of a development editor differently, and development editors also vary among themselves in how they define their role.

Understand the DE's Role

The DE represents both the publisher and the customers for your textbook and in that capacity helps to answer the questions in the ten domains of development. Working with a development editor usually involves frequent contact, collaborative or consensual decision making, and adherence to manuscript length requirements and schedules for submitting work. Working with a DE also involves trying to have a positive attitude and an appreciation for what the editor needs from you and what he or she can do for you and your book. This editor traditionally and normally is, above all, your ally, your champion, and should be treated accordingly.

Inexperienced authors sometimes assume that development editors' only allegiance is to the publisher and that their job is solely to guarantee a salable product. Publishers, no doubt, would like to think so, too. The truth is, however, that the professional development editor's chief allegiance probably is to your book and the people who will use it. For as little as a few days to as much as a year or more, the DE works for them as well as for you and the publisher. Making an excellent book that will achieve its full market potential is the goal. And the process can be arduous, so much so that the metaphor of pregnancy and birth for publishing a book has entered the canon of cliché.

Establish a Good Working Relationship

For a variety of reasons, authors and editors typically experience some tension in their relationship. Author and editor need each other to achieve their goals but have differing agenda. When author-editor relationships are unsatisfying or stressful, their book is at risk, much as a child is at risk when parents bicker or separate. Some sources of this tension are suggested in the following examples of sources of tension between authors and editors.

Some Sources of Tension in the Author-Editor Relationship

Schedule, Length, and Mechanics:
Editor has unrealistic expectations about schedule; nags about

deadlines; asks for or dictates "impossible" cuts for length; requests nitpicking formatting changes.

Author cannot be reached or does not return calls promptly; sends manuscript late without notice; does not draft to length; does not attend to manuscript preparation; does not attend to permissions correctly or in a timely way.

Effort and Commitment:

Editor requests changes that involve too much time or effort; requests extra rounds of revision or causes more work by changing the book plan in mid-stream.

Author is too busy (or out of town) or insufficiently committed to get the job done; does not update sources sufficiently; submits manuscript with elements missing or treated inconsistently; avoids responsibility for pedagogical features.

Evaluation and Ego:

Editor expects too much or too little, is overly critical, focuses on weaknesses; edits too heavily and is too heavy-handed or else fails to provide sufficient feedback.

Author cannot take valid criticism, is unresponsive to reviewer concerns and sound editorial suggestions, and accepts or insists on mediocre output.

Ownership and Control:

Editor dictates cuts and changes but refuses to assist with (or to desist from performing) authoring tasks; acts like this is his or her book. Whose book is it anyway?

Author makes unnegotiated changes to text at the last minute without notice; expects the editor to perform the author's responsibilities or overdepends; has to be bailed out through unbudgeted help or unscheduled overtime.

Editors, like authors, vary greatly in their personalities, knowledge, abilities, professional commitments, standards, strengths, and needs. They vary greatly in education, subject area knowledge, and publishing experience, not to mention motivation and skill. In failing to deal with tensions, if and when they arise, authors and editors can become unmotivated, suspicious, antagonistic, or alienated. Straightforward communication and a spirit of cooperative problem solving are the antidotes.

You would be wise to respect the editor's recommendations, as he or she understands the textbook publishing business. One thing to remember is that for every editorial request, however grand or trivial, normally there is a reason relating to publishing needs and realities. The first rule of thumb, therefore, is never to ignore an editorial request. Good development editors hesitate to confound authors routinely with the many technical details of publishing needs, but will gladly explain reasons or argue a case. It is the editor's job to anticipate and address your questions and concerns—you need only ask.

The second rule of thumb is to carefully establish the boundaries and ground rules for your working relationship early on in a positive manner, starting with mutual appreciation for the many personal and professional sacrifices both author and editor may make in creating a textbook. Ask the DE precisely what his or her role on the project will be and what will be expected of you.

The third rule of thumb is not to complain about your development editor without confronting her or him first, because publishing houses, like academic departments, are political working environments. That is, if you have a grievance about the way development is going, the development editor has a right to know about it directly and to have an opportunity to amend the process. Smart DEs ask their authors for feedback on their work to ensure mutual satisfaction with the manner in which development is done.

Doing Your Own Development

Since the mid-1980s the role of the development editor has been changing drastically—from that of author's alter ego, mentor, critic, muse, market analyst, creative consultant, advocate, and interpreter of the culture of publishing to that of product manager. Some publishers have found it in their interest to reduce the cost of development by having DEs handle as many books as possible, and the more titles they handle, the less time and care they can spend on each one. Correspondingly, publishers are placing a greater burden of responsibility for books on their authors. Thus, costs that were once assumed by publishers as author perks are being passed back to authors, along with tasks that restructured development editors may no longer have time to perform.

Even if you are assigned development help, in other words, you might find yourself pretty much on your own, which is the reason for this book. Lacking substantive collaboration with editors, you need to be able to do your own development. A major advantage of doing your own development is that you retain more control over your product and what goes into it. The disadvantage is that you need to devote more time and resources to planning your book with a view to commercial success.

Following are guidelines for performing development tasks to ensure that success. These tasks guide you in developing your table of contents, prospectus, and sample chapters described in Chapter 2. If you already have signed with a publisher, the information will guide you in further drafting and revising. And if you already have published and are working on a revision, the following practices will help you to increase your market share. These practices include getting publisher input, charting the competition, professional networking, and working with reviews.

Get the Input You Need

Request information from the publisher about your book's market. How large is this market? What are the current top sellers? What percent of the market do they control? Who orders those books? Why are those books successful? What are customers looking for now? Acquisitions editors and marketing managers have their ears to the ground, constantly searching out market trends, consumer demand, and competitive edges. Ask them about their market research in your subject area and to send you the results of any pertinent marketing surveys. Also ask for information about competing texts.

Acquire examination copies of the current leading competing books and compare their contents. Or study the relevant product information on competing companies' web sites. Then perform a competition analysis, including tallies of types of chapter elements. The aim is to ensure that your book will be competitive enough to succeed in the marketplace. The matrix on page 60 provides categories for a simple comparison grid.

Chart Your Comparative Survey of the Competition

Some authors resist looking at their competition, for a variety of reasons: fear of being influenced unduly, fear of unconscious imitation, professional pride, professional jealousy, fear of invading turf, and fear of feeling outgunned. Natural fears such as these are worth overcoming, however, because a close examination of competing books will help you avoid spending a lot of time writing something that the publisher cannot sell because (a) it's a clone of all the other books out there, or (b) it's an alien from outer space—unlike any other book out there—that instructors can't use.

So, how many chapters do other art history books have on the European Renaissance? Is it significant that all the other introductory psychology texts devote at least 40 pages to cognition? Should you also plan to have embedded calculus problems for students to solve as they read? In what primary context do the other health books discuss AIDS in detail? Do the other books in criminal justice cite Smith and Jones on their controversial new research? Should you consider adding maps showing frequency distributions in every chapter of your sociology text? Should engineering applications be treated in a separate chapter or integrated into every chapter? Should you think about converting some concepts in business law into flow charts or graphics? Does your social problems text have enough global and comparative coverage to be competitive?

At the same time as they are unique, successful books also selectively match or top the characteristics that make competing books successful. These characteristics include the organization of the book, the length, the topical coverage, the pedagogical features, and so on. Also, anything you discover about the competition is ammunition for getting your publisher to invest more in your textbook, because textbooks must be competitive to sell. Perhaps you can make a good argument for going two-color, having more photos, or putting up a companion web site.

Charting Your Comparative Survey of the Competition

	Top Competitor 1	Top Competitor 2	Top Competitor 3
Book Author, Title, Edition Publisher, Year			
Market Authors' Mission Text Themes Unique Features or Special Coverage			
Organization and Content # Parts & Chapters (Attach TOC) # Chapters/Pages on Key Topics			
Apparatus and Pedagogy Chapter Openers Chapter Closers Pedagogical Features			
Presentation # Pages Trim Size/# Colors Casebound/Paper # Figures/Tables # Photos			
Supplements Instructor Student			

Networking

Use your own professional network, professional meetings, or resources such as
the *Higher Education Directory* to contact instructors who teach the course for
which you are writing your text. These people are potential adopters of your
book. Select schools with large enrollments in the course you are writing for. Find
out what books they are using, why they chose them, what they think the
strengths and weaknesses of the books are, what pedagogical features they use or

don't use, what they need in a book that existing ones lack, and what supplements they would like to have. Also try out some of your ideas. Without giving away the whole show, ask them if they would be interested in a book that does what you are planning to do.

Within reason, maintain strict confidentiality in your contacts. You are working on an introduction to African-American literature, and that is all anyone really needs to know. More than one book has been scooped in its market because word of it reached rival publishers. If your book is a revision, keep the new copyright date to yourself. Keep a log of what you learn from your networking contacts and discuss the information with your sponsoring editor for further feedback and follow-up.

Transform your informal mail or phone survey into an online search. The possibilities are limited only by your imagination. Browse web pages and databases for information on your subject or field that might enhance your book's currency and appeal. Start or join a discussion group, asking colleagues about their courses and instructional concerns and about the books they use. This kind of information gathering gives you a broader insight into the instructional needs, hot topics, research developments, academic movements, patterns, and trends that your book might profitably reflect or represent. Also look for online information resources for yourself as a textbook author. Appendix A at the end of this chapter lists resources for academic author networking and some examples of what you will find online. Lists of other online resources also appear in Chapters 2, 3, 5, 11, and 13.

Use information from the publisher, your competition analysis, and your networking to refine your table of contents and to draft or revise your manuscript. Your final book plan should especially include the numbers and types of pedagogical features you plan to have for each chapter and samples of what they will look like. Chapter 7 guides you in the specifics of developing your table of contents, and Chapters 8, 9, and 10 guide you in developing your apparatus and pedagogy.

Getting and Using Helpful Reviews

The next step in development is to send out revised draft chapters for professional peer review, which the publisher should manage for you. The acquisitions editor has already had your book prospectus, table of contents, and sample chapters reviewed and has available a ready database for selecting reviewers. For each chapter of your manuscript, develop a list of specific questions you would like your reviewers to address. The editor can include these questions with the general reviewing guidelines that go out to cover the publisher's concerns. Your questions should reflect your informed concerns and should be worded neutrally; that is: no leading, loaded, or rhetorical questions. Would the reviewer assign this chapter for students to read? Why or why not? Does it cover all the topics it should? What should be added? Dropped? Is it current? Accurate? Balanced? Coherent? Clear? If your book is a revision, develop two sets of questions, one for past users of your book and one for nonusers (potential new customers). A sample set of general reviewing guidelines that you can adapt to your particular needs is provided in this chapter's Appendix B.

Also identify chapters that you think should go out for expert review, aside from the general reviews by professors who teach the course. As described in Chapter 2, expert reviews are critical reviews by specialists in a field. Especially in an introductory or survey text, you would be wise to select a chapter or two at the edge of your range of expertise that a specialist could check for you.

Number of Reviews. Be an advocate for publisher responsibility to have your book reviewed adequately and reviewers sufficiently remunerated. In some houses, skimping on reviewing is a solution to overstretched editorial budgets. Ask how many reviews are being commissioned and what the honorarium will be. As a rule of thumb, every chapter should have an absolute minimum of three generalist reviews, and selected chapters should have additional expert reviews. Five to eight reviews per chapter are more typical. The more reviews you have to work with, the easier it is to identify areas of critical consensus, and the surer you can be of crafting a successful book. Your publisher usually pays the honorarium for each review and should not disclose to you the identities of reviewers until your book is in print.

Authors signed with university, scholarly, association, or academic presses sometimes are asked to arrange their own reviewing. These authors might be tempted to ask friends and like-minded colleagues to review their work, with the object of collecting positive testimonials for the publisher's promotional campaign. This focus is not appropriate for textbook publishing, however. If you are sincere about providing intellectual and educational value to instructors and students, you will want critical reviews.

For commercial textbook publishers, reviews are everything. Editors typically are not content experts, though they may become so, but count on reviewers to give them an idea of whether or not to publish or revise a manuscript. You do want positive reviews, therefore, in addition to critical ones. Helpful reviewers both guide you in improving your manuscript and also make you look good in the eyes of the publisher, and finding and cultivating these reviewers is an art. You can help yourself best in the process by providing reviewers with complete manuscript—no missing pieces—that you have at least spell-checked.

Review Analysis. When the reviews come in, perform your own analysis of them as objectively as possible. Analyzing reviews can be difficult. It is natural to focus on laudatory remarks, tempting to dismiss criticism, easy to become defensive and to discard wholesale the comments of people who seem to disagree with you philosophically. Reviewers do sometimes have axes to grind and may not communicate in ways that are helpful or kind. Focusing too much on criticism also is a fault.

Review analysis also can be confusing. Positive and negative reviews have a way of canceling each other out, leaving you with no clear direction. However, your natural resistance must be balanced with openness to the possibility that the chapter is imperfect and can be improved, that improvements can be made without compromising your views or intellectual integrity, and that such improvements can lead to greater success for your book. At the same time, avoid joining the small minority of "knee-jerk" authors who attempt to accommodate every stray comment that every reviewer has to offer. Often, theirs may be the books that critics call "vacillating and bland."

As with your competition analysis, you can use your analysis of reviews to further refine your book plan, beginning with issues of writing style and voice, the subjects of Chapters 5 and 6, and moving on to issues of structure, organization, and content. If the publisher has conducted the reviewing for you, you should receive annotated copies of the reviews and a review summary or analysis. Your editors will use the reviews to request changes that they think will affect sales and to make final decisions about when and how to publish your book. Your final draft should accommodate proven publisher concerns and also should fairly address reviewer concerns. Chief among those concerns is whether you are reaching your true audience, the subject of the next chapter.

Appendix A: Online Resources for Textbook Authors

- Visit the web pages of textbook publishers. Also visit the web pages of professional organizations and publications in your academic discipline and survey their indexes for information and contacts you could use. Just type in the name of the organization or journal in a keyword search.

- Contact colleagues via email to discuss your project or solicit feedback. Create an online discussion group as a focus group or forum for textbook development in your field.

- Use higher education directories such as those listed below to locate new colleagues and departments where your course is taught. Also survey course syllabi and bibliographies in your field. You also will find interesting instructional materials developed by members of college faculties for classroom use and for distance learning courses (but remember that everything you see online is copyright protected).

  American Universities: **www.clas.ufl.edu/CLAS/**
  U.S. Universities by State: **www.utexas.edu/world/univ/state/**
  U.S. Two-Year Colleges: **www.sp.utoledo.edu/twoyrcol.html**
  Yahoo's University Listing:
  www.yahoo.com/Regional/Countries/
  United_States/Education/Colleges_and_Universities/

- Survey publishing industry sites for information on textbook publishing. The Association of American Publishers, for example, publishes an Author's Guide to College Textbook Publishing.

  Association of American Publishers (AAP): **www.publishers.org**
  Publisher's Weekly (PW): **www.bookwire.com/pw**
  Association of American University Presses (AAUP):
  www.aaup.pupress.princeton.edu/
  Book Industry Study Group (BISG): **www.bisg.org**
  Educational Paperback Association (EPA): **www.edubook.com**
  Publishers' Catalogues:
  www.library.swt.edu/alkek_lib/acq/pub_catalogs.html

- Sample local and national library resources, services, and directories, e.g.,

  American Library Association (ALA) : **www.ala.org/**
  Library of Congress (LOC): **www.loc.gov/**

Textbook Publisher Directory:
   www.lib.clemson.edu/links/publishing.html
Literary Market Place (LMP): **www.lmp.bookwire.com/**
Bibliofind (rare and out-of-print books): **www.bibliofind.com**
Library Spot (library of libraries, with links): **www.libraryspot.com**

- Survey higher education sites and periodicals for current research, news, and discussion on curricular and instructional issues in higher education and in your field, e.g.,

   ERIC Clearinghouse for Higher Education: **www.ericsp.org**
   Education Week: **www.edweek.com/**
   Chronicle of Higher Education: **www.che.com/**

- Critically survey sites that serve as advocates for textbook authors. The best known of these is Text and Academic Authors (TAA): **www.TAAonline.net.**

- Order books through **Amazon.com, Barnes & Noble College Bookstores, Borders Books & Music Online, Blackwell's,** or other online booksellers. These sources have many titles on authoring and publishing as well as textbooks in your field.

Appendix B: Guidelines and Questions for Peer Reviews

Your critical review of this manuscript will greatly help us revise it for publication. Using the following questions as a guide, please comment in some detail.

Organization and Content

1. Does the manuscript organization match the way the course is taught in your department? How, if at all, would you change the sequence of parts and chapters? Are there chapters you could drop? add? combine? Are there chapters you would not assign? Why?

2. Does topical coverage in the manuscript match syllabi for this course at your school? What topics, if any, would you drop? add? How, if at all, would you change topical emphasis or improve topical balance?

3. Is this manuscript current enough and accurate? What chapters and topics are most in need of updating? Does it cover appropriate research and trends in the field and provide appropriate examples? Is it sufficiently documented? What source citations or references do you think should be added?

Writing Style and Presentation

4. Is the manuscript written at an appropriate length and intellectual level for the students taking this course? Are the writing style and tone appropriate and motivating? Is the exposition clear? What sections, if any, may need to be revised for greater unity, clarity, or coherence? Which chapters and sections would hold the most and the least interest for students?

5. Are the figures and tables appropriate, clear, and useful to students? Which figures and tables in each chapter would you identify as the most and the least valuable to learners? Which, if any, would you drop? add?

Apparatus and Pedagogy

6. Are the chapter opening and chapter closing elements inviting to students and useful as learning tools? What, if anything, would you change about the way chapters open and close and other aids to student learning?

7. Are the features or boxes appropriate in themes, interesting to students, and useful as learning tools? What are some examples of features you regard as especially strong? weak? What, if anything,

would you change about the feature strands? How else, if at all, would you improve the pedagogical value of each chapter for students?

Overall Assessment

8. What do you identify as the three greatest strengths of this manuscript? What, if any, weaknesses do you identify? How well does this manuscript compare with other texts you have used for this course? How well does this manuscript achieve its mission, set out in the Preface? Would you adopt this text for use in your course?

Thank you in advance for your help.

Write to Reach Your True Audience

In writing, your voice is the way you "speak" to your audience, and it includes your "tone" of voice. Style is the way you use words to express yourself in writing. A second meaning of style is the system of conventions you adopt to format your writing for your subject area, such as the APA, MLA, CBE, or Chicago A or B styles. These editorial styles are discussed further later in this chapter. Voice, the subject of Chapter 6, and style are important matters in textbook publishing. By themselves, your writing style and voice can make or break your book. Making decisions about style and voice involves reflecting on your mission, understanding your audience, choosing how you will represent yourself and your subject, and monitoring your tone. This chapter focuses on audience and intentions.

Reflecting on Your Mission

A good way to ascertain if you are ready to write your textbook is to draft a working preface. The preface sets out your mission—the reason you wrote it (other than the potential status, security, and income) and what you hope it will accomplish. Textbook authors might have any of the following goals or a combination:

- Correct misconceptions, myths, and stereotypes.
- Expose students to the subject.
- Assist instructors teaching the course.
- Enable mastery of the subject.
- Fill a need for more, less, or different content coverage.
- Share love of subject and attract students to the field.
- Get students to think differently about the subject.
- Introduce new facts, ideas, models, or paradigms.
- Show students how to use or apply subject knowledge and skills.
- Share professional knowledge, skills, and experiences.

However, authors with the following mission or goals (intentional or latent) enter a shady or risky area, especially if they are writing an introductory text:

- Advance an argument.
- Expose falsehoods or misconduct.
- Discredit a person, theory, or point of view.
- Promote a particular paradigm or approach to the subject.

- Indoctrinate students.
- Discourage induction into the field.
- Change the way the course is taught.

Take a moment, then, to reflect on your mission. Frame a mission statement to keep before you as you draft. What will students come away with when they have finished reading your textbook? Who is your real reader anyway?

Identifying Your Real Reader

What students will read your textbook? Identifying and successfully addressing your readership is a complex enterprise. Even then, many authors forget who their true audience is as they draft. Magnetic shifts occur in which the writer draws away from the student toward his or her peers: the faculty member, adoption committee, professional review board, journal editorial committee, colleague, doctoral student, reviewer, or critic. Authors writing for experts, on the other hand, by some reverse compulsion tend to creep toward treating the expert reader as a neophyte. Keeping the real reader firmly in mind requires mindfulness and self-discipline.

Who is your true audience? In the case of introductory college textbooks, the real reader might be eighteen or nineteen years old, semi-permanently away from home for the first time, heavily invested in peer culture, and not yet transformed from late adolescence into adulthood. This reader has not declared a major, is uncertain about career options, and is not, for now, planning to enter your field or follow in your footsteps. Probably your textbook is this student's first substantive exposure to your specialty. This reader also is naive in the sense that he or she has few assumptions about your subject and little direct experience with it; might harbor misconceptions; does not recognize the big names you cite; and is not aware of the in-group issues, controversies, histories, personalities, debates, agendas, and nuances that rivet the attention of professionals in your field.

This student brings few or many skills to the classroom, depending on background and preparation at the secondary level. He or she might be in a two-year college, a technical school, a small private four-year college, an adult education night school, or a large state university—wherever your course is taught. Regardless of preparation, your undergraduate readers are still developing reading comprehension skills and critical thinking skills. They are still learning to distinguish fact from opinion and to evaluate evidence. They still tend to treat constructs as real, and they are still concrete thinkers (Piaget aside), who need concrete examples to grasp abstractions. Most important, few of these students have learned to question what they read.

Thus, on unfamiliar ground, your undergraduate readers, however smart, often struggle to construct meaning from text. The majority will not recognize irony, for instance, at least not your idea of it. Nor will they distinguish well among irony, sarcasm, cynicism, humor, sexual innuendo, and opinion in a textbook on French composition, neurophysiology, sociolinguistics, or political science. Irony, sarcasm, cynicism, and sexual innuendo especially have no place in textbook writing. Authors of textbooks at any educational level need to provide straightforward, unnuanced, expository prose.

Avoiding Undeclared Bias

Your introductory audience also is diverse. Nationally, at least a third of your readership will be members of racial, ethnic, religious, and language minority groups. As many as ten percent will be students with disabilities and another ten percent will be senior citizens. As many as half will come from single-parent, blended, and low-income inner-city and rural families. And more than half will be women. Textbook authors, most often in the past white males in middle age from comparatively affluent suburban backgrounds, easily forget these facts about their readers, which is why editors remain constantly vigilant about political correctness.

Political Correctness and the Mainstream Text

Political correctness is not about politics, nor is it necessarily about making books politically neutral. In textbook publishing, the term "politically correct" is a borrowed euphemism for language that does not offend readers who happen to be members of minority groups, to have disabilities, to be elderly, to come from economically disadvantaged environments, or to be female, etc. Condescension toward the young or inexperienced also is taboo. Some authors have disdain for publishers' concerns about political correctness. However, it makes a good deal of practical sense not to offend your intended reader if you can avoid it. An offended reader will stop reading—will not learn from you. In addition, your publisher will be handicapped in attempting to sell your book successfully.

Guidelines for making your textbook culture- and gender-fair are presented below, and there are many resources for writers on this subject. The classic source is *The Handbook of Nonsexist Writing: For Writers, Editors and Speakers,* 2nd edition (Lippincott 1988) by Casey Miller and Kate Swift. Be aware, however, that rules and labels are constantly changing in the world of political correctness. Check with your editor about this as well as about house style preferences in the naming of social aggregates, attributes, and groups.

Guidelines for Making Your Textbook Culture- and Gender-Fair

- Balance your representation of people, places, and activities so that all your readers can identify with your textbook examples.
- Use examples that relate to the prior experience or future expectations of all your potential readers.

- Include ethnically diverse given names and both males and females in examples.
- Scrupulously avoid all stereotypes, unless stereotyping is itself the subject of discourse.
- Use nonsexist language, including occupational designations.
- Use "he or she" and "his or her," etc., rather than shortcuts such as "he/she," "s/he," or "him- or herself." Alternating sexes in examples, such that an example about "Fred" is followed by an example about "Becky," and so on, as in the naming of hurricanes, may seem fair, but this strategy confuses readers.
- Use formally correct names and labels for categories or aggregates of people, especially racial and ethnic designations, and for groups and organizations.
- Use "people first" language for individuals with disabilities (e.g., "students with mental retardation," "child with hearing impairment," etc.)
- Refer to "low-income" vs. "poor" or "disadvantaged" people or groups, unless the subject of discourse is poverty or "the poor."

Unfortunately, political correctness sometimes can extend to matters involving (a) reality and (b) the truth, and in these matters concerns about censorship can be quite valid. In textbooks the Vietnam War was for years not a "war" but a "police action," for instance; publishers only recently gave up insisting on referring to "the United States" versus "America" on grounds of actual political geography; and after September 11, 2001, sympathetic or self-critical responses to terrorism are, for better or worse, not especially welcome. A survery of schoolbooks through time reveals racist moralizing in McGuffey's Readers of the 19th century and political chauvinism in early-twentieth-century editions of Muzzy's *American History*. There are countless other examples. Textbooks enter an already made world that changes, and publishing as a social institution is no less influenced by political and economic factors than other social institutions, such as the family, education, or medicine. As a textbook author of your time and place, it is up to you, your editor, and your publisher to decide where to draw the line regarding political correctness.

Pitfalls of Unintended Bias and Unwarranted Assumptions

As simple and sensible as ideas about political correctness and the guidelines above may seem, authors frequently violate them, usually unintentionally. Instances of insensitivity are not always obvious. In the following examples from college textbooks, which shall remain anonymous, put yourself in the place of any intended reader. How might you feel about the passages? How might you feel if the passages described you (or did not describe you)? How might you feel toward learning the subjects of these passages?

Example A: Suppose a person jumps from the top of the Sears Tower in Chicago. The scientific law of gravity leaves him little choice: He will fall swiftly to the ground, most likely to his death. However, should he choose to equip himself with a parachute, he would foil the law of gravity by exploiting other laws of physics.

Example B: The essential characteristic of physical experience is the abstraction of the physical properties of objects encountered in the environment. For example, by setting a spinnaker, playing the oboe, or cultivating freesias, one comes to know that spinnakers are "billowy," oboes are "reedy," and freesias smell "sweet."

Example C: Restricted language codes are associated with short, simple, and grammatically uncomplicated sentences, which are usually devoted to actions and things in specific contexts. Language codes have a strong correlation with parenting styles, with restricted language codes being more characteristic of authoritarian, power-centered families or neglecting, ignoring families. In such families questions are rarely asked. Children from this type of language environment are behind when they enter school and their deficit grows as they continue through school. Elaborated language codes, on the other hand, are most often found in middle- and upper-class, educated families. Parents who exhibit elaborated language codes tend to socialize their children. Speech is used for communication and discussion when children are asked to comply with parental wishes, not as an element of control.

In Example A, personhood involves being male, knowledge of a specific cultural landmark is assumed, and the scenario evokes an image of suicide. In Example B, the assumption that readers have the kind of background and social environment that would have enabled them to experience spinnakers, oboes, and freesias is unwarranted. Example C is even more classist and by extension racist. Lower- and working-class families are authoritarian or neglecting; they do not have elaborated language and do not socialize their children! In addition, naive readers might not notice or understand the significance of the fact that passage C is undocumented. Source citations, in addition to their other functions, are important clues for readers' reasoned judgments about what you are saying and what you are telling them to think.

The Place of Ideology

Unlike different theoretical perspectives in your academic discipline, political ideologies have no place in introductory textbooks unless they are themselves the subject of discourse or are presented in a balanced way. Contrary to critics' complaints, this does not mean that authors must avoid taking a stand on issues, only that they must refrain from doing so secretly, claiming that theirs is the only stand, or misrepresenting other stands.

If your liberalism, conservatism, Marxism, feminism, deism, positivism, existentialism, or other "ism" unavoidably informs (or contaminates) your content, it is your duty to declare it. Depending on the level of investment in your textbook, your publisher may prevail upon you to eliminate the need for a declaration of this kind, because it inevitably shrinks the market for your book and reduces sales. Even with only a particular single-focus theoretical perspective, you risk becoming the author of a niche book, more so if you are authoring an introductory undergraduate textbook. Niche books may not earn enough to be revised (and to sales reps the label "niche" can be a kiss of death—realistically, they won't want to spend a lot of time trying to sell a niche book). Besides, how can readers taking their first college-level course in your subject possibly be in a position to detect your stance on their own, to compare and contrast it with other stances, and to evaluate critically what you are asking them to believe? On both mercantile and moral grounds, therefore, authors must be mindful of inappropriate ideological biases in instructional materials.

In many ways, then, understanding your readership and avoiding undeclared bias is more complex than you might expect. "Respect your audience and meet their needs as learners" is the prime directive. If you find you have difficulty remaining mindful of your readers and their needs, take a snapshot of your students or a class in which your book might become the assigned text. Mount the picture on your computer monitor and glance at it as you draft. See if you can develop a liking for those students and sympathy for their individual journeys to enlightenment. Write for them.

Writing to Reading Level

Your vocabulary, sentence length, sentence construction, paragraph length, and level of conceptual abstraction determine the reading level of your book. Other commonly used terms for "reading level" are "cognitive level," "comprehension level," and "difficulty level." In elementary and secondary textbooks, various mathematical formulae are applied to determine reading levels, which are critical for successful adoption by state-run textbook adoption committees. In college publishing, however, tests of reading level usually are commissioned only when the publisher needs to prove that a book is too far above or below reading level for the course for which it is intended. As a rule of thumb, introductory undergraduate textbooks should be written at a grade 12 level; the reader is a high school graduate.

A system commonly used for checking post-secondary reading level is the Fry Readability Formula, which is readily available for free online. For example, see **http://school.discovery.com/schrockguide/fry/fry.html**. Your wordprocessing program probably also will calculate readability based on the statistics it tracks on the number of pages, words, characters, paragraphs, and lines in your chapter files. This function usually is an option in the spelling and grammar check utility. Note, however, that wordprocessing programs use different calculi, such as the Flesch scale (general), the Flesch-Kincaid (grade school), and the Coleman-Liau or the Bormuth scales, which both use only word length and sentence length to determine a grade level and so are not optimal for calculating readability in college textbooks.

If you find that your reading level is too high, the following rules of thumb will help you improve readability without compromising content.

Rules of Thumb for Improving Readability

- Avoid strings of polysyllabic words.
- Reduce sentence length. (Using active voice automatically reduces the number of words in a sentence.)
- Avoid interrupting compound verb forms—including infinitive phrases—with adverbs.
- Keep the verb as near as possible to its subject. Keep the object as near as possible to its verb.
- Eliminate unnecessary prepositional and appositive phrases.
- Eliminate unnecessary nonrestrictive (usually relative) clauses (e.g., large dogs, not dogs that are large in nature).
- Break long compound and complex sentences into separate sentences. Keep sentences that are both compound and complex to a minimum.
- Avoid stringing together independent clauses with colons, semicolons, or dashes.
- Do not place key content in parenthetical expressions, and eliminate parenthetical asides.
- Break long blocks of narrative text into separate shorter paragraphs.
- Increase the number of subheadings and reword them to guide reading comprehension.
- Add clear transitions between paragraphs and sections of text.
- Define technical terms fully in narrative context where they first appear.
- Operationalize concepts by giving concise concrete examples.

Principles of Reading Comprehension

Some authors mistake simple straightforward language and sentences of modest length for accessible reading. They oversimplify language in hopes that this will make their thought more comprehensible. However, writing for readability does not involve this kind of "dumbing down." Contrary to popular misconception, your college textbook publisher hopes that you are not writing *Anthropology for Dummies* or *Physics Made Easy as Pie*. Enriched vocabulary and suitable complexity actually are desirable in a college textbook. These characteristics usually are not the problem in reading comprehension, especially when a glossary is provided. What matters in reading comprehension is your progression of thought, connections between one thought and the next, and support of abstractions using concrete examples. Your heuristic devices, intellectual assumptions, undefined jargon, unsupported general-izations, and leaps of logic (or of faith) leave readers in the dust.

Consider the reading levels of the following fair-use excerpts from (unnamed) introductory college textbooks. Which is easier both to read and to comprehend, and why?

Example A: Readability

The table indicates a difference of 1.8 percentage points between the proportion of the Indian population living in urban places in 1972 and 1980, a span of eight years. Given this fact, it may be surprising to learn that there is great concern over urban growth in India, while there is not much concern in Spain where the urban population shows nearly 7 percentage points difference between 1972 and 1980. To understand the concern over the Indian rate, one has only to look at the actual numbers involved. In the eight years between 1972 and 1978, through migration *and* natural increase, India increased its total number of urbanites by over thirty-one and a half million people (note that in contrast to indus-trializing Europe, where urban growth was typically solely the product of migration, Third World cities were experiencing additional growth due to an excess of births over deaths within the urban population). The number of *new* urbanites in India in the span of those eight years was just five million less than the *total* population of Spain in 1978. [Paragraph continues for another 7 sentences.]

Example B: Readability

Hypothermia is arbitrarily defined in humans as a condition in which the core temperature of the body falls below 35° C. It is a major cause of death in boating accidents, in mountaineering and polar expeditions, and in aged people living in cold climates in homes with no central heating. Table 12.2 lists the symptoms asso-ciated with various levels of hypothermia. It illustrates two impor-tant points. The first is that manifestations of cerebral dysfunction (i.e., apathy, amnesia, confusion, poor judgment, and hallucina-tions) are among the earliest overt signs of hypothermia as the temperature of the body core drops. As a result, the idiosyncratic behavior of people under dangerously frigid conditions often increases the hazardousness of the situation. The second point is that humans can recover from core temperatures below 27° C, although they appear to be dead at such temperatures, with no detectable heart beat, respiration, or EEG (e.g., Niazi & Lewis, 1958). The only certain sign of death in hypothermia is failure to recover when warmed (Lloyd, 1986). [Paragraph ends.]

You no doubt chose Example B as the easier text to read and comprehend. It starts with a definition, provides a concrete context for learning about the subject, and systematically and without digression explains the behavioral significance of the data in the table, thus linking the subject to the course. At the same time the passage retains an enriched vocabulary with many multisyllabic descriptive and technical words. The subject is as equally complex as the passage on India's urbanization, yet easier to acquire.

Example A, in contrast, contains only one vaguely interesting word (*urbanites*), yet makes a hash of the reader's effort to construct meaning. For example, the author assumes that the reader will understand what is meant by the conventions of the first sentence, despite the incorrect grammar, and that the significance of a span of eight years will be understood implicitly (i.e., the reader will realize that this is a significantly long or short time). For readability, the first sentences could have been better stated as follows:

The table indicates a 1.8 percentage increase in the proportion of the Indian population living in cities between 1972 and 1980. This percentage increase is remarkable for the comparatively (short) (long) span of eight years.

Example A goes on to say prematurely, "Given this fact," before any fact has been made clear. The author then immediately introduces a comparison between India and Spain, suggesting we might be surprised. But we are baffled. Why Spain? In what way is Spain comparable to India? Why not Italy or Pakistan? Then we are asked to believe that urbanization in Spain is not so great a concern as urbanization in India, despite the fact that Spain's rate of urbanization is so much greater than India's.

At the very next sentence, most readers will stop struggling with text and will study the table instead or will skip to the next paragraph, for in the next sentence the span of "eight" years changes from "1972-1980" to "1972-1978"! Readers who try to read on may start to feel stupid as they come to the long digression in parentheses (which obliquely suggests the point of the comparison between India and Spain) and the italicized words *and, new,* and *total.* These words have been singled out for emphasis, and the author assumes emphasis alone will cue readers as to significance. Pondering that significance, an intelligent reader might wonder why the text is making such a big deal of a simple matter of scale. Why should we be surprised if a pond concentrates proportionally more fish through natural increase and migration than does an ocean? But what reader has the time and level of commitment to extract or construct meaning from page after page of abstruse text?

The proof is in the learning, and learning is what it is all about. If you think now about what you read, you will find that you remember more about hypothermia than about urbanization in India.

What Is Clarity?

Part of the reason that Example A was difficult to read and comprehend is that it lacked clarity of expression. Clarity is clearness; there is no doubt as to what is being said and what is meant by it. Writing for clarity in exposition, like writing for readability, also does not involve "dumbing down." It involves crafting your writing style. As Strunk and White pointed out so famously so long ago, being clear, coherent, and concise (the three Cs) are the foundations of good writing. Here are some avoidable writing problems that interfere with clarity.

What Makes Writing "Not Clear"?

- Wordiness
- Convoluted sentence structure in which the subject, verb, and predicate are separated by too many words, phrases, and clauses
- Overuse of passive voice, forms of the verb be
- Overuse of the past perfect and conditional tenses (e.g., had had, would have had)
- Lack of grammatical agreement in tense and number
- Inappropriate uses of personal and relative pronouns; unclear referents for pronouns
- Lack of transitions
- Lack of concrete examples or illustrations
- Archaic and formal usages unrelated to the purpose of exposition
- Undefined or unnecessary jargon
- Skipped steps in logical development, progression of ideas, or cause and effect
- Statements of the obvious, causing readers to doubt their comprehension
- A focus on accuracy before basic comprehension has been achieved, e.g., premature presentation of alternatives, disclaimers, and exceptions
- Digression
- Repetition or redundancy

If you find you tend to write above or beyond the reading comprehension level of your audience, as an alternative to using readability analyses, enlist the aid of one or more student readers. Give them copies of a chapter of your manuscript and ask them to mark any passages they find are "Not Clear." Your analysis of those passages should help you identify and overcome patterns of exposition that reduce comprehension and learning rate in your readers. Also keep in mind, by the way, that when editors mark passages "Not Clear," they are basing their judgments on the perceived needs of your audience.

Writing Well

Writing well is discussed further in Chapter 11, where you will find a list of selected references on academic writing and editing. In composition all good writing for any audience at any educational level has the same basic qualities, including clarity, concision, unity, coherence, and emphasis. Just as poor writing habits and habits of thought compromise clarity, wordiness compromises concision.

What Is Wordiness?

Wordiness is the habitual practice of using more words than are necessary to convey information or an idea or a feeling. Passive constructions and optional adjectives, adverbs, and prepositional phrases cause the greatest offense. In addition, wordiness comes from uncertainty and self-regard. That is, authors tend to use more words when they are unsure of the information they are attempting to convey, or the points they are trying to make, or their efficacy in communicating on the page. Self-regarding authors, who like to hear themselves talk and extemporize on the page, also use more words. Whatever the reason for it, wordiness is to be scrupulously avoided. However careful or fascinating you believe you are in your writing, in reality your wordiness bores readers to death and interferes with their learning. Consider the following unedited passage for a college textbook on criminal justice.

Example of Wordiness:

Rehabilitation and restorative justice are more contemporary philosophies defining the purpose of criminal sanctions. Rehabilitation and restorative justice philosophies argue that criminal sanctions should provide for a "cure" of the criminality of the offender. The rehabilitation model is often referred to as the medical model in that it views criminality as a "disease" to be "cured." Rehabilitation of the offender is considered to be impossible by some. For those who believe that it is possible to rehabilitate the offender through rehabilitation and restorative justice models the most common approaches involve psychology, the biological/medical approach, self-esteem treatment, and programs aimed at developing ethical values and work skills.

Here is the same passage with 35 fewer words. Note that in "tightening" the paragraph the editor preserved, even improved, the author's intention and meaning.

Improved Version:

Rehabilitation and restoration are contemporary philosophies of obtaining justice through criminal sanctions. Rehabilitation calls for sanctions that "cure" the offender of criminality. Because criminality is seen as a disease to be cured, this model often is referred to as a medical model. Some believe that rehabilitating offenders is impossible. Others, however, believe that effective rehabilitation is possible through psychological approaches, medical treatment, self-esteem counseling, and programs promoting ethical values and work skills.

Eliminating unnecessary words and phrases helps control manuscript length as well as improve clarity in exposition. Following are some tips on eliminating wordiness.

Wordiness Elimination Guide

Example: One of the most important factors that ambiguity is caused by that is often ignored is wordiness.

1st Pass: Change the sentence to active voice.
One of the most important factors that causes ambiguity that is often ignored is wordiness.

2nd Pass: Eliminate unnecessary articles and prepositional phrases.
An important factor that causes ambiguity that is often ignored is wordiness.

3rd Pass: Eliminate unnecessary words and relative phrases and clauses, including parenthetical asides.
An important, often ignored cause of ambiguity is wordiness.

4th Pass: Delete additional adjectives or adjectival forms that do not directly advance the purpose or point of the sentence.
An often ignored cause of ambiguity is wordiness, OR, An important cause of ambiguity is wordiness, OR A cause of ambiguity is wordiness.

5th Pass: Change the word order so that the subject comes first, directly followed by an active verb. Isn't the following statement the point?
Wordiness causes ambiguity.

6th Pass: Beyond the sentence level, delete every sentence that does not directly support the paragraph in which it is embedded.

What Are Unity, Coherence, and Emphasis?

In addition to clarity and concision, all good expository writing exhibits unity, coherence, and emphasis. Unity is the quality of centrality and relevance, or belongingness. That is, all the paragraphs in a section relate to the purpose of that section, and all the sentences in a paragraph relate to the point set out in the paragraph's topic sentence or thesis statement. In prose, irrelevancies, tangential remarks, digressions, sudden insights, flashbacks, cosmic syntheses, and brainstorming on the page can all compromise unity.

Coherence is the quality of sequentiality and integrity, or togetherness. Sentences and paragraphs progress in a logical or natural order, flowing smoothly from one to the next while sticking together in meaning. The writing and the meanings it conveys have direction and thrust. Coherence is compromised most by lack of transitions, derailment of logic, stagnation of thought, and non sequiturs (statements that do not follow what has just been said).

Emphasis in writing is the quality of focus, interest, and control. Words, ideas, and images are subtly weighted or ranked such that the most important word, idea, or image in each sentence, paragraph, and chapter stands out. Emphasis guides the reader in constructing meaning from text by distinguishing what is to be regarded as important. Emphasis is compromised when words, ideas, and images are all given equal importance or when the reader's attention is focused inappropriately.

The above section of text, "What Are Unity, Coherence, and Emphasis?", exhibits the qualities described in it. The three paragraphs all address the same implied purpose (to define and illustrate these qualities), which is unity. The progression of thought within and between paragraphs facilitates sense making (through the repetition of a pattern of exposition), which is coherence. And the section ends with the application in this paragraph, which reinforces the emphasis introduced in the first sentence of the section. Good writers and editors evaluate writing in terms of these qualities of unity, coherence, and emphasis.

What Is Style?

The elements of style are word choices, word usages, sentence constructions, paragraph constructions, writing rules and conventions and formats, and your personal distinguishing communication values and expression of self. Read a list of the standard rules of style in English composition in the table of contents of Strunk and White, *The Elements of Style*, originally published in 1935. Read the complete 1938 edition online at **www.bartleby.com/141/.** You also may read the table of contents of the Longman 4th edition of Strunk and White at **www.ablongman.com/professional/catalog/academic/**

Keep in mind, however, that many elements of style are arbitrary conventions and matters of taste. These vary among publishing houses and change over time. Items in a series may or may not require a comma before the last item, for instance; certain abbreviations may or may not be allowed, and so on. Rules that you learned in school (and disobeyed only at your peril) may no longer apply, so it serves to be flexible on matters of style.

Ask your editor about "house style"—the publisher's style guidelines. You might find it helpful to consult the house style sheet as you draft. The copyeditor assigned to vet your manuscript will work to these guidelines as well. House styles are built from manuals of editorial style based on the publisher's list needs, publishing experience, and idiosyncrasies of powerful editors. Preferences include simple matters, such as capitalization and punctuation, and larger decisions, such as using endnotes rather than footnotes. You can save yourself, any coauthors, your editors, and the people who will produce your book a great deal of anguish by choosing and consistently using one agreed-on style.

As mentioned at the beginning of this chapter, editorial styles most commonly used in college textbooks are the Modern Language Association (MLA) style, the American Psychological Association (APA) style, Council of Biology Editors (CBE) style, and Chicago style (The Chicago Manual of Style), and several others. These styles differ mainly in their treatment of headings, source citations, notes, references, bibliographies, and technical notational or symbol systems used in the respective disciplines.

Any college handbook on English composition will contain information on these styles for documenting research, but the best source is the current style manual for your discipline. You also can find most style guides online. For your convenience the chapter appendix lists the standard editorial style manuals used in academic and higher education writing and where they reside online.

In both the broad and the narrow sense, then, your style is a key ingredient in reaching your true audience and accomplishing your mission in writing a textbook. The other, closely related, key ingredient is your authorial voice, the subject of the next chapter.

Appendix: Academic Style Manuals, by Discipline

Anthropology
The American Anthropological Association uses *The Chicago Manual of Style* and *Merriam-Webster's Collegiate Dictionary* (10th edition, 2000).
> Official web site: **www.aaanet.org/pubs/style_guide.htm**
> Explanatory web site: **www.usd.edu/anth/handbook/bib.htm**

Biology
Council of Biology Editors. *CBE Style Manual: A Guide for Authors, Editors, and Publishers in the Biological Sciences*. Washington: American Chemical Society, 1986.
> Official web site: **www.councilscienceeditors.org/**
> Explanatory web site:
> **www.lib.ohio-state.edu/guides/cbegd.html**

Chemistry
American Chemical Society. *The ACS Style Guide: A Manual for Authors and Editors*. Washington: American Chemical Society, 1986.
> Official web site: **pubs.acs.org**
> Explanatory web site: **pubs.acs.org/books/references.shtml**

Chicago Style (used in many disciplines)
The Chicago Manual of Style. 14th ed. Chicago: University of Chicago Press, 1993.
> Official web site: **www.chicagomanualofstyle.org/cmosfaq.html**
> Explanatory web site:
> **www.wisc.edu/writing/Handbook/DocChicago.html**

Engineering
Institute of Electrical and Electronics Engineers. *Information for IEEE Transactions and Journal Authors*. New York: IEEE, 1989.
> Official web site: **www.pubs.asce.org/authors/index.html**

English (and some disciplines in the humanities)
Gibaldi, Joseph. *MLA Style Manual and Guide to Scholarly Publishing*. 2nd ed. New York: The Modern Language Association of America, 1998.
Gibaldi, Joseph. *MLA Handbook for Writers of Research Papers, Theses and Dissertations*. 5th ed. New York: The Modern Language Association, 1995.
> Official web site: **www.mla.org**
> Explanatory web site:
> **owl.english.purdue.edu/handouts/research/r_mla.html**

Geology

Bates, Robert L., Rex Buchanan, and Marla Adkins-Heljeson, eds. *Geowriting: A Guide to Writing, Editing, and Printing in Earth Science*. 5th ed. Alexandria, VA: Amer. Geological Inst., 1995.

United States Geological Survey. *Suggestions to Authors of the Reports of the United States Geological Survey*. 7th ed. Washington: GPO, 1991.

> Official web site: **www.usgs.gov/**
> Explanatory web site: **www.agu.org/pubs/contrib.html**

Government

Gapner, Diane L., and Diane H. Smith. *The Complete Guide to Citing Government Information Resources: A Manual for Writers and Librarians*. Rev. ed. Bethesda: Congressional Information Service, 1993.

> Explanatory web site:
> **exlibris.memphis.edu/govpubs/citeweb.htm**

History

Gray, Wood. *Historian's Handbook: A Key to the Study and Writing of History*. 2nd ed. Boston: Houghton Mifflin, 1991. Most historians use either Chicago style or Turabian style.

> Official web site: **www.chicagomanualofstyle.org/cmosfaq.html**
> Explanatory web site:
> **www.bedfordstmartins.com/hacker/resdoc/history/**
> **bibliography.htm**

Information Sciences and Computer Science

American National Standard for Information Sciences. Scientific and Technical Reports: Organization, Preparation, and Production. New York: ANSI, 1987.

> Official web site: **www.computer.org/author/style/cs-style.htm**
> Explanatory web site:
> **www.computer.org/author/style/refer.htm**

Journalism

Goldstein, Norm (ed) and Associated Press Staff. *The Associated Press Stylebook and Briefing on Media Law*. Cambridge, MA: Perseus Books, 2000.

UPI Stylebook: *The Authoritative Handbook for Writers, Editors & News Directors*. 3rd ed. Lincolnwood, IL: National Textbook Company, 1992.

> Official web site: **www.ap.org**
> Explanatory web site:
> **www.usu.edu/~communic/faculty/sweeney/ap.htm**

Law and Legal Studies

The Bluebook : A Uniform System of Citation. 16th ed. Cambridge, MA: Harvard Law Review Association, 1996.

Official web site: **www.legalbluebook.com/**
Explanatory web site: **www.law.cornell.edu/citation/**

Linguistics
Linguistic Society of America. *LSA Bulletin*, December issue (annually).
Official web site: **www.lsadc.org/web2/dec99bull/langstyl.html**

Mathematics
American Mathematical Society. *Manual for Authors of Mathematical Papers*. 8th
ed. Providence, RI: American Mathematical Society, 1990.
Official web site: **www.ams.org**

Management
American Management Association. *The AMA Style Guide for Business Writing*.
New York: AMACOM, 1996.
Official web site:
www.amanet.org/books/catalog/0814402976.htm

Medicine
American Medical Association. *AMA Manual of Style*. 8th ed. Chicago:
American Medical Association, 1990.
Official web site: **www.ama-assn.org/**
Explanatory web site:
healthlinks.washington.edu/hsl/styleguides/ama.html

Physics
American Institute of Physics. *Style Manual for Guidelines in the Preparation of
Papers*. 4th ed. New York: American Institute of Physics, 1990.
Official web site:**www.aip.org/pubservs/style/4thed/toc.html**
(download the manual free of charge)

Psychology (and other social sciences)
American Psychological Association. *Publication Manual of the American
Psychological Association*. 5th ed. Washington: American Psychological
Association, 2001.
Official web site: **www.apastyle.org/index.html**
Explanatory web site:
owl.english.purdue.edu/handouts/research/r_apa.html

Political Science
American Political Science Association Committee on Publications. *The Style
Manual for Political Science*. Washington, DC: American Political Science
Association, 2002.
Official web site: **www.apsanet.org/**

Explanatory web site:
www.wisc.edu/writing/Handbook/DocAPSA.html

Sociology
American Sociological Association. *ASA Style Guide*. Washington, DC:
American Sociological Association, 1997.
> Official web site: **www.asanet.org/pubs/style.html**
> Explanatory web site:
> **owl.english.purdue.edu/handouts/research/r_docsocio.html**

Turabian Style
Kate Turabian's A Manual for Writers of Term Papers, Theses, and Dissertations.
Chicago: University of Chicago Press, 1996.
> Explanatory web site:
> **www.lib.usm.edu/~instruct/guides/turabian.html**

Source: Adapted from Erin Karper, June 2001. Updated May 2002.
(**owl.english.purdue.edu/research/r_docsources.html**).
Used with permission.

Establish an Effective Authorial Voice

An authorial voice is achieved through (1) your attitudes toward your subject as revealed in the language you use and your carefully disclosed philosophical or political orientations; (2) your attitudes toward the reader as revealed in the style and tone you use; and (3) elements of your personality that inevitably leak through your prose. Voice is tricky. If voice is missing, your textbook is likely to fail. If readers are put off by the voice, it will fail faster.

Reflecting on Your Voice

As you read in Chapter 5, a common complaint is that textbook writing can go overboard in avoiding offending or being too difficult for anyone, with the result that a textbook lacks a true authorial voice. Exposition becomes anonymous, noncommittal, sanitized. However, the best textbooks are not, need not, and should not be "soulless and bland." They do have distinctive authorial voices. A person and a teacher, not just an expert, is talking to us. Who are you as a person and a teacher? Who will you be to your readers? To begin with, how do you feel about what you are saying?

Your Attitudes Toward Your Subject

A surprising number of authors write as if they were bored by their subject. An effective authorial voice uses language that conveys respect for the subject, focuses attention on it, arouses curiosity about it, and generates excitement for learning it. Education research supports the importance of these ingredients in preparing readers to "listen and learn." Compare the following paragraphs from two world history texts introducing chapters on the scientific revolution, for instance. Which one would you prefer to read? Why?

Sample Voice A:

The foremost cause of the change in world view was the scientific revolution. Modern science crystallized in the seventeenth century. Whereas science had been secondary and subordinate in medieval intellectual life, it became independent and even primary for many educated people in the eighteenth century.

Sample Voice B:

The sixteenth and seventeenth centuries witnessed a sweeping change in the scientific view of the universe. An earth-centered picture of the universe gave way to one in which the earth was only another planet orbiting about the sun. The sun itself became one of millions of stars. This transformation of humankind's perception of its place in the larger scheme of things led to a vast rethinking of moral and religious matters as well as of scientific theory.

Both samples are perfectly clear, but Sample B presents a more positive attitude toward the subject, as the following comparison shows:

	Sample A:	Sample B:
Verb Forms	was	witnessed
	crystallized	gave way
	had been	became
	became	led to
Adjectives	foremost	sweeping
	subordinate	earth-centered
	secondary	larger
	intellectual	vast
	primary	moral
	independent	religious
	educated	scientific
Key Nouns	cause	change
	change	universe
	world view	picture
	science	earth
	life	planet
	people	sun
		stars
		transformation
		humankind
		perception
		place
		scheme
		rethinking
		matters
		theory

You undoubtedly chose Sample B. Sample B contains more interesting verbs in an active rather than a passive voice (*witnessed* vs. *was*). Sample B also provides adjectives that are distinctly more compelling; that is, you would probably prefer to read about something that is *sweeping* and *earth-centered* rather than about something that is *foremost* and *subordinate*. Sample B also contains a number of engaging concrete nouns (*planet, sun,* etc.) in contrast to Sample A's more abstract nouns.

Consider also the subtle differences in attitude toward the subject that are revealed in the language. Sample A interprets the subject as *science,* which is reinforced through the use of the pronoun *it. Crystallized* conveys the idea that science was in a muddle until the scientific revolution made it right. The relevance of science is confined to "medieval intellectual life" and "educated people." The net effect is stuffiness. The author of Sample A seems to want us to feel inferior to the subject.

In Sample B, on the other hand, relevance is extended to "humankind's perception of its place in the larger scheme of things." Sample B interprets the subject as a "change." *Witnessed* focuses attention on the impact of the change. Sample B further identifies knowledge of planets and stars as the basis of the change. The author of Sample B seems to want us to feel a bit in awe of the subject, the experience of which we are being let in on. We can feel connected to the subject, as we are a part of this universe.

Your Philosophical and Political Orientations

Philosophical orientation consists of your beliefs and values concerning your subject, including your professional judgments and personal political, religious, or ideological biases. These beliefs and values come though in subtle ways in your writing, much like the fabled subliminal images and messages in advertising. Like truth in advertising, intellectual honesty is an entitlement of the consumer.

Intellectual honesty requires including ideas with which you do not agree. Authors of an introductory psychology textbook who reject Freud must nevertheless discuss Freud and his followers in their book and must manage to do so evenhandedly. Intellectual honesty is expressed not in avoiding a point of view but in clearly identifying a point of view for what it is, perhaps identifying strengths and weaknesses of that view, and providing information about the existence of other points of view, all the time using fair, value-free language. "Value-free" does not mean that you must not convey a point of view, simply that your point of view must be expressed openly and defended, and that readers must be allowed to evaluate it for themselves.

As mentioned in Chapter 5, an undergraduate introductory textbook also is not the place for liberal, conservative, radical, reactionary, or feminist posturing, grandstanding, or proselytizing. Achieving balance and objectivity in exposition is easier said than done, however. In writing, as in life, honesty and authenticity are a struggle.

Let us continue with the example from world history.

Sample Voice A:
The emergence of modern science was a development of tremendous long-term significance. A noted historian has even said that the scientific revolution of the late sixteenth and seventeenth cen-

turies 'outshines everything since the rise of Christianity and reduces the Renaissance and Reformation to the rank of mere episodes, mere internal displacements within the system of medieval Christendom.' The scientific revolution was 'the real origin both of the modern world and the modern mentality.'[1] This statement is an exaggeration, but not much of one. Of all the great civilizations, only that of the West developed modern science. It was with the scientific revolution that Western society began to acquire its most distinctive traits.

Sample Voice B:
The process by which this new view of the universe and of scientific knowledge came to be established is normally termed the 'Scientific Revolution.' However, care must be taken in the use of this metaphor. The word revolution normally denotes fairly rapid changes in the political world, involving large numbers of people. The Scientific Revolution was not rapid, nor did it involve more than a few hundred human beings. It was a complex movement with many false starts and many brilliant people with wrong as well as useful ideas. However, the ultimate result of this transformation of thought revolutionized the manner in which Europeans thought about physical nature and themselves. This new outlook would later be exported to every other major world civilization.

Sample A is full of value statements. Author A says that the subject is "tremendous" and that we don't have to take Author A's word for it, because others, such as the footnoted historian, claim that the subject is even more important than that, that it "outshines everything since [Christ]." Author A doesn't buy this entirely; it's a slight exaggeration. In the last two sentences, Author A concludes that we should value the subject because it was unique to Western civilization—a conservative, somewhat Eurocentric, view. It is important to Author A that we correctly interpret the degree of importance of the subject. Meanwhile, the material reveals (a) a belief in the absolute ranking of historical events in terms of importance, and (b) the value judgment that the rise of Christianity should receive the highest rank. The quoted historian also has a metaphysical stance (defining a selected origin as the "real" one) and assumes that the notion of a "modern mentality" has validity as a construct.

In the second sample, Author B is not so much concerned with our interpretation of the subject's importance as with our definition of it, our conceptualization. The name for the subject is a metaphor, Author B says, and we should value accuracy in our use of metaphors. The subject's importance is qualified in terms of the rate of change, the number of people involved, the degree of complexity, and the degree of continuity. The qualifiers further encapsulate the views that being brilliant doesn't make you right and that right ideas are ones that are useful. Author B offers a liberal conclusion that the metaphor is appropriate because the subject resulted in a new outlook, and that we should value the subject because it affected not only Europeans but the world.

Few readers analyze what they read in this critical way, however. They simply acquire your undeclared assumptions and attitudes toward the subject. This fact imparts to you a grave responsibility.

What Is Tone?

The stinginess or stuffiness of Sample A in the history examples, and the generousness or openness of Sample B, are aspects of tone. Tone refers to the quality of voice that reflects how an author feels about the subject and the reader. Thus, tone is your affective response as revealed through the words and phrases you choose. These choices have a cumulative and subtle psychological net effect on readers. Consider, for example, these examples of positive and negative tones.

Examples of Positive and Negative Tone

open	stuffy
respectful	disparaging
earnest	insincere
honest	defensive
enthusiastic	neutral
down to earth	imperial
warm	cold
pleasant	cranky
forthright	sneaky
excited	bored
friendly	mean-spirited
intimate	hostile

Viewed this way, few authors would consciously choose a negative tone. However, negativity can creep into the writing of authors who are inwardly angry or resentful or have private agenda. Be aware that regardless of subject matter, any audience at any age and level of educational attainment is more motivated to read and learn text that has a positive tone.

Your Attitudes Toward the Reader

Your tone and the language you use should convey respect for your audience as well as for your subject. Authors sometimes convey negative expectations of readers or imply that readers are deficient, ignorant, immature, inexperienced, inferior, stupid, dumb, lazy, repulsive, pathetic, helpless, or irrelevant. Other messages are that readers need the author to enlighten them; to parent, counsel, patronize, chastise, or reform them; to put them in their place, show them a thing or two, or trick them into learning something. Authors who convey these negative messages often do so unintentionally.

The most common faults in authorial tone involve language that is avuncular and gratuitous, seconded by the frosty, stern, or authoritarian voice of the taskmaster. Third is the neutral or "pure" voice, devoid of affect—the android's synthesized voice. Fourth is the manipulative voice of the propagandist or spinmaster. The fifth most common fault is ambivalence toward the audience, at times championing the readers and at times criticizing them. You may recognize this fifth fault as a tendency of the voice of this book—and of editors in general. The chapter Appendix attempts to offer examples of "bad-voice" problems in the form of archetypes.

Your Personality or Persona

Because of its duration and intensity, writing a textbook is unavoidably a self-defining endeavor. Authors working with development editors sometimes feel a bit exposed. In any case, authors often unintentionally reveal interesting self-concepts and personal character traits in their writing. "I am omniscient" or "I am brilliant" is the commonest message. "I'm plain folks just like you" or "I'm just a good ole boy" are close seconds.

Intellectual arrogance, however subtle, tips us off to authors who regard themselves as brilliant (and who among us does not?). Our narratives might contain self-congratulatory nuggets, arguments or dialectics with the self, highly competitive judgments of others, self-conscious claims of authority, self-promotion, self-justification, and summary condemnations of others' views or works. "Of course," "Obviously," "In fact," "Clearly," and "Perhaps," are identifying markers, along with prodigious use of jargon.

Often, textbooks with ego also are peppered with "I" and "we," sometimes in the form of "the author(s)." In some textbooks, authors' first-person accounts of their experiences or research are an asset. Authors of a textbook on archaeology who describe their most challenging digs and amazing finds, for example, might be serving their readers and mission. The problem with *we* is that usually it has too many referents, confusing the reader as to which "we" is meant—these authors, paleontologists or criminologists as a group, Americans or Westerners, or human beings in general.

In addition, the use of *we* can establish a power and control issue that distracts the reader and detracts from the instructional content. In the following excerpt, for example, the authors appropriate the information and make themselves the subject of the paragraph instead.

Example: Inappropriate (Plus Ungrammatical) Use of First Person

If multicultural education efforts are to be successful as the school accepts the growing diversity among its student body, we see a multitude of social, cultural, and educational issues that need to be addressed. We present here what we believe some of those major issues to be. As prospective teachers, we suggest that you examine these issues with us and build them into your concerns about education as you embark on your career. We no longer accept that the problems of cultural differences are so great that the school cannot respond to them. There must be a beginning and we believe it should start here with the major point we have attempted to stress in this chapter: the school we know today will become vastly different as we enter the next century.

As you can see, "we" becomes the subject of the paragraph. While the use of personal pronouns is accepted, even expected, in professional journals, "the author(s)" is not an appropriate focus for a textbook. In introductory textbooks especially, the student reader ("you") and the subject are paramount.

Achieving a Voice Through Style

Inexperienced authors who have not yet felt the copyeditor's lash often try to establish a distinctive voice through the use of colloquialisms, regionalisms, clichés, dialect, or slang, often in the mistaken belief that a "Prairie Home Companion" presentation makes their textbook more accessible. In exposition these usages cannot substitute for authorial voice, however, and in most contexts constitute bad style as well. Distinctive authorial voices come through in subtle choices among words and expressions that cumulatively create an impression of the author as a person and as a teacher in the reader's mind. Following are three passages from different older textbooks on the same subject, suggesting the diversity, subtlety, range, and effectiveness of authors' voices.

Example: Voice A

As an educational reform movement, multicultural education seeks to change the effects described above. Exactly *how* to do this is the topic of heated debate. Should education emphasize the similarities *or* the differences among people? Some reformers urge schools to focus on improving human relations so that students will learn to respect *all* people. Other educators press for in-depth studies of various racial and ethnic groups as part of the curriculum. But critics believe this is not enough. They want to *infuse* the entire curriculum with material written by and about minority group members. Still another approach to multicultural education is to *transform* the entire educational system so that students learn to be politically effective in reshaping society.

Voice A briefly but persuasively describes alternative approaches to addressing problems that have been presented previously. The writing conveys the feeling that the subject is important. Without going into detail the voice wants us to advance our appreciation of a complex matter by considering degrees of response to the problems. The tone is sincere and informal, even personal and warm. The use of italics (which actually is not good style) emphasizes comprehension through oral rhythms, as if this author-teacher were speaking to us directly.

Example: Voice B

General disagreements about multicultural education have followed some of the same lines as the specific arguments about Afrocentric and other minority-oriented curricula. For example, critics contend that multicultural education may divide society by emphasizing ethnic separatism rather than developing citizens who will work together to accomplish common goals.[70] Some believe that multicultural education will fragment and overload the school curriculum, reinforcing tendencies for teachers to stress memorization and regurgitation of disconnected facts and concepts.[71] Furthermore, critics argue that multicultural concerns may be misused to justify second-rate education for economically disadvantaged or minority students.[72] If "ethnic studies" programs do not make great efforts to maintain a high quality of instruction, the diplomas or degrees students receive may be viewed as second-rate.

Voice B struggles to present fairly an issue on which he or she has strong views. In this passage those views are largely conservative or negative, but perhaps the writing will go on to present the complement. The language is straightforward and precise but mildly shocking, edgy with implied harsh judgments. The tone is authoritative, hard-edged, and aggressive, and statements are supported by source citations through which this author-teacher perhaps seeks to overwhelm us. Nevertheless, although admonitory, Voice B is not about to claim that he or she has all the right answers.

Example: Voice C

Why is multicultural education so controversial? The debate about multicultural education is neither new nor faddish. It is part of the larger, continuing dialogue about the meaning of e pluribus unum. As one country composed of many states and many peoples, the nation continues to struggle to define itself. How is America to

> conceptualize and deliver a public education that is appropriate for all its people? This question arises in many forms and many languages in political forums, churches, social organizations, and schools across the country.

Voice C conveys the feeling that the subject is important but should not be taken too seriously because it is a perennially unresolved issue. The tone is inflated or passionate, depending on your point of view, and the language can be taken as pretentious or imitative of stump speeches. This author does not seem as knowledgeable about the subject as the others. This voice is easy to listen to, the prose stirring but empty.

Consider now the readers of these three passages. What relationship to the text and to the subject might they develop based on their experience of Voice A, Voice B, or Voice C? In each case how does the voice invite learning or motivate the learner to read? Most important, what would readers learn from these passages?

Integrating Coauthors' Voices and Styles

Because introductory undergraduate textbooks are by nature far-ranging, many have two or more coauthors whose overlapping areas of expertise can cover the subject adequately. Too often, however, each coauthor does things his or her own way. The author of Chapter 1 decides to underline everything that seems important, the author of Chapter 2 writes verbosely above grade level, and the author of Chapter 3 provides 25 figures and tables thinly connected by text. In addition, Chapter 1 is warm and inviting, Chapter 2 is distinctly contemptuous in tone, and Chapter 3 admits no affective response at all. The reader, meanwhile, is doomed. Random differences and mixed messages from chapter to chapter foil any attempt at coherent learning. As a result, whatever first-year sales the publisher can garner quickly slip away and the book fails, never to see royalty, reprint, or revision.

In professional circles it is common practice for a group of colleagues to put their names to a journal article authored principally by only one of their number. The order of their names in bibliographies and references rotates as each "partner" takes a turn at authoring an article, thus avoiding the lack of recognition implicit in et al. In textbook publishing, however, silent partners are rare. They include original authors who are too far into retirement to contribute or who are deceased, and new recruits to author teams who have minor or highly specialized roles in a revision. In cases of multiple authorship, therefore, integrating authoring styles is critical.

Integrating authoring styles is difficult, because authors usually have strong and unique personalities, attitudes, backgrounds, and professional agendas. The object in integration is not to bury the individual voices but to provide a consistent style and "metavoice" for the book as a whole.

There are three ways to make a metavoice: (1) The publisher hires an editor at your expense to "smooth" the book, rectifying styles and rewriting narrative as necessary, an expensive project and one that many authors find painful; (2) One of the authors on the team is chosen consensually to make a final edit of the whole manuscript for the purpose of smoothing; or (3) The authors collaborate in advance to decide the ground rules for style, format, and voice, based on the publisher's input concerning house style and the book's market. If carried out, the third option usually is best for all concerned.

Whether you are sole author or coauthor, establishing, integrating, and monitoring your authorial voice is a key to your book's instructional and commercial success. As you can see, establishing an effective authorial voice involves far more than merely expressing one's individuality and putting one's best foot forward in print. However experienced you may be as a professional and a human being, take time to reflect on yourself in your role as author.

Appendix: Some "Bad-Voice" Archetypes

UNCLE
Tip-offs: low-level ("dumbed down") language, overexplanation, over-use of personal or down-home anecdotes or homilies, oversimplified examples, the use of repetitions and refrains as in storytelling, and use of statements that go without saying.
Message to Readers: You are children (and all that being a child implies).

Example: Unlike scientific theories, intuitive theories come from personal experience. For example, you probably have an intuitive theory about crossing the street. Crossing the street is a daily event in most people's lives. I have an intuitive theory about crossing the street in downtown Boston. As Figure 1.1 shows, many cars turn onto Boylston Street from Massachusetts Avenue, the intersection I cross on my way to work. As a result, many cars occupy the space I must use. Through reflection on my experiences at the intersection, I have developed an intuitive theory that explains how I cross the street. At the heart of my theory is a hypothesis: if I make eye contact with the driver, the driver goes and I have to wait, whereas if I avoid making eye contact, the driver waits while I cross. My theory works fairly well. After all, here I am to write about it. Your intuitive theory about crossing the street must work well too, for here you are to read about it.

Possible Reader Response: Give me a break! (or, Get over yourself!)
Reader Motivation: Don't bother; this is a gut course.

TASKMASTER
Tip-offs: lots of rules, conditions, and injunctions; extensive use of "should" and "must;" moralistic or legalistic overtones.
Message to Readers: You are bad and had better shape up.

Example: As a teacher, you should make it your business to learn how to use the computer to instructional advantage in your classroom. Unfortunately, teachers often resist this kind of change. If you do not overcome resistance to educational technology, however, your students will go into the world without the background they need for success in the world of the future. Increasingly, as schools must devote more resources to acquiring equipment and training teachers in their use, teachers will be expected to fulfill society's mandate for technologically literate graduates.

Possible Reader Response: Shame on me! (or, Bug off!)

Reader Motivation: Feel righteous (or, Seek to avoid further punishment).

ANDROID
Tip-offs: slavish devotion to logic, precision, and rigor; lack of warmth; impersonal tone.
Message to Readers: You are unworthy as human beings and unlovable.

Example: An organization is a group of people, working toward objectives, which develops and maintains stable and predictable behavior patterns. These behavior patterns persist over time, while the individuals who make up the organization may change. The two factors that determine behavior patterns in organizations are organizational structure and organizational culture. Organizational structure is determined by the tasks the organization performs. Organizational culture is determined by the beliefs, values, attitudes, and norms that are the basis for the behavior patterns in the organization.

Possible Reader Response: What a bore! (or, Who cares!)
Reader Motivation: Skip the book; get the study guide.

SPINMASTER
Tip-Offs: evocation of strong feelings through media formats, including tendency to write in sound bites; use of present tense in descriptions of past events; exaggerated claims, overuse of hypothetical scenarios; dramatic or inaccurate language used purely for effect.
Message to Readers: You are not sufficiently intelligent or motivated and cannot be trusted to learn.

Example: It's 1862 and a curious young biologist is moving mollusks. He moves them from the calm water they are used to to a turbulent shore. What will happen? Will they be dashed to bits? Will they survive to reproduce? If they survive, will their descendants be adapted to the new environment? The biologist, who will become known as the greatest scientist of his day, watches. Mollusks, he muses, like other life forms, must evolve.

Possible Reader Response: What a joke!
Reader Motivation: Read for pleasure; I'm not going to learn anything from this.

Heading Structure and Why It Matters

The steps outlined in Chapters 4-6—getting information from competition analysis, market research, instructors who are potential users of the book, and professional peer reviews; reflecting on your mission; identifying your audience; choosing and developing your style and voice—form the foundation of textbook development. The next steps involve organizing your course content into a sequence of parts and chapters and then developing a system of text headings for each chapter. Your final writing outline is the basis for text headings, which you will use to develop your table of contents.

Because headings have high visibility, and because your book will be sold largely on the basis of its table of contents, it is worth whatever time it takes you to get the organization and headings right. This task should be done at the very beginning, not after you have written your manuscript. Authors who try to insert headings after drafting and while rushing to revise often discover that they need to rearrange their chapters. Textbooks are written to outlines rather than outlined after the fact.

Thus, you should know what is going to be in every chapter of your book before you even start. This point cannot be stressed enough. Your publisher probably will require that you provide a whole-book working table of contents (TOC) with your prospectus. That TOC goes out for review along with your prospectus before your book is even signed, and your revised TOC may be printed in your publisher's sales catalogue before you have even finished drafting. Take care to develop your TOC on the basis of your mission, market research, and competition analysis.

The Organization of Your Book

In the planning stage, begin with a brief TOC, which sets out the proposed organization of your book in terms of parts and chapters. Textbooks commonly have a Part I that serves as an introductory or foundational unit. Chapters in Part I typically cover core concepts and background information necessary for studying the subject. For example, a Part I in an introduction to archaeology might define and describe the basic subdivisions within the field, identify the underlying assumptions or basic theoretical orientations, or briefly survey the history and philosophy of the field. Try to have three to six parts, and organize the content so that each part has two or more chapters.

Parts in a textbook represent units of study. Parts and chapters may progress in a chronological, hierarchical, or horizontal topical fashion, depending on your subject and what you are intending to accomplish. For instance, if your textbook's mission is to empower readers to find and evaluate information on the Internet efficiently and effectively, chapters in Part I might provide background information on the Internet and might explain why it is useful or important to be able to find and evaluate information on the Internet. Chapters in Part II might then go on to describe how to find and evaluate information on the Internet. Part III chapters might follow by laying out the knowledge and skills readers need to find and evaluate Internet information efficiently and effectively. Chapters in Part IV might demonstrate reader empowerment through specific applications to selected careers or subject areas. Thus, the TOC (completely hypothetical) might look something like this:

Part I The Internet
        Chapter   1 Internet Technology and the Information Age
        Chapter   2 Living and Working Online
Part II Navigating Cyberspace
        Chapter   3 How to Locate Information on the Internet
        Chapter   4 How to Read Screens and Web Sites
        Chapter   5 How to Evaluate Online Information
Part III   Becoming an Information Expert
        Chapter   6 Improving Your Efficiency and Effectiveness on the Internet
        Chapter   7 Knowing Where to Go
        Chapter   8 Using Databases
        Chapter   9 Using Subscription Services
        Chapter 10 Taking Advantage of Information Software
Part IV Applying Internet Skills
        Chapter 11 Doing Online Academic Research
        Chapter 12 Doing Online Market Research
        Chapter 13 Being a Smart Online Consumer
        Chapter 14 Using Online Resources at Work

Giving titles to parts and chapters requires some thought and flexibility. It is not unusual for titles to change from draft to draft as editorial advice comes in and messages and market concerns become clearer. Following are some tips on giving titles to parts and chapters.

Tips on Writing Titles

- Give clear, brief, simple names to parts and chapters.
- Pack as much specific information as possible into titles without making them too long.
- Avoid making part and chapter titles too long through formal

usages or subtitles.

- As a rule of thumb, make titles one to eight words in length, inclusive of articles and conjunctions. No chapter or part title needs to exceed ten words.
- Identify the core concept, subject, or theme of the part or chapter.
- As much as possible, use concrete nouns.
- Within reason, use parallel structure in wording the names of parts and chapters.
- Most important, write straightforward titles without attempting to be coy, cryptic, clever, or comic.

Writing Outlines vs. Tables of Contents

Your topical outline (writing outline) or system of headings (table of contents) then lays out the contents of each chapter listed in your brief TOC. Note that a writing outline is not the same as a table of contents. A writing outline formally lists the sequence of topics in a way that is hierarchical and logically exhaustive. A system of text headings and subheadings, on the other hand, are functional and natural for learning a subject rather than for expressing a form. Rather than defining a class of ideas, headings provide words or labels for salient chunks of copy that will help the reader to construct meaning from the sequence of text. You can develop a working table of contents from your writing outline.

The difference between writing outlines and tables of contents often confuses even experienced authors and editors. That this whole chapter is devoted to the subject of headings testifies to their importance in exposition, however, as well as in textbook publishing. As you will see, headings also play a significant role in learning, topical balance, textbook packages, and marketing and sales.

A writing outline expresses the book's logical development and the author's progression of thought, using a conventional outline format with Roman numerals, the Roman alphabet, Arabic numbers, etc. The product is layers of logically differentiated subtopics that are exhaustively subsumed under larger topics. Some items serve only as abstract or analytical categories—umbrella concepts that are inclusive of the topics that actually will be addressed in the writing. The outline, then, is a system of classifying information, a taxonomy.

In contrast, the headings in a final chapter outline in a table of contents group information in a functional, informational way. All the headings are real and all have actual content under them; that is, they are not empty pegs or logical abstractions. Every heading is followed preferably by three or more paragraphs of text. Your table of contents, therefore, is more like a road map or a concept web than a taxonomy.

The following examples illustrate the difference between a writing outline and a corresponding chapter outline. The example assumes that the topic of motivation is intended as one main section of text within a chapter that contains other topics as well.

Example: Writing Outline and Corresponding Chapter Outline

Writing Outline:

I. Motivation
    A. Definition
    B. Types
        1. Extrinsic
        2. Intrinsic
    C. Sources
        1. External
        2. Internal
    D. Theoretical Perspectives
        1. Behavioral
        2. Humanistic
        3. Cognitive
        4. Social Learning

Headings in the Chapter Outline in the TOC:

<A> What Is Motivation?
    <B> Extrinsic and Intrinsic Motivation
    <B> External and Internal Sources of Motivation
    <B> Theoretical Perspectives on Motivation
        <C> Behavioral Views
        <C> Humanistic Views
        <C> Cognitive Learning Theory
        <C> Social Learning Theory

As you can see, the writing outline guides the author, while the chapter outline serves the reader. The headings in the chapter outline convey relationships among core concepts, and these headings are organized in levels different from but no less logical than the formal writing outline. You no doubt will agree that in the TOC the chapter on motivation should read like the chapter outline in the above example and not like the writing outline.

Levels of Heading

Textbooks can have up to five levels of heading, but three is optimal in most subjects and standard practice in introductory texts. The levels of heading are differentiated through book design using different sizes, styles, and colors of type. A-heads (<A>) are the most general and inclusive and also the most prominent visually; B-heads (<B>) are subsumed under A-heads, are next most prominent visually, and appear on their own lines. C-heads (<C>) are subsumed under B-heads and, like D-heads, often start on the same line as their copy. D-heads (<D>) are also distinguished typologically but are the least prominent heading on the page. Glance at pages in textbooks sitting on your bookshelves to see the way levels of heading are differentiated. Notice how different levels of heading use space on the page. You might also see topical subheadings used as marginalia.

Proper headings, like elements in a formal outline, follow the "rule of two"; that is, if an A-head has B-heads, there must be two or more B-heads, and if a B-head has C-heads, there must be two or more C-heads, and so on. A singleton A-head, B-head, or C-head is not good practice. Also, at every level, headings must have sufficient copy under them to warrant their separate existence and the space they take on the page. Having a one-paragraph A-head section, for instance, is not good practice and usually indicates either topical underdevelopment or inappropriate use of headings as logical pegs.

The style of headings in textbooks differs from styles dictated by professional organizations for journal writing. For example, American Sociological Association guidelines might require that you make A-heads all caps or that you underline and indent A-heads and have B-heads flush left on their own line, etc. However, textbook headings normally are never all capitals, underlined, or indented, and if your book is being designed rather than going to print as camera-ready copy, then all your efforts in formatting will be wasted. A copyeditor must pencil changes or reformat your disk—an unnecessary expense that is charged to your book. For this and other reasons, instead of clinging to formatting guidelines for journal articles, you would be wise to consistently follow your publisher's Author Guidelines for differentiating among levels of heading and keyboarding them.

Unless instructed not to do so, use the <A>, <B>, and <C> notational system to identify levels of heading (the carets indicate you do not intend the actual letters to be set into type). That way, publishing personnel always will be able to tell consistently which level of heading you intend. Alternatively, supply a chapter outline that clearly shows intended levels of heading that your copyeditor can use as an authoritative guide. Inconsistency in heading structure that finds its way into print can destroy the organizational integrity of your book.

Wording Headings and Developing Text Sections

The best way to develop your writing outline into a system of headings (and by extension into your table of contents) is to convert your Roman-numeraled items into questions. These questions are your A-heads. They focus the reader's attention on a particular quest for enlightenment and identify your broad theme or unifying concept. The paragraphs you write under an A-head should introduce the theme, define the concept, or provide background or context for the discussion to follow. The last sentence or two of an A-head section can briefly forecast your answer to the question by identifying the topics in your B-heads. This gives the student readers what they need to begin learning what you want them to know.

The question-answer approach to heading development is challenging and works better for some subjects than for others. Initially, however, this approach is worth trying. The question-answer structure is pedagogically sound for exposition, helpful to students, and especially appropriate for instruction based on objectives or learning outcomes, a subject of the next chapter. Students are trained to use headings for reading comprehension and review study. To that end, they are coached to convert text headings into questions to answer.

The next level of items in your formal outline (those that are real versus purely logical), become your B-heads. B-heads should be worded to answer directly the question posed in the A-head under which they are subsumed. The paragraphs under B-heads elaborate their function of answering the A-head question. All the B-heads should consistently have wording parallel in structure and grammatical agreement; that is, the wordings should not switch from one form or part of speech to another. Headings also should be worded to provide straightforwardly the most solid and specific information possible in the least possible space. A heading that simply says, "Introduction" or "Research" or "Criticisms" conveys insufficient information.

Based on the discussion so far, what is wrong with the following example of headings?

Example: Poor Headings

<A> What Are the Stages of Cognitive Development?
  <B> Theories of Cognitive Development
  <B> Sensorimotor
  <B> Observing the Preoperational Child
  <B> Poured Concrete Operations
  <B> What Are the Hallmarks of Formal Operational Thought
       and How Can You Encourage Formal Operational
       Thinking in Children?

In the example the first B-head does not directly serve its A-head question; that is, "theories of cognitive development" are not "stages of cognitive development." The reader is confused at the outset. In addition, the B-heads lack parallel grammatical agreement and style; that is, the B-heads switch between noun phrases, verbal phrases, and additional questions. The wording of the fourth B-head contains a distracting, not-so-clever, pun. The last B-head is too nonconforming compared with the other B-heads and would unnecessarily take up a lot of space on the page. The net effect of the headings is that students' efforts to make sense of information are compromised.

Example: Corrected Headings

<A> What Are Theories of Cognitive Development?

<A> What Are Piaget's Stages of Cognitive Development?
    <B> Sensorimotor Stage
    <B> Preoperational Stage
    <B> Concrete Operational Stage
    <B> Formal Operational Stage

In the first A-head of the corrected version, the concept of stage theories could be defined and contrasted with nonstage theories. Then, key theorists and background information on their work could be identified in added B-heads. In the B-heads under the second A-head of the corrected version, "observations" and "hallmarks" and other conceptual organizers for each stage could be taken up in added C-heads.

Avoid repeating the same headings in similar contexts from chapter to chapter. Each heading in a textbook should be unique. In headings, repetition is not "system" but monotony, and readers intuitively count on your headings to get a clue about the topical differentiations you are making. In exposition, obscurantist headings are mean-spirited. It bears repeating that headings should be straightforward, economical, informative, unique, and strong. They articulate the bones to which the sinews and flesh of your prose attach.

The C-heads in your chapter outline are derived from Items in your writing outline denoted by Arabic numbers. C-heads give the details, examples, or other elaborations that directly support their B-head. The "rule of two or more" applies throughout, and for every heading, you must have something substantive to say.

What Headings Really Mean

There is no one right way to construct a system of headings. Depending on your goals and emphasis, for example, you might recast your lesson on cognitive development in other ways:

Example A: Alternative Heading Structure
<A> What Are Some Theories of Cognitive Development?
    <B> Piaget's Theory of Cognitive Development
    <B> Neo-Piagetian Theories
    <B> Vygotsky's Theory of Cognitive Development
    <B> The Constructivist View
<A> What Are Piaget's Stages of Cognitive Development?
    <B> The Sensorimotor Stage
    <B> The Preoperational Stage
    <B> The Concrete Operational Stage
    <B> The Formal Operational Stage

Example B: Alternative Heading Structure
<A> What Is Cognitive Development?

<A> What Is Piaget's Theory of Cognitive Development?
    <B> Developmental Processes
        <C> Schemes
        <C> Accommodation
        <C> Assimilation
        <C> Equilibration
    <B> Developmental Stages
        <C> Sensorimotor Stage
        <C> Preoperational Stage
        <C> Concrete Operational Stage
        <C> Formal Operational Stage
<A> How Is Piaget's Work Viewed Today?
    <B> Criticisms of Piaget's Stages
        <C> Limitations of Theories Based on Stages
        <C> Impact of Culture on Development
        <C> Relationship of Gender to Development
    <B> Influences on Neo-Piagetian Theories
        <C> Information Processing
        <C> Constructivism
        <C> Ecological Models of Development
    <B> Piaget's Influence on Education
        <C> Developmentally Appropriate Education
        <C> Focus on the Learning Process
<A> What Is Vygotsky's Theory of Cognitive Development?
    Etc.

Notice that the differences between these two examples reflect differences in both organization and emphasis. Your heading structure, in other words, reflects the amount of information you are providing, the amount of differentiation you are making within and between topics, and each topic's relative importance in your scheme of things. How much do you have to say? About what? At what level of specificity? And how important is it?

The levels of heading thus signify their function as conceptual organizers. In Example A, for instance, the author regards "The Constructivist View" as a stand-alone B-level topic equal in importance to the other B-head topics in that section. Author A wants us to remember constructivism as a major theoretical orientation in the study of cognitive development. In Example B, in contrast, constructivism is a C-head subsumed under Neo-Piagetian Theories, which the author has chosen as the more important conceptual organizer. Author B wants us to remember constructivism as only one of several neo-Piagetian theories of cognitive development.

The relative importance you give to your topics in this way becomes a road map to your beliefs and values as an author in your subject area, a blueprint to your philosophical stances on the topics you consider. Intentionally or otherwise, your headings reveal what learning you feel is most important for your readers to acquire and retain.

Role of Headings in Topical Development

A- and B-head sections are the most important conceptually and thus should contain the longest copy, or the most paragraphs. C- and D-head sections, while they contain important details, are briefer. Avoid consigning the meat of your chapters to long C- or D-head sections. At the other extreme, three sentences are regarded as the minimum for copy under a C-head. The following hypothetical example shows an inappropriate treatment of sections in terms of level of heading and length of copy as indications of relative importance:

Example: Inappropriate Topical Development

<A> What Are the Stage Theories of Cognitive Development?
Stage theories postulate that individuals progress in their cognitive development through a specific number of defined stages.

    <B> Piaget's Theory
        Jean Piaget, a Swiss psychologist, studied children's learning behavior at different ages and concluded that there are specific stages of cognitive development, shown in Table 2.1.

<Insert Table 2.1>

    <B> Vygotsky's Theory
        Lev S. Vygotsky, a Russian psychologist influenced by the work of Piaget, conducted experiments to clarify Piagetian stages and study how children move from one stage to another.

    <B> Neo-Piagetian Theorists
        In the decades following Piaget's contributions to cognitive psychology and the study of child development, new research led to criticisms of Piaget's stage theory. It was found that children do not all move through all the stages by certain ages and may not even move through the stages in the same sequence. Piaget's conclusions were also criticized because they did not seem to take into account the impact of culture and enculturation on child development. Neo-Piagetian theorists revised the definitions of the stages to attempt to account for these factors.

<A> What Are Piaget's Stages of Cognitive Development?
    <B> The Sensorimotor Stage
        The first stage, from birth to two years of age, is called the sensorimotor stage. Etc.

In the foregoing example, the narratives under the first A-head and the first two B-heads are too brief, consisting of single sentences. The length of copy under the third B-head suggests that the topic is more important than the others. The second A-head, meanwhile, is used purely logically with no copy at all. The example also reveals a serious lack of explanation below the level of highest abstraction—that is, sections lack the specific examples and concrete applications that readers need to make meaningful sense of the information. Without concrete examples, your subject, however worthy, cannot come alive for readers.

Underdevelopment of topics is a serious flaw in exposition because it does not provide sufficient information for comprehension to take place. With overdevelopment, in contrast, readers always are tempted to skip over unneeded passages once they have achieved comprehension. Overdevelopment also may make your book too dense and long, so that is not really a solution to the challenge of topical development.

When developing sections in terms of your chapter outline, take care not to chop up text too finely. A surfeit of headings followed by brief copy particulates information, becomes visually confusing to readers, and also eats up valuable space on the page. Some authors go the other way, however, and spin out page after page of narrative without providing enough subheadings for the reader to organize the material conceptually or to gain some visual relief. As a rule of thumb, chapters in most content areas ideally have a minimum of three and a maximum of eight A-head sections of text.

This book has three to six A-head sections per chapter. The A-heads address implied questions, and the B-heads elaborate the implied answers consistently in the form of either statements or gerund phrases. The function of C-heads is fulfilled in the form of the many examples and models this book provides. To examine the organization and heading structure of this book, review the Table of Contents in the frontmatter.

Following is a list of guidelines for providing good topical structure and organization.

Characteristics of Good Topical Structure and Organization

- Each A-, B-, and C-head section of text begins with a thesis statement or includes a thesis question or statement in the introductory paragraph. Avoid making the purpose of taking up a topic a mystery for the reader to solve or a surprise.
- Ideas or points are grouped or clustered into meaningful chunks or categories of information. Avoid logically exhaustive or taxonomic development.
- Categories of information embrace a reasonable amount of meaningful information. Avoid imbalance or inconsistency in topical development; for example, with topics of equal importance, avoid

developing some too little (too narrow or brief) and others too much (too broad or long).

- Categories of information lead naturally and coherently from one to the next. Avoid encyclopedic exposition in which each topic is treated without reference to any others. This unhelpful kind of organization is known variously in the trade as the "recipe card," "scattershot," or "encyclopedic" approach to disseminating information.

- Transition from one idea or topic to the next is clear. Avoid abrupt endings and unclear connections between sections of text. Also avoid leaps of faith in which you assume the reader is filling in logical steps (or gaps) in your progression of thought.

- Each main idea or point is supported by specific examples, data, or evidence, or by arguments containing examples, data, and evidence. Avoid underdevelopment of ideas and unsupported claims.

- Topics are treated fully in the context of their greatest relevance. Avoid reiterating topics repeatedly in all relevant contexts. Also avoid introducing a topic that is not taken up substantively until later in the book. Key terms and concepts should be defined and explicated fully in the context where they are first used meaningfully.

Role of Concrete Examples in Supporting Topical Development

Editors of college textbooks often are amazed to find manuscripts with page after page of unrelentingly abstract prose, paragraph after paragraph on constructs with no hint that empirical analogs exist in the real world. What are these authors thinking? Why should readers care to learn anything about stratigraphy, for instance, even when defined, if they cannot imagine what that might look like or where in the world they might see it? How much better it would be to read about archaeological excavations at Ceren, El Salvador, or Harappa, Pakistan, and how the stratigraphy at those sites revealed interesting facts from successive cultural depositions. Or to read about geological surveys in which stratigraphy revealed the history of vulcanism in the Pacific rim or iridium in Italy or pollen in Greenland ice cores or drought in Yucatan or, frankly, anything empirical. Readers then might be motivated to wade through a closely reasoned, technical, and conceptual argument about stratigraphy as a research tool.

Concrete examples help readers to operationalize concepts—make them into something they can use. They can imagine, visualize, or identify with representations or exemplars of the concept. Vicariously experiencing an exemplar, in turn, engenders self-confidence in the reader, who then becomes more motivated to tackle the difficult or complex idea in aid of which you advanced a concrete example. Offering concrete examples is more than a courtesy to the reader; it is essential to learning.

When asked to provide an example, lazy authors often write abstract examples rather than concrete ones. The following "example," for instance, actually is little help. Why should we the readers care about A, B, or C?

Example: Concrete Example Gone Abstract

For example, imagine stratigraphy in which layer A is overlain by layer B, which was laid down on top of layer A at a later time. Then, layer C was deposited on top of layer B, and, assuming the depositions were not disturbed, layer C is the most recent or represents the present-day surface.

Example: Improved Version of Concrete Example Gone Abstract

At Harappa, the living floors and material culture of the earliest Stone Age inhabitants were overlain by the cultural remains of early farmers of the Indus Valley. On top of those deposits, later farmers built a small walled city with a sophisticated sanitation system. Still later Harappans expanded the amount of land under cultivation and built extensive irrigation networks, which remain visible at the present-day surface. As you can imagine, excavating down through Harappa's stratigraphy is a way of going back through time.

"Inhabitants," "farmers," and "Harappans" are inherently more interesting to readers than "A," "B," and "C." Notice that concrete examples typically take up more space on the page, however. Choose them carefully to support topical development and the most important constructs you are trying to teach.

Another refuge of the lazy or unmindful author is hypothetical examples, which in most contexts are not as good as real ones. Readers are keen judges of credibility and tend to have less confidence in nonauthentic examples. Readers also often have unpleasant memories of hypothetical examples from earlier schooling (Mary has two oranges and Jim has three apples. How can they share the fruit equally with Larry and Sandra?) When they directly involve the reader, concocted fictions also can backfire and convey wrong messages that thwart learning, as in the following example:

Example: Hypothetical Example Gone Wrong

As an example of crime profiling, imagine you are a serial killer. You choose your victim, say a grocery clerk, and assemble your weapons of choice—a cord for strangling, perhaps, and a switchblade for carving your initials in the corpse. You plan the time and place of your attack (behind the grocery store after closing) and *also the details of your escape (on foot). You don't bother to disguise your appearance because you will be killing your victim and making sure there are no witnesses.*

Whatever is happening here, the reader is not thinking about the concept of crime profiling.

Role of Headings in Marketing and Sales

Frontmatter tables of contents may not contain all levels of heading, so you would be wise to ensure that the hot topics and buzz words your customers will regard as most important all appear in A- and B-heads. For the publisher, the TOC is an important sales tool. It will be published in the sales manual and used to instruct the sales force on how to sell your book. It will be published in the company's catalogue and will appear on the company's web site. It may be compared to the TOCs of competing texts to highlight your book's superior organization and content. It may be printed in full on direct-mail advertising brochures sent to faculty members nationwide. Your TOC may be printed in both long and short forms on the endpapers or frontmatter of your book, and portions of the TOC might be reproduced on acetate transparencies or on PowerPoint slides as lecture aids for adopters.

The TOC also is the key to correlating any supplements planned to accompany your text, such as an instructor's manual, test bank, and study guide. Your supplements authors must use your heading system to organize their content. The test bank author, for example, constructs items for each level of heading, assessing students' mastery at each level of conceptual organization and detail that you have laid out. In an Annotated Instructor's Edition, margin annotations next to each heading might indicate which test items cover the information in that section of text. Your study guide author likewise relies on your system of headings to guide the students through your material and to structure their opportunities for self-assessment. In your instructor's manual, lecture notes or instructional strategies may be keyed to specific sections of text. Your headings, in other words, are the scaffolding for your whole textbook package.

As mentioned at the beginning of this chapter, inexperienced authors sometimes wait until they have finished a chapter and then go back to line out the contents according to whatever headings they can stick in or seem to fit. This strategy often leads to extra time and effort, however, for this is when they find out that they have only one A-head for the whole chapter or that they have singleton B-heads and C-heads, or that they have overdifferentiated or underdifferentiated in topical development. It bears repeating, therefore, that the time you spend retrofitting your chapter to make the headings work is better spent in figuring them out in the first place.

Experienced authors and those who grasp the functionality and importance of the table of contents often skip the writing outline and go straight to developing a system of headings. As mentioned in Chapter 2, submitting a real working table of contents with your curriculum vitae, prospectus, and sample chapters will win the respect and confidence of your editors. In drafting, exposition flows naturally from your heading structure. Heading structure also provides a convenient mechanism for staying in control of length and schedule, as you assign value, space, and time to each portion of your TOC. With your working heading structure in place and drafting underway, you can turn your attention to the apparatus and pedagogy of your chapters, the subjects of the next three chapters of this book.

Pedagogy and What It Does for Your Textbook

Pedagogy is the name given to all the written elements of your book that are neither narrative text nor the figures and tables that directly support narrative text. These pedagogical elements include the apparatus—chapter openers and chapter closers; systematic study aids, such as mid-chapter reviews, marginal annotations, or boldfaced key terms—and intext features, such as thematic boxes, which are distinguished from the narrative through design.

The Functions of Pedagogy

The idea behind pedagogy is that a textbook acts as an instructor—a teacher—and that learning theories and research-based principles of effective instruction therefore apply. For instance, research supports the theory that people learn more, better, faster, if information is given in ways compatible with what is known about cognitive processing—the way people think: the way the human brain operates in the learning process. Without resorting to jargon, this means that information should be delivered or presented for discovery in proven ways. These ways include teaching sequences in both direct and nondirect instruction.

Principles of Direct Instruction

Textbooks contain expository writing most often in the form of direct instruction—the direct transmission of information that all students are expected to master. During past decades, different researchers have identified similar elements and events in this process (Gagne, 1977; Good et al., 1983; Evertson et al., 1984; Rosenshine & Stevens, 1986; Gagne & Driscoll, 1988). Most research giving rise to models of direct instruction has been done on behalf of elementary and secondary education. Because the studies draw upon general learning theories, however, the findings are equally valid for learners at the college, graduate, and postgraduate levels. All the models can be summarized in terms of the following general sequence (Slavin, 2002). Will your chapters perform the following tasks, reflecting students' instructional needs?

Events in a Direct Instruction Lesson

1. State objectives and expectations.
2. Review prerequisite knowledge and skills.

3. Present new material.
4. Question to check for comprehension.
5. Provide opportunities for independent practice.
6. Assess performance and provide feedback.
7. Provide opportunities for outside application.

In many ways, the events in direct instruction relate to what is known about cognitive and psychological processes involved in learning. Event or Step 1, for example, activates motivation by telling learners what to expect and what will be expected of them. This first step also suggests how the information is relevant to learners personally or professionally and how it relates to their prior knowledge and experiences.

In Event or Step 2 students' attention and perception are directed selectively to (1) the topic and (2) to concepts students need to acquire to understand the new information. In Steps 3 and 4 the learner acquires the new information, makes sense of it, and retains it in memory through cognitive processes that encode stimuli and connect responses to those stimuli in neural networks. Steps 5, 6, and 7 reinforce learning, the application of learning, the motivation to learn, and the transfer of learning to new contexts or to the real world. An effective textbook does exactly the same things.

This is not to say that a textbook literally is a series of direct instruction lectures. Many an author has attempted to produce a textbook by having his or her lecture notes or tapes transcribed. These efforts fail, because spoken words do not transfer well to print and the nonverbal communication that takes place in the classroom is lost. The colloquial language, body language, shock tactics, personal fables, Socratic monologues, ironic observations, nostalgic anecdotes, rhetoric, panegyrics, polemics, and folksy or mordant humor that you use to attract students' attention—and that might make you a spellbinding lecturer—will make you look gratuitous, silly, egotistical, dated, eccentric, politically incorrect, and intellectually unsound on the printed page. In print, the events of direct and nondirect instruction occur through skillfully structured narrative and sound pedagogy.

Principles of Nondirect Instruction

In education, nondirect instruction includes all the planned learning experiences by which it is intended that students will acquire information on their own or through interaction with their peers and others. Students at all ages and at all levels of educational attainment learn actively and indirectly through observation, inquiry, discussion, modeling, progressive skill approximation, critical thinking, problem solving, decision making, and hands-on experience. Pedagogical features give you an opportunity to build some of these learning experiences into your textbook. Consider, for example, what pedagogical features you could develop that would encourage students to use some of the following critical thinking skills (Kneedler, 1985). Will your textbook encourage readers to exercise the following skills?

Examples of Critical Thinking Skills

1. Define and clarify the problem.
   a. Identify the central issue.
   b. Compare similarities and differences.
   c. Distinguish relevant from irrelevant information.
   d. Generate appropriate questions.
2. Judge information pertaining to the situation.
   a. Distinguish among fact, opinion, and reasoned judgment.
   b. Evaluate consistency.
   c. Identify unstated assumptions.
   d. Recognize stereotypes and clichés.
   e. Identify factual inaccuracies, misleading information, and false claims.
   f. Identify fallacies in arguments.
   g. Recognize bias, manipulation, propaganda, and semantic loading.
   h. Distinguish between verifiable facts and value claims.
   i. Recognize different value systems and ideologies.
3. Solve problems and draw conclusions.
   a. Evaluate the credibility of a source.
   b. Recognize the adequacy of data.
   c. Weigh competing evidence.
   d. Make inferences from evidence.
   e. Hypothesize and predict probabilities.

Students as Active Learners

Higher education faculties and critics frequently decry the lack of independent thinking and critical thinking skills among college undergraduates. Yet, a glimpse in undergraduate classrooms and textbooks suggests that students generally are expected to be the passive recipients of bodies of knowledge. Both live and in print, higher education faculties often unintentionally discourage learners from interacting with information sources, constructing meaningful knowledge actively, or thinking critically. Thus, the student's right to make reasoned judgments about what to believe and do—the whole point of learning—is preempted.

Part of the reason for this situation is the persistence of the historical role of college instructors as didacts and their lack of education as teachers. One could predict that few college professors would readily identify themselves as "teachers" at all. A "teacher" is the person who terrorized or nurtured them in second grade. Another part of the reason is that college instruction generally centers on the subject and on the instructor as the subject expert. Today, however, the trend in education at all levels is to place the student at the center of learning and to actively involve the student in acquiring the subject. As a result, the "I" or "we" implicit in author-centered, subject-centered textbooks now becomes "you"—the student, the person whose learning is at stake.

Effective instruction no longer rests on the lecture model in which the instructor is the "sage on the stage" "telling it like it is" to passive, note-taking students who occasionally are invited to ask questions (but had better be careful not to betray any real curiosity or ignorance). The best textbooks are made to guide the reader through a self-directed learning process. This is the purpose of having pedagogical features in your textbook. Pedagogical features give readers opportunities to construct, monitor, apply, and extend their own learning through interaction with text.

The following links will guide you to more information about learning theory and instructional models.

Educational Research on Models of Instruction

Summary of Principles of Direct Instruction:
chiron.valdosta.edu/whuitt/col/instruct/dirprn.html

University of Colorado at Denver's encyclopedia of instructional models:
carbon.cudenver.edu/~mryder/itc_data/idmodels.html

Educational Resources Information Center (ERIC), Clearinghouse on Higher Education:
www.eriche.org/

Resources on Critical Thinking

North Central Regional Educational Laboratory's Summary of Critical Thinking Skills:
www.ncrel.org/sdrs/areas/issues/envrnmnt/drugfree/sa3crit.htm

Critical Thinking Consortium. Click on links under "College."
www.criticalthinking.org/

Mission: Critical—San Jose State University's Critical Thinking Page:
www.sjsu.edu/depts/itl/graphics/main.html

Longview (MI) Community College, Critical Thinking across the Curriculum Project:
www.kcmetro.cc.mo.us/longview/ctac/corenotes.htm

Thinking Critically about World Wide Web Resources (UCLA):

www.library.ucla.edu/libraries/college/help/critical/index.htm

Tutorial on Evaluating Web Resources (Harvard):
www2.widener.edu/Wolfgram-Memorial-Library/webevaluation/webeval.htm

Role of Pedagogy in Marketing and Sales

Another reason you need pedagogy is purely practical. Your publisher's sales force needs pedagogical features to sell your book. Assume for the sake of argument that your text is not one of those extremely rare, if not mythic, titles that "sells itself." The publisher's representatives are out on campus carrying it around to academic departments to show to potential customers. These salespeople are not content experts in your field, and few can "talk shop" with college professors for very long. To interest professors in trying your book, the salesperson needs to be able to open it and point to something besides the table of contents. Advertising and promotional materials also depend on identifying the pedagogical benefits of your book to instructors and students.

Forms of Apparatus and Pedagogy

Chapter apparatus consists of your opening and closing pedagogy. The chapter opener expresses the subject, theme, aims, topics, and organization of a chapter. Inexperienced authors often resist chapter openers as "taking up space" or "giving away the show." They want to delight and surprise or intentionally confuse the reader temporarily. Readers, however, have a right to know at the outset what they are reading and why or to what end. Also, readers learn the material better if they are mentally prepared for it. Chapter openers perform the functions of the first steps in models of direct instruction. They arouse curiosity, motivate, direct attention, and activate prior knowledge.

Openers and Closers

Chapter openers may include one or more of the following kinds of pedagogical elements, discussed in more detail in Chapter 9:
- chapter overview or introduction
- chapter outline
- focus questions or anticipation guide
- learning objectives or outcomes
- graphic organizer
- scenario or vignette
- quotation or epigram
- photo or illustration

Chapter closers—all the elements following the chapter narrative—provide psychological closure and give students opportunities to review, reinforce, or extend their learning. Chapter closing pedagogy always includes some kind of a conclusion and summary and commonly in introductory textbooks a list of terms and concepts with page cross-references. Closers might also contain review questions, self-assessment quizzes with answers, content applications, field or lab or Internet activities, research assignments, annotated bibliographies assembled expressly for student use, or features such as chapter closing reflections or case analyses.

Integrated Pedagogical Devices

Other pedagogical devices to consider as regular internal elements in each chapter include the following possibilities:

- boldfaced key terms
- cross-references to relevant material in other sections or chapters
- highlighted statements of main points
- call-outs of embedded subtopics
- margin notes, such as glossary annotations, background notes, examples, or applications
- side bars with key facts
- study or review questions, reflection or discussion questions, or critical thinking questions
- reminders of appropriate operations or formulae

When well planned and well written, integrated pedagogical devices such as these aid student learning.

Interior Feature Strands

Intext features, whether boxes or portions of text set off through design, function pedagogically to attract attention; arouse curiosity; increase motivation to read; stimulate critical thinking; and provide opportunities for reflection, application, or problem solving. You might consider including one of more of the following kinds of feature strands in your textbook.

- case studies
- profiles
- debates
- primary sources
- models
- reflections
- thematic boxes

The development of feature strands is discussed in more detail in Chapter 10.

Pedagogy Pitfalls

Pedagogy has pitfalls. Some authors, readers, and textbook critics complain that features "dumb down" a text, are gimmicky, interrupt the narrative flow, create a boxy appearance, or cause confusion about what is important to know. Others claim that features serve only as window dressing or filler, the publisher's hype, and that students don't bother to read them unless they are on the test. These complaints can be valid and usually stem from one or more of the following problems:

- poor design of features
- poorly written features
- features that are too long
- too many features (or too few)
- inconsistent types or uses of features
- lack of fit between features and chapter content
- lack of clear purpose or relevance in using features
- strained or insincere features based on the latest buzz in the field

Some textbook features obviously pander to marketing directives rather than educative value and look and sound like television infomercials. Other pitfalls stem from authors' lack of enthusiasm in supplying pedagogy or publishers' lack of investment in commissioning contributions to it. Plugging in two pages of boring or irrelevant prose per chapter to fulfill a marketing plan calling for an emphasis on diversity or technology or global perspective, for example, does not help to put your book on the road to success. You can avoid the pitfalls of pedagogy by observing the general rules of thumb outlined below.

Tips for Avoiding Pedagogy Pitfalls

- Choose a small number of specific chapter opening and chapter closing elements and use them consistently in every chapter.
- Develop at least one but not more than four types of feature strands.
- For each type of feature have a clear purpose that reflects both key market concerns and real concerns in the course.
- Try to have one of each type of feature in every chapter or every other chapter as a regular way of maintaining feature strands throughout the text.
- Ask to have some features designed as boxes and others as portions of text embedded in the narrative flow but set off through design.
- Establish a consistent standard for the desired length and content of each feature type.
- In most cases, keep features to less than one book page in length. In most subjects a two-page spread (a comprehensive, often illus-

trated, feature on facing pages) might be regarded as a maximum.

- Build in opportunities for readers to respond to feature content, for example, by adding comprehension, critical thinking, reflection, or discussion questions.
- Take responsibility for writing the pedagogical elements and features yourself or for checking the quality of material written by contributors or freelancers.

If done right, features can greatly enhance both the salability of your text and its instructional value to readers. Doing pedagogy right involves planning, selecting, creating, integrating, and designing chapter apparatus and feature strands.

If a development editor is assigned to your book, the development plan will contain a pedagogy plan. This plan will be based on what you already have provided in your draft manuscript, what competing texts have to show, what reviewers say, and what marketing research suggests is desirable. You will receive guidelines and models for drafting or subcontracting the agreed-upon features. The development editor might provide models for some pedagogical elements for you, or your publisher might have features written by contributors or freelance writers on a work-for-hire basis.

Lacking editorial assistance, you will need to make all the decisions about apparatus and pedagogy yourself and supply all the elements and features. The next two chapters are intended to help you in this task. In addition, these chapters direct you to actual examples of pedagogy in sample chapters of textbooks posted on publishers' web sites.

By going to selected places on the Internet you can see how effective pedagogical features look and work. Sample chapters of textbooks can be downloaded and viewed as pdf files, and publishers typically provide for free whatever self-extracting software is needed to read them, such as Adobe Acrobat Reader, if you do not already have this program in your hard drive.

To begin using the Internet to get ideas for apparatus and pedagogy for your textbook, try the following or similar sites, which may be archived on some companies' servers and open to the public. Note, however, that site names and locations may change each year as the newest books are highlighted on publishers' web sites. You also may check the web site of the publisher of this book for postings of updates, as all the URLs in *Writing and Developing Your College Textbook* are checked regularly (see **www.atlanticpathpublishing.com**).

Online Examples of Effective Apparatus and Pedagogy

In a history textbook at **www.ablongman.com/html/nashtour/**

- See sample Chapter 8 for an effective chapter opener. Note the photo and outline as standard chapter opening elements.
- In the sample chapter, "Technology Changes the American People" is an example of a long topical feature that works. Note the critical thinking questions at the end and the contextual reference to the

feature in the chapter narrative.

- The same chapter also has a long methodological feature that works: "Recovering the Past." Note the way the feature invites interaction with text and the suggestions for application at the end.

In a child development textbook at
www.ablongman.com/html/fabestour/

- See sample Chapter 2 for another example of a chapter opener. Note how the opener relates to the closer.
- The sample chapter (p. 49) also has an example of how even a brief box can add rigor or precision. Note how the box is not optional reading in the context. Students skip over it at their peril.
- Scroll through the chapter to see how the heading structure works with A-, B-, and C-levels of heading (recall Chapter 7 of this book).

Find other sample chapters in your discipline to survey. For example, see Wadsworth's or Prentice Hall's online product tours and select your discipline to explore titles relevant to you and your textbook.

www.wadsworthtours.com/ptours/company.cfm?company_id=1: For example, see sample Chapter 6, "Eating Patterns and Problems," in Hales' *An Invitation to Health*.

http://vig.prenhall.com/catalog/academic: For example, see sample Chapter 4, "Life's Home: The Cell," in Krogh's *Biology: A Guide to the Natural World*.

Chapters 9 and 10 of this book suggest other sites as well. Because web pages are archived or removed, the URLs in this book may not lead you to the examples cited. Although it is likely that information about the textbooks will remain somewhere on the publisher's web site, new sample chapters will replace the old with each year's frontlist, and you will have to find your own examples.

As you survey publishers' college textbooks, continue thinking about your apparatus and pedagogy. You may wish to record your ideas using the following Appendix, Developing Your Pedagogy Plan.

Appendix: Developing Your Pedagogy Plan

In this chart, list your ideas for your textbook's apparatus and pedagogy. For each item in your list, identify the pedagogical function it will serve in relation to the principles of instruction, students' learning needs or thinking skills, and your teaching goals or writing purposes.

APPARATUS AND PEDAGOGY	PEDAGOGICAL FUNCTION
Chapter Opening Elements	
Chapter Closing Elements	
Internal Pedagogical Devices	
Feature Strands	

Create Truly Useful Chapter Apparatus

The following sections describe some options and suggestions for the structural aspects of your chapter pedagogy, such as your chapter openers and chapter closers, introduced in Chapter 8. Suggestions are based on educational research and principles of effective direct and nondirect instruction, discussed briefly in Chapter 8. Suggestions also reflect standard practice in college textbook publishing and the author's professional experience in this field. As preparation for reading this chapter, examine several textbooks on your office shelves and observe how chapters begin and end. Notice page layout and design elements that both distinguish and tie together these parts of the chapter apparatus. Notice the kinds of pedagogy used in the apparatus. What kinds of teaching go on?

The Chapter Opener

The chapter opening elements or devices that you and your editor choose will be applied consistently at the beginning of every chapter. Your publisher will incorporate the elements into a design for the page or spread that begins each chapter. Through their consistency in type and design and their appropriateness to your mission, these elements will become a distinguishing feature of your text. In addition, they will connect both to chapter content and to the chapter closers in a way that will unify your instruction.

The Overview and Introduction

An overview and introduction collectively explain what the chapter is about, why readers should learn about it (or how they should begin thinking about it), and what kinds of information are involved (or what topics will be taken up).

Chapters may be organized into parts, or units, and presented in part-opening overviews in addition to separate chapter overviews. In other instances, part divisions are indicated in the table of contents as a window on the textbook's organization, but the parts do not have actual text pages devoted to them as openers. Part openers take up space in a book, so their use should have clear justification.

In addition, introductions and overviews introduce the chapter theme and central concepts and also relate each chapter or part to the previous one, showing how the readers are advancing their knowledge by connecting intelligently to what they already have studied or already know. Well-considered and well-wrought overviews and introductions give your book integrity. How, then, do overviews and introductions differ?

Notice in the following examples that the overview and the introduction, while interrelated, are not the same thing. The overview gives the big picture, and the introduction prepares readers for acquiring the details offered in the chapter at hand. The last sentence of the introduction briefly foreshadows the six A-head sections in terms of which the chapter is organized.

Example: Chapter Overview

Chapter 9 outlined the main financial institutions that affect companies doing business internationally, including institutions for raising capital, managing debt, making investments, and facilitating the flow of funds. Now, Chapter 10 explores in greater depth the flow of direct foreign investment, in particular the efforts of both home and host countries to influence that flow to regulate multinational enterprises. You have seen how the actions of MNEs affect nations and individuals as citizens, as consumers, and as producers. Now, what efforts are made to control the actions of MNEs, and what impact do those efforts have on international business?

Example: Chapter Introduction

The reasons that MNEs engage in direct investment ownership are to expand markets by selling abroad; to acquire foreign resources, such as raw materials, inexpensive labor, and expertise; and, at a government level, to attain some political advantage. MNEs pursue these goals and seek to extend their control mainly through trade and direct investment. Home and host countries, in turn, control MNEs principally through trade restrictions, investment incentives, government ownership, regional economic cooperation, commodity and trade agreements, and foreign exchange rates.

Overviews and introductions often are slighted by authors who treat them as nuisance writing or as mere obligatory or pro forma gestures. Inexperienced authors often save them for last or leave them out entirely. Yet these elements are more than a matter of good exposition or sound instructional practice. They serve as self-monitoring devices, an author's best weapons against incoherence and a host of other follies. If you cannot write a two or three paragraph description of your chapter, encapsulating an explanation of why anybody should read it, then you are not ready to draft it.

Overviews should not be first-person catalogues of authors' intentions, however: "In this chapter, first we talk about this; next we take up this other thing; then we cover that, that, and that; and finally we close with a consideration of this." In such an introduction, the focus is on the authors, secondarily on the subject, and not at all on the learners and the state of their knowledge. You are talking only to yourself. Rather, good overviews invite the student to read and learn the material.

The Outline and Focus Questions

Other than providing an overview or introduction, or both, the simplest way to prepare the reader for what is to come is to provide a chapter outline or a list of focus questions, or both. An outline at the beginning of each chapter presents the chapter headings and subheadings in the order they appear—a table of contents without page references. Outlines can present all the levels of headings or just the main ones (see Chapter 7 on heading structure) and can include titled pedagogical features.

As a chapter opening element, a list of questions at the beginning of a chapter or with a chapter outline alerts readers to what is most important to learn and thus guides their reading. If you conceptualize or frame your main headings as questions, then they automatically will suggest or serve as focus questions. In the following example of an outline as a chapter opening element, the focus questions are embedded in the chapter's A-heads:

Example: Embedded Focus Questions
Chapter 6 History of the Bantu to 1497
        What are the origins of the Bantu?
                The Bantu Homeland in Western Africa
                The Bantu Migrations
                Bantu-Speaking Peoples Today
        What were the economic impacts of the Bantu migrations?
                Farming and Herding
                Cattle and Taro
                Copper and Iron
        What Bantu kingdoms arose by the 15th century A.D.?
                The Luba States
                The Kongo Empire
                Great Zimbabwe
        How did trade link the Bantu states with other peoples?
                The East-West Central African Trade
                African Trade in the Roman Era
                The Arab and Asian Trade
                The Portuguese

Alternatively, list focus questions or study questions after the outline, or key them to sections of the outline, letting readers know in more detail what they should expect to learn.

Example: Chapter Outline Followed by Focus Questions
Chapter 6 History of the Bantu to 1497
        Origins of the Bantu

The Bantu Homeland in Western Africa
The Bantu Migrations
Bantu-Speaking Peoples Today
Economic Impacts of the Bantu Migrations
Farming and Herding
Cattle and Taro
Copper and Iron
Bantu Kingdoms by the 15th Century A.D.
The Luba States
The Kongo Empire
Great Zimbabwe
Trade Links Between the Bantu States and Other Peoples
The East-West Central African Trade
African Trade in the Roman Era
The Arabs and Asian Trade
The Portuguese

FOCUS QUESTIONS

1. What are the geographic and ethnic origins of Bantu-speaking peoples in relation to their present-day distributions?
2. What were the patterns and trends of Bantu migration?
3. How did the Bantu migrations affect demographic, economic, and technological developments in sub-Saharan Africa?
4. What factors contributed to the rise and spread of Bantu states?
5. How were the Luba, Lunda, Kongo, and Mwenenmutapa states alike and different?
6. How did trade link the Bantu states with peoples of Africa, the Middle East, Asia, and Europe?

As you can see, focus questions provide a basis for Steps 4, 5, and 6 in the model of direct instruction presented in Chapter 8. That is, students can assess their own levels of knowledge and comprehension by answering the questions independently, and instructors can assess students' learning by asking the questions in class or adapting them for use as test items. Thus, focus questions aid the instructor who assigns your chapters as well as the student readers.

Learning Objectives or Outcomes
An alternative to focus questions, also useful to both students and instructors, is a list of learning objectives—another chapter opening device with multiple functions. Learning objectives specify precisely what students are expected to know or be able to do after reading the chapter and studying the information—a pedagogical device especially appropriate for introductory textbooks.

A traditional approach in education is to make statements describing the information, tasks, and behaviors students should master. Such statements of objectives often are written according to rules developed through venerable educational theory and research (Mager, 1975). These rules were developed for elementary and secondary education to ensure functional interrelatedness between the planning and delivery of instruction and the assessment of learning based on measurable performance. Classically, the desired behaviors, the conditions of performance, and the criteria for mastery are included in learning objective statements, as in the statement, Given 10 complete sentences containing 20 nouns, students will correctly circle 18 or more nouns. Naming measurable indicators of learning is important in this scheme. To identify, to list, to trace, to compare, to solve, to write, or to argue are directly measurable, for example. To learn, to reflect, to understand, or to appreciate, however, are not directly measurable.

In college-level texts, specific measurable behaviors, conditions of performance, and levels of mastery often are omitted. Instead, authors express objectives more generally as goals of learning or learning outcomes that students should keep before them as they read and should anticipate on tests. Learning outcomes identify the knowledge and skills that will result from student learning.

Example: Learning Outcomes

After reading this chapter [in a U.S. government text], you should be able to:

1. define public opinion and identify the forces that shape it.
2. trace the process of political socialization in American life.
3. analyze the role of technology and the media in shaping public opinion.
4. explain and illustrate how demography shapes political participation.
5. list and describe six basic forms of political participation.
6. evaluate protests, political action groups, and lobbies as expressions of American political participation.

Notice, however, that these statements of learning outcomes retain the semantics of behavioral objectives by specifying in behavioral terms what students will do.

College-level texts also emphasize learning objectives in the cognitive domain. Cognitive objectives address internal or conceptual changes in the learner, for example, by asking students to recognize, to create, to interrelate, to apply, to demonstrate comprehension, to hypothesize, to predict, or to transfer learning to real-life situations.

Example: Cognitive Learning Objectives. Students will:

1. demonstrate an understanding of the relationship between mass communication and public opinion.
2. create advertising copy for and against a particular political

action committee.

3. apply their knowledge of political socialization to plan increased participation in student government.
4. present hypotheses explaining the institutionalization of dissent in a democracy.

Educational theorists have classified behavioral objectives to reflect a progression from simple to complex, factual to conceptual knowledge, and lower to higher levels of cognitive functioning. Historically, a six-part taxonomy of educational objectives has been the most influential (Bloom et al., 1956). The following six different types of learning performance are all appropriate for college students for different purposes.

Taxonomy of Cognitive Objectives

1. Knowledge (memorizing and recalling factual information)
2. Comprehension (translating, interpreting, inferring, extrapolating, predicting)
3. Application (using abstractions to solve novel or real-life problems)
4. Analysis (identifying main points, breaking down complex information to explain how the parts are related or organized, comparing and contrasting)
5. Synthesis (creating something that did not exist before, e.g., writing an essay, designing an experiment)
6. Evaluation (judging something against given or stated standards)

How might you classify the U.S. government examples given above in terms of Bloom's taxonomy for the chapter on political participation? Here are the objectives again, this time showing how they call for different levels of cognitive functioning.

1. Define public opinion and identify the forces that shape it. (Knowledge)
2. Trace the process of political socialization in American life. (Comprehension)
3. Analyze the role of technology and the media in shaping public opinion. (Analysis)
4. Explain and illustrate how demography shapes political participation. (Comprehension)
5. List and describe six basic forms of political participation. (Knowledge)
6. Evaluate protests, political action groups, and lobbies as expresions of American political participation. (Evaluation)
7. Demonstrate an understanding of the relationship between mass communication and public opinion. (Analysis)

8. Create advertising copy for and against supporting a particular political action committee. (Synthesis)
9. Apply knowledge of political socialization to increase participation in student government on campus. (Application)
10. Present hypotheses explaining the institutionalization of dissent in a democracy. (Synthesis)

Authors also often have unexpressed affective objectives; that is, they want students to care enough to vote, to become entrepreneurs, to love chemistry, to change their health habits, or to appreciate art, for example. Affective outcomes such as these involve the reader learning to value something or feel differently about something. Affective outcomes often are embedded or implied in behavioral and cognitive objectives.

Some authors reject the use of instructional objectives as too elementary, utilitarian, or restrictive. They claim that learning objectives and outcomes guide the student to acquire only the specified knowledge and skills, without extension. However, although objectives were developed for elementary and secondary school applications, educational research clearly supports their use with students at any age or level of educational attainment and in any field of study. Research also suggests the importance of engaging the full range of cognitive abilities in both directing and assessing all students' learning (Slavin, 2002).

In any case, stating learning objectives or outcomes in your chapter openers is optional—an alternative to using focus questions. Like focus questions, objectives can have multiple functions. Together with your system of text headings, learning objectives can integrate your pedagogy and drive your supplements. Objectives also provide you with clear goals for creating text features to support what you want your readers to gain from reading your textbook. Whether you state them or not, as you draft each chapter you should know what outcomes or objectives are guiding your efforts as an author-educator.

Scenarios and Vignettes

Another chapter-opening device is the scenario, also sometimes called a vignette. Scenarios and vignettes are brief descriptions of simulated or real-life situations, usually involving named characters or the reader. The situation is expressed in the form of a description, account, news clipping, dialogue, or story problem. Technically a *scenario* (Italian) is an outline of a plot or hypothesized chain of events, and a *vignette* (French) is a borderless image that blends decoratively into the page—a metaphor for writing that produces the same effect; that is, the situation merges seamlessly with text.

Example: Scenario
Imagine that you are being interviewed by a government census-taker, who is asking you questions—how many people live in your

household, what are their relationships to one another, and so on. Then the census-taker asks you about your race and gives you five choices: White, Black, Asian/Pacific Islander, American Indian/Alaskan Native, and Other. You hesitate to answer. Although you are listed officially as White on your birth certificate and your mother's parents were from Western Europe, your father's grandparents included a Chinese, a Filipino, and an African American. What does that make you? You decide not to answer the question, but on the basis of your appearance and your name the census-taker records you as "White" and "of Spanish/Hispanic origin." You've been counted.

Example: Vignette

The facts of U.S. racial diversity were acknowledged in the 2000 census, which permitted multiracial classifications for the first time in American history. Previously, census-takers gave respondents only five choices: White, Black, Asian/Pacific Islander, American Indian/Alaskan Native, and Other. (Persons of Spanish/Hispanic origin can be any race.) But what if your unofficial racial identity were a combination of these categories. Say you were listed officially as White on your birth certificate—your mother's parents were from Western Europe. But your father's grandparents included a Chinese, a Filipino, and an African American. How would you be classified according to the old census? How might you feel to be "Other?" The Census Bureau's addition of the category "Multiracial" in the 2000 census signaled an important change in American cultural perceptions of race.

Both scenarios and vignettes present situations, and situations stimulate interest. The situations let readers activate any prior knowledge or experience they have with the subject and enable them possibly to identify with the subjects. The situations also call attention to key issues the chapter will address and suggest the relevance of those issues for readers.

In some subject areas, chapter opening biographies, profiles, case studies, or product samples can serve the same purpose as scenarios. The value of scenarios and vignettes depends almost entirely on their reality or authenticity and their interest to readers. Here are some tips for writing effective scenarios.

Tips for Writing Effective Scenarios

1. Be as authentic and true to life and credible as possible.
2. Avoid logically abstract scenarios (unless logic is the subject).
3. Prefer real to hypothetical examples.
4. Make hypothetical scenarios relate closely to the actual subject

of the chapter.

5. Use language to engender some excitement, but avoid tabloid style.
6. Use present tense for immediacy, as appropriate.
7. Use natural-sounding dialogue, as appropriate.
8. Avoid stereotyping or bias in characterization.
9. Include characters of both sexes who accurately reflect cultural diversity.
10. Consider first-person accounts of your own or others' experiences.
11. Edit verbatim accounts for audience appropriateness in print form.
12. Refrain from prurient subjects and manipulations of readers' emotions.
13. Avoid voyeurism, gratuitousness, excessive morbidity, and righteousness in tone.
14. Include the outcome or result of the action or situation.
15. Tie in the situation or example to the chapter's opening exposition.

To be effective, vignettes and scenarios must link directly to the content in the chapter introduction or the first A-head section of text. Vignettes by definition are embedded in relevant text, but for scenarios you need to call attention to how they link to chapter content rather than assume that students will make the connection automatically. For example, the following report of a school homicide could open a chapter about issues and trends in criminal justice, causes of violent crime, or juvenile justice.

Example: Scenario

On April 20, 1999, in Littleton, Colorado, Columbine High School students Erik Harris and Dylan Klebold walked into their school with a semi-automatic pistol, a carbine, and two sawed-off shotguns. They laughed as they shot at people, ultimately killing twelve students and a coach. They also planted at least thirty pipe bombs and other explosives, discovered later, around the school. The pair often wrote and talked about killing people. They even made a video for class that showed them walking down the halls of their school, pretending to shoot friends dressed as hated classmates who had taunted or insulted them in the past. Then it all took a terrible turn into reality. Several copycat school homicides occurred—and some were prevented—in the weeks following the Columbine massacre.

This scenario could be tied to text quite simply by beginning the narrative exposition with a sentence of transition, as in the following examples:

Examples: Transitions for linking the Scenario to the Chapter Narrative

- Public reaction to school homicides like this one in Colorado includes heightened fear of victimization, which often is heightened further by media coverage. The role of the media in public perceptions of crime is a major issue in criminal justice today. What is that role?
- The Colorado massacre described at the beginning of this chapter raises serious issues for contemporary society and the criminal justice system. What causes this type of crime? How can mass murders in schools be prevented? Who, or what, is accountable for the shocking rise in youth violence?
- Today, school homicides—unheard of a century ago—and other violent crimes perpetrated by juveniles challenge the U.S. criminal justice system. School shootings topped the list of trends in crime in the 1990s. What are some of those trends?

Without a direct tie-in to the chapter content, the opening scenario is just a gimmick floating in the space allotted for chapter openers.

Ending a scenario or vignette or its transition with a question to the reader enhances its pedagogical value, especially if you refer to the vignette again within your narrative as chapter concepts come to apply. A chapter closing application can then ask students to answer the scenario question (or to solve the problem or correct the sample), using what they have learned in the chapter. Used in a functional, integrated way, then, scenarios can add pedagogical value to your book by reinforcing learning and permitting self-assessment. Examples of effective integrated scenarios follow.

Example A: Effective Scenario
Chapter 3 Language and Politics
In the opener: Bruce, a journalism student, researched and wrote a story on Christopher Columbus. His piece has been rejected without comment, however, by every paper he has sent it to. One editor drew a red X through the following paragraph:

> Columbus discovered the Caribbean islands, but he was slow on the uptake when it came to understanding where he was. Seeing near-naked redskins cowering behind the treeline, he realized he could not be in China. That he nevertheless named the natives Indians shows just how badly he wanted to believe that he was somewhere in the Orient.

After reading Chapter 2, you no doubt can spot Bruce's stylistic errors—his colloquialisms, euphemisms, and cliches, such as "slow on the uptake," "when it came to understanding," and "shows just how badly." However, even if Buce edited the paragraph to eliminate these expressions, no really responsible editor would publish it. Why? What else does Bruce have to learn about appropriate usage in professional journalism?

In the body of the chapter narrative: Elements of Bruce's paragraph are reiterated in connection with the concepts of attributions, racial and ethnic representations, and political correctness.

In the chapter closer:
1. As the editor who crossed out Bruce's paragraph, write Bruce a letter explaining why you are not publishing his piece.
2. Using what you have learned in this chapter, rewrite Bruce's paragraph.

Example B: Effective Scenario
Chapter 11 TEACHERS' RIGHTS AND RESPONSIBILITIES IN SCHOOL LAW
Mr. Wilson is a tenured physical education teacher at a suburban high school. He has been a teacher in good standing there for the last ten years. Lately, however, school administrators have received three complaints from parents of the girls' varsity basketball team that he has used offensive language and has invaded the privacy of team members in the girls' locker room. On the basis of these complaints, he has been given notice of dismissal. Can Mr. Wilson be dismissed legally for these reasons? What are his rights in the matter? What procedures must the school board follow in seeking to dismiss him?

In the narrative: The case of Mr. Wilson is reiterated in connection with the concepts and provisions of tenure, dismissal, and due process, and the outcome of the case is explained.

In the closer: A related or parallel case is presented, and readers are asked to address the same questions, applying what they have learned.

Example C: Effective Scenario
CHAPTER 18 ALCOHOLS
Lara and Hector are following all the steps that lead to the synthesis of complex alcohols. They have a firm grasp of the chemical

properties and preparations involved, but their sequence of reactions keeps leading them deeper and deeper into a labyrinth of possibilities, and they are running out of time. Here is what they have so far.

<Figure 18.1, diagram of faulty chemical formula>

What is the source of their problem? How would you approach this challenge?

In the first section of narrative text: In the example at the beginning of this chapter, Hector and Lara forgot that organic synthesis of complex compounds involves working backwards. They knew the chemistry of the individual steps, but did not plan the most efficient route from their goal. In almost every organic synthesis it is best to begin with the molecule you want—the target molecule—and work backwards from it. In reality, there are only a few ways to make a complicated alcohol. For example, there are comparatively few ways to make a Grignard reagent or an aldehyde or ketone, and so on—back to your primary starting materials. Working the other way around, your starting materials can undergo so many different reactions that you discover a bewildering number of paths, few of which take you to where you want to go.

In the closer: Lara and Hector were attempting to make tricyclopropylmethanol, although you wouldn't know it from their partial formula. Using the basic principle of organic synthesis, draw your own formula for achieving this product.

As you can see, scenarios or vignettes take a little thought. They are, however, among the most effective chapter openers in any subject, which is why they are so common in textbooks. As another example, take a look at the chapter opening vignette in the online sample chapter for a sociology textbook at **www.ablongman.com/henslintour/.** Note the unorthodox use of first person, by the way. This very successful textbook author gets away with it. Scroll down to the chapter conclusion, "A Concluding Note," and see how the closer relates to the opener.

Epigrams

Epigrams—brief quotations—ready the reader in a more reflective way and can be very effective when combined with chapter opening photographs. The use of chapter opening photos is an industry standard in introductory textbooks. With or without photos, however, epigrams can set the tone of a chapter and reinforce its principal theme.

Epigrams should be more than merely inspirational or decorative. Authors too often leave epigrams floating without narrative or pedagogical context, as if the clever, witty, coy, cute, ironic, telling, acerbic, harrowing, or nostalgic little nuggets of thought were themselves entirely sufficient. For follow-through, the chapter closer might reiterate the quotation and ask students to reinterpret it in terms of what they have learned.

Example A: Epigram
FOR A CHAPTER ON "GETTING STARTED" IN A TEXTBOOK ON WRITING:

> "The great enemy of clear language is insincerity. When there is a gap between one's real and one's declared aims, one turns, as it were instinctively, to long words and exhausted idioms, like a cuttlefish squirting out ink."
> —George Orwell

In the closer: Review the epigram at the beginning of this chapter and clarify its meaning in light of what you have read. Then write three paragraphs using specific examples to answer each of the following questions:

1. How does clarity of expression depend on clear intentions?
2. How does Orwell's statement reflect his claim?
3. What problems of style other than "long words and exhausted idioms" can develop when writers are "insincere?"

Example B: Epigram
FOR A CHAPTER ON "PRAGMATISM" IN A PHILOSOPHY TEXTBOOK:

> "The philosophy which is so important in each of us is not a technical matter; it is our more or less dumb sense of what life honestly and deeply means. It is only partly got from books; it is our individual way of just seeing and feeling the total push and pressure of the cosmos."
> —William James

In the closer: To what philosophy does William James refer in the quotation at the beginning of this chapter? According to James, what is the basis of this philosophy and what is its source? How does the quotation suggest the influence James had on the educational philosophy of John Dewey and his followers?

The epigram is an old-fashioned but timeless device. It is suitable not only for the arts and humanities, but for any textbook in which the intended primary learning objective is to reflect on ideas. For an online example of the effective use of epigrams, see sample Chapter 11 in an introduction to philosophy textbook (*Archetypes of Wisdom* by D. Soccio) at **www.wadsworthtours.com/ptours/**. This chapter also shows an effective use of embedded critical thinking questions as internal pedagogy.

Internal Apparatus

Introductory college textbooks often have internal pedagogy as part of chapter apparatus. Each A-head section may begin with a thesis statement or main point, for example, and each A-head section may end with a summative statement or review question. These regular elements of internal apparatus may be distinguished from the regular text through book design.

As noted in Chapter 8, another common treatment is to boldface key terms in the narrative and define them in margin glosses. Regular marginalia, such as definitions, topical headings, cross-references, URLs, or other kinds of information, may contribute to the internal structure of chapters, especially if your textbook will be an annotated instructor's edition or an interactive edition.

When choosing elements of internal apparatus, consider how much structure, direction, assistance, and convenience your readers need to learn what you want them to know most quickly and most efficiently. Too many elements will clutter the page and confuse the reader. Too few will raise the difficulty level and reduce the learning rate.

Some college instructors, unsympathetic toward learners, believe that internal apparatus "spoon-feeds" readers, who should be struggling for learning. The assumption seems to be that only hard-won knowledge will be retained. However, removing obstacles to learning, rather than creating them, should be your goal as a textbook author-educator.

Chapter Closers

Much has already been said about the pedagogical value of chapter closers (see Chapter 8). Among the most useful closers—and often the most underrated by authors—are the conclusion and the summary. In structure and function, the conclusion and the summary at the end of a chapter mirror the overview and the introduction at the beginning.

The Conclusion

Just as the introduction is not a list of intentions, the conclusion is not a rehash of what you covered or tried to accomplish in the chapter. Such a rehash focuses on yourself as an author and subject expert rather than on knowledge. Some conclusion is needed, however. Consider the following paragraph, which ends a chapter on millenarian movements in a comparative religion textbook and is immediately followed by a new chapter.

> Finally, an example from nineteenth-century North America is the ghost dance cult, a millenarian movement among Native Americans of the Great Plains. This religious movement had two spreads in the 1870s and the 1880s at times of increasing population pressure and dislocation through contact with westward-migrating Anglo-Europeans. The second movement began among the Paiutes in Nevada, initiated by the prophet Wovoka, and quickly spread to the Arapaho, Cheyenne, Dakota, and others. Wovoka received from the Great Spirit a vision of the resurrection of the dead and the restoration of traditional ways of life. He returned to his people with a message of hope and a dance ritual to be performed for five consecutive days at frequent intervals. His message was reinterpreted and added to wherever it was carried. In some groups, it included the return of buffalo—slaughtered by plainsmen for sport or to supply railroad builders—and the destruction of the white man. The cult was expressed through religious symbolisms as well as through the trance-inducing collective dancing. The ghost dance cult did not die out until after the massacre of more than 300 Sioux at Wounded Knee Creek, South Dakota, in 1890.

What will the reader make of the information in this chapter? Not much. There is no conclusion, no interpretation of significance, no unifying thought. The reader clearly is intended merely to acquire information as discrete bits for their own sake and for no other apparent reason than that the author regards these bits as important for them to know. This is the "flash card" or "encyclopedia" approach to education, evident in many college textbooks. While flash cards and encyclopedias have their place, educational research shows that students taught this way never learn to connect up information or even to ask or wonder, "So what?" The chapter needs a conclusion. Consider the value of even a brief conclusion such as the following for the chapter on millenarian movements:

Example: A Chapter Conclusion
Thus, the spread of religious ideas in response to conquest, missionary activity, and other intercultural contact has occurred throughout the ages and throughout the world. As you have seen, whatever form they take, millenarian movements constitute an adaptive response to changes that have led to real or perceived

cultural inadequacy or that have resulted in profound physical, cultural, or psychological loss.

Conclusions and the ability to draw conclusions are indispensable to learning. At the same time, conclusions and summaries are not appropriate places for introducing new information or adding new details.

The Summary

Experienced authors look forward to writing their chapter summaries. These are moments of truth. While drafting a summary you find out if your chapter has everything in it that should be, progresses logically, and makes sense as a whole. If the summary proves a difficult task or takes more than 20 minutes to draft, then something is wrong with the way the chapter has been conceived and executed. In a textbook, a chapter summary is a test of teaching effectiveness.

Ideally, your main headings for each section are in the form of questions or are convertible to questions or imply them. Your summary, whether in the form of paragraphs or a numbered list of main points, should answer those questions in a clear, concise way. Some authors even restate the questions as subheadings as a way to structure the summary. Answers then emerge naturally as you review the content in each section.

In the following example, a five-page A-head section from an introduction to teaching textbook is summarized using one sentence (more or less) per heading for an average of less than two lines of type per page of text.

Example: Summary for a Section of Text

Outline of Section:
<A> What Is Taught in the Schools?
    <B> Kinds of Curriculum
        <C> Explicit Curriculum
        <C> Hidden Curriculum
        <C> Null Curriculum
        <C> Extracurriculum
    <B> Curriculum Content

Summary of Section:
What is taught is called the curriculum—the subject areas, course content, learning outcomes, and planned and unplanned experiences that affect student learning. Four curricula that all students experience are the explicit curriculum, the hidden (implicit) curriculum, the null curriculum, and extracurricular programs. In all four forms, curriculum content reflects what communities and the wider society believe is important for students to learn.

A summary should be a content review, not a catalogue of what has been covered, which is sure to be boring and unhelpful to learners. Compare the following poor summary to the one above for the section on curriculum in the education textbook.

Example: Summary in an Inappropriate Style

In this chapter we first discussed the problem of defining what is meant by curriculum, pointing out the lack of universal agreement on what the concept of curriculum should entail. We then offered a broad definition that takes into account all the experiences that affect students and their education. We discussed the explicit curriculum, the hidden curriculum, the null curriculum, and the extracurriculum. Last, we turned our attention to curriculum content.

A summary such as the above might be reassuring to you in your role as author, but it does not bespeak your role as teacher, and it imparts little of value to the reader.

Other Chapter Endmatter

Chapter closers also can include activities for application or extension, such as problem sets or Internet activities, chapter quizzes, annotated recommended readings for students, topical cross-references, chapter notes or references, key terms and glosses, or other pedagogical devices.

For other examples, see the chapter closing elements in the online sample chapter for S. Tan, *Finite Mathematics for the Managerial, Life and Social Sciences* (Brooks/Cole)—Chapter 3, "Linear Programming: A Geometric Approach," at **www.wadsworthtours.com/ptours/.** Note how the closer offers self-assessment and application activities in which students use linear programming to solve real-life problems in production scheduling, shipping costs, asset allocation, crop planning, mining production, diet planning, and other applications in fields as diverse as transportation and advertising.

The intended functional interrelationships among elements in chapter apparatus often can be seen in a textbook's design. As an example, see online sample Chapter 2, "Power Politics" in *International Relations* by J. Goldstein at **www.ablongman.com/goldsteintour/.** Notice how the design motif of the open-gridded globe opens and closes the chapter and is echoed in the internal features strands, such as the "Thinking Critically" feature on p. 25 and the "Changing World Order" box on p. 26. Note also how the margins are used to link text to supplements, including an atlas CD, and to the Internet.

The number of elements in chapter closers and their length depends on your audience, your subject, your teaching goals, the relative need for independent practice or concept transfer on the part of learners, and, as always, your market and competition. In mathematics and English composition textbooks for required undergraduate courses, for instance, chapter closers can run several pages. Chapter closers in textbooks with built-in readings, annotated book lists, study guides, or practice tests also run long. Regardless, all pedagogical elements add to the length, bulk, weight, and cost of a book—more reason for choosing wisely. Use the planning sheet in the chapter appendix to start choosing and defining your apparatus.

In keeping with the message of this chapter, here is a brief conclusion. In this case, however, it is you who must draw the conclusions, based on your answers to the following questions: What will be the right mix of functionally interrelated chapter openers and chapter closers for your book? What are you providing to students to aid their active learning and to make your textbook indispensable to them?

Appendix: Planning Your Apparatus

Part Opening Elements	Possible Text Applications
Part Overview	
Part Outline	
Other	
Chapter Opening Elements	**Possible Text Applications**
Chapter Overview	
Introduction	
Chapter Outline	
Focus Questions	
Learning Objectives/Outcomes	
Scenario/Vignette	
Epigram	
Other	
Internal Apparatus	**Possible Text Applications**
Section Openers	
Section Closers	
Terms and Definitions	
Marginalia	
Other	
Chapter Closing Elements	**Possible Text Applications**
Conclusion	
Summary	
Key Terms/Vocabulary Review	
Discussion/Review Questions	
Chapter Quiz/Study Guide	
Applications/Problems	
Activities	
Annotated Readings	
Chapter End Notes	
Part Closing Elements	**Possible Text Applications**
Part Summary	
Other	

Develop Successful Feature Strands

Pedagogy only begins with the chapter apparatus, the subject of Chapter 9. Regularly occurring pedagogical features within the body of each chapter, often called feature strands, also contribute to the educative value and visual appeal of your textbook. The features described in the following sections—case studies, debates, primary sources, models, reflection and critical thinking questions, thematic boxes, and supplement tie-ins—need not be restricted to internal use, however. In some textbooks they are successfully located at the beginning or end of a chapter. Features such as case studies, reflections, primary source documents, and biographical profiles are especially adaptable as chapter openers or as material on which chapter-closing activities are based. As a rule of thumb, place each feature where it will do students the most good—that is, in its most relevant context in relation to chapter content and to what you are trying to put across.

Types of Internal Text Features

The types of features you choose should be guided by what your market requires or prefers, what your competition has, what your publisher suggests, and your own ideas. Whatever features you choose you must carry out systematically in every chapter, or at least regularly and not just here and there. Authors sometimes resist this kind of consistency, especially when they think certain features are more suitable for some chapters than for others. Consistency is needed, however. In the following promotion for a biology textbook revision, imagine the impression the new feature strands might make:

Example: Poor Impression Caused by Inconsistent Feature Strands

The following text features, new to this edition, were designed to capture the interest of your students and help them integrate the knowledge they gain in this course.

- BIOLOGY IN SPACE: A news feature that links chapter content to NASA research, including findings from the Space Shuttle program and SpaceLab experiments. This feature appears in Chapters 2, 3, and 7.
- PIONEERS IN BIOLOGICAL SCIENCE: An illustrated biographical

feature that briefly tells the stories of the people and events behind historically significant developments in biology. This feature appears in Chapters 1, 14, and 15.

Feature strands by definition are carried out regularly throughout a textbook, ideally in every chapter. You can overcome the problem of consistency and fit by conceptualizing a feature strand in broad enough terms to remain applicable in every chapter. For instance, in the above example, if relevant information were insufficient to have a BIOLOGY IN SPACE box in every chapter (not likely), you could call the feature strand BIOLOGY IN LIFE instead (pun intended) and include your NASA examples among others.

Each type of feature has a name or title (sometimes called a tag line) and is distinguished from the basal text through design. A real title and a design help unify a feature strand throughout your book and generate readership. Titles such as Box 1.1, Box 1.2, and Box 1.3 do not invite readership, but feature strands called SOCIOLOGY IN ACTION or ASTRONOMY'S GREATEST DISCOVERIES do. Subtitles then identify the specific subject of each box. Titled feature strands also help your publisher to promote your book and the sales force to sell it.

As mentioned in Chapter 8, some authors and instructors scorn all "boxes" and do not provide or assign them. Critics claim that features make the text too boxy or jumpy, distract the reader from the "real" reading, or compromise intellectual rigor for interest or popularity. These are the authors and instructors who believe strongly that textbooks should not "spoon feed" or pander to students and that students rightly should struggle to decipher text. When properly done, however, boxes are integral parts of the chapter, not dispensable frills or add-ons. Good feature strands help fulfill your mission in writing a textbook, can add rigor as well as interest, and often provide the in-depth concrete examples that students need to grasp or apply core concepts. Consider the following feature strands with an open mind, therefore. What kinds could you use in your textbook?

Case Studies

Case-based instruction is a mainstay in fields such as business, advertising, management, law, education, social work, and others, in which the particulars of an actual circumstance are used to test or demonstrate chapter concepts or principles in action. The best cases are real and situational, consist of accurate reportage, and end with questions for the reader. The questions invite readers to reflect on, analyze, compare or contrast, apply, or evaluate the information in the case. Case studies engage readers in cognitive processes that are desirable in active learners, such as critical thinking and problem solving. They also give instructors the option of using case analysis as a basis for class discussion or course assessment. In some courses, such as law, cases are regarded as mandatory.

Following are two examples of case studies, one for a chapter on the impact of cultural environments on multinational business and one for a chapter on assimilation and pluralism in a textbook on multicultural education.

Example A: Case Study

CASE TO CONSIDER: Cultural Assumptions
In the 1970s, a publishing house set up an operation in Bahrain to edit the first telephone and business directories for thirteen Arab states. Problems began when the company could not find sufficient qualified personnel on or near the Arab peninsula to work on the project. The publisher filled four key positions through ads in newspapers, including a young single woman as editor and three salesmen.

None of the new hires had visited the Middle East before, and all expected to conduct business as usual. The salesmen, on commission, expected to make the usual number of calls in a 9 to 5 day. They also expected to have appointments at scheduled times, the undivided attention of potential clients, and efficient business transactions. These expectations were not met, however. After many complaints from Arab businessmen, the salesmen were replaced, but the damage to sales could not be recovered.

The editor found that she was not free to travel unaccompanied in Arab countries and could not easily hire freelance assistants from hotel rooms during her travels. She had assumed that collecting the data for the telephone directories would be a simple, cost effective task. The publisher had quoted prices on the assumption that all streets would have names and that all residences and businesses would have street numbers, which proved not to be the case.

After two years, the company had to sell its floundering Bahraini operations. What, exactly, went wrong? What factors contributed to failure there, and how might the problems have been prevented or addressed? What guidelines would you propose for multinational firms planning to conduct foreign operations?

Example B: Case Study

THE CASE OF MARIA GONZALEZ
Maria sits proudly in the student lounge of a prestigious Eastern university. She thinks how if had not been for her mother and grandmother her life would be completely different now. She recalls her mother's immigrant stories about her childhood: the move from Mexico City; the humiliation of not speaking English;

the move to the suburbs and becoming American at all costs. Then her mother was introduced to Carlos Gonzales, rediscovered her roots and the joys of Latin dancing, music, and poetry. There were feasts with grandmother's cooking and trips back to the old village for the Day of the Dead. Maria and her brothers were taught to be proud of their Mexican heritage, and all are fluent in Spanish and English. Maria wonders about the other students in the student lounge and if they will expect her to be like them. She vows that will succeed at the university while still maintaining her roots.

As with chapter openers, the pedagogical value of case studies increases when they are reiterated in some way within the chapter narrative and in the closing elements. The case of Maria, for example, might employ any of the following strategies:

Examples: Linking Cases to Instruction
In the chapter introduction: The case of Maria Gonzalez suggests the pressures and conflicts that students from microcultures often confront as they try to adjust to the macroculture of a school. Maria determines to retain her Chicana identity as a U.S. citizen. Her decision reflects the process of cultural pluralism or accommodation, as distinct from assimilation or absorption into the host culture.

In the body of the narrative in a discussion of degrees of assimilation:
Recall Maria Gonzalez' story at the beginning of this chapter. If cultural assimilation is at one end of the continuum and cultural suppression is at the other, where would Maria's position fall on the continuum?

In the body of the narrative in a discussion of Mexican-American race relations:
The story of Maria Gonzalez illustrates the tension between cultural pluralism and assimilation felt by many Mexican-Americans who are bicultural. She is pulled in two different directions and must adjust to two different needs: the need to keep her identity as a Chicana with a rich culture and history and the need to be accepted by her classmates.

In the chapter conclusion:
Students like Maria Gonzalez experience cultural conflict. Most American schools have students who, like Maria, feel the pressures of a dual identity as a result of living within two cultures simultaneously. Multicultural education has developed in recognition of this reality.

As a closing activity or an item in the test bank or study guide supplement:
Contrast the case of Maria Gonzalez to that of Isaac Washington. What are the essential differences in their experiences as members of microcultures? What are the essential differences in their responses to biculturalism?

Case studies are not suitable for all subject areas. Consider them for your textbook, however. Like scenarios and vignettes, cases often are easily and appropriately adaptable for both "soft" and "hard" academic courses.

Profiles

Profiles offer detailed descriptive accounts of particular examples (or exemplars) of chapter content. Like case studies, profiles explore a selected topic in greater depth. Business, management, and marketing texts, for example, often highlight the success stories of particular individuals, firms, or advertising campaigns. An archaeology text might profile excavations of particularly important sites. A professional book might have career profiles. Literature surveys might have biographical or historical profiles to provide context for selections of literature; and texts on government, international politics, urban sociology, or cultural geography might offer chapter-by-chapter cartographic and statistical profiles.

In addition to providing data, profiles most often feature positive exemplars, such as famous or successful people, places, products, or events. Positive real-life profiles in each chapter can provide strong motivation to read. A marketing textbook might profile the founders of Ben and Jerry's ice cream and other entrepreneurs. A teacher education textbook might profile winners of the national Teacher of the Year award. An American architectural history textbook might profile the F. W. Woolworth building, and so on.

As with other kinds of feature strands, the pedagogical value of profiles increases with opportunities for students to interact with the information beyond simple comprehension. Applications at the end of the marketing profiles might ask students to find other current examples of the kinds of success shown or to visit the profiled companies' home pages on the Internet. Applications at the end of the teacher profiles might ask students to identify positive attributes or to find out more about the subjects.

Debates

Some textbooks lend themselves to features that present opposing views on chapter-relevant issues. Pro/Con or Point/Counterpoint features are especially appropriate for textbooks in the social sciences and related fields and for introductions to the professions. The keys to successful debate formats are balance, fairness, and credibility, so some care must be taken in selecting spokespersons for opposing views. Identify those persons by name and source, and give their views equal space. Again, end the features with questions for the reader.

> **Example: Topics for a Debate Feature**
> **For a one-half page, two-column feature in a behavioral psychology text:**
> **Chapter 3** Biology and Behavior
> DEBATE FORUM: Are there sex differences in the way people think?
> **Chapter 5** Environment and Behavior
> DEBATE FORUM: Can environmental controls on behavior solve social problems?
> **Chapter 8** Motivation and Behavior
> DEBATE FORUM: Do people fear success as much as they do failure?

The design formats for a debate feature may be based on polarization, with a "PRO" or "YES" column juxtaposed beside a "CON" or "NO" column. Another option is to present the feature in three parts: Part one states the issue, part two describes the debate, and part three asks readers about a solution. Debate features might end with specific versions of some of the following generic questions:

- With which view or combination of views do you agree most?
- Which evidence or argument did you find most persuasive, and why?
- How do your own past experiences relate to these opposing views?
- What further evidence or argument might you add to the debate?
- How does the information in this chapter relate to this debate?
- What are the implications of each view for practice or policy?
- What questions would you ask, and what answers would you need, to strengthen or change your view?

To make effective debate features, choose current and authentic issues and avoid insulting the reader's intelligence. The best debates represent true dilemmas in which both or all positions on an issue can be believably defended. Above all, avoid the language of high-minded sentiment or propaganda and offer documented evidence and arguments based on facts. Note that values clarification typically is not a goal of debate features in college textbooks today, but ethical or professional dilemmas may be entirely appropriate along with policy debates.

Primary Sources
Excerpts from documents, first-person accounts, artifacts or exhibits of evidence, and passages from literature are examples of the use of primary sources in

textbooks. Primary source material is all but indispensable in some arts and humanities—including history, philosophy, and literature—and also in the social sciences. If your field is document-based, why not build the need for primary source material into a regular chapter feature?

Examples: Primary Source Feature Strands

A. SNAPSHOTS OF THE PAST (in an undergraduate U.S. history textbook, 1865 to the present): a one-half page per chapter feature on the interpretation of photographs as historical evidence. Each photograph relates to the period or theme of the chapter and supports a main point. An extended caption identifies the link between the photo and the chapter, provides background information on the event captured, guides the reader through the image, models the historiographical process involved in treating the image as evidence, and asks questions pertaining to all the above.

B. THE PHILOSOPHER'S STONE (in a textbook on philosophy for a survey course): two one-page features per chapter with excerpts from classic works by noted philosophers representative of the chapter's period, theme, or main point. Excerpts end with questions to readers to stimulate reflection, aid comprehension, or guide analysis. This model is also commonly used in literature surveys.

C. FIELD NOTES (in a textbook on cultural anthropology): a one-page feature in each chapter with a transcription of a noted ethnographer's first person account of his or her field experiences. Students are asked to interpret the field notes or to explain their significance in relation to chapter content.

D. TEACHER TALK (in a textbook on becoming a teacher): one-page first-person accounts by practicing master teachers on how they deal with situations pertaining to main chapter topics.

Substantive excerpts are best for primary source features, because they enable readers to examine critical material in some depth or detail. An in-depth feature also can serve as an antidote to a common complaint about survey texts—that in attempting to cover too much they merely "mention" everything superficially. If your textbook is for a survey course, therefore, consider that primary sources, cases, debates, or profiles might systematically permit more depth.

Arguments against using primary source material are the time it takes to find them and the permissions costs, which in some cases can be prohibitively high. Whatever the course, in addition to primary source documents consider the role that brief first-person accounts or documentary excerpts might play in your exposition. Anecdotes, famous quotations, unusual newspaper headlines, or provocative government statistics might contribute to your pedagogical aims as well as your publisher's marketing campaign.

Models

Models in any field are applications or demonstrations of practices, principles, theories, or laws expressed in form or function. Models are examples of perfection, therefore, or at least of excellence or ideal cases (all other things being equal). The implicit message of models of any type is that they should be followed.

English composition textbooks, for example, model good writing. An emphasis on decision making processes in marketing could be translated into a feature strand in which a model marketing decision is presented in each chapter. A textbook on research might model steps in the scientific method. A textbook on law enforcement or on accounting might model professional routines or procedures. A primatology or climatology textbook might present predictive models that readers run to answer questions. A chemistry textbook might contain diagrams of reactions and compounds, an example of models in the most literal sense as illustrations. Textbooks on chemistry, mathematics, photography, and architectural design typically rely on physical models in the form of graphical representations.

Related to models are "how-to" features, usually presented as numbered lists set off from the narrative. The lists briefly call out the sequence of steps to take to accomplish something or to apply a method. In some textbooks, the lists give reminders or tips for successful practice. Eye-catching how-to boxes offer the reader a resource for quick reference or immediate access to what you are attempting to teach in each chapter. How-tos are especially appropriate if your textbook and its market have a practical or applied orientation. This book contains many such lists, for instance. In any field, however, educational research strongly supports the use of modeling as a method of instruction. Activities calling for applications to new contexts are an ideal way to maximize the pedagogical value of models.

As an example of effective pedagogy of this type, examine the online sample chapter at **www.ablongman.com/slavintour/**. This educational psychology textbook by R. Slavin zeroes in on teaching standards and teaching practice as the purposes of study in the course. All the chapter pedagogy directly supports these purposes, beginning with the opening case and including self-checks relating to the INTASC and PRAXIS II standards, the "Theory into Practice" feature (pp. 266-68), the "Teacher Action Checklist" feature (p. 276), and the self-assessment in the closer. Textbooks in the professions with this type of practical pedagogy tend to have much higher retention rates.

Reflection and Critical Thinking Questions

Reflective features present situations and invite readers to perceive, think about, and respond to those situations in relation to themselves as individuals. The goal is to engage the reader's personal identification with the subject, prior knowledge, thought processes, and affective responses. Reflections often are built around questions and include an activity such as recording thoughts and feelings in a journal or filling out a rating form. Questionnaires, opinion polls, and self-assessments also are forms of this type of feature. Reflection questions are geared to the individual learner and often are not well suited for class discussion.

In an introductory American government text, for example, chapters might contain reflection features built on the following questions.

Example: Reflection-Based Feature Strand

Chapter 1 Understanding American Government

REFLECTION: What are three questions you have about American government to which you wish you had answers?

Chapter 2 The Constitutional Foundations

REFLECTION: As a participant in the Constitutional Convention, what part of the Constitution might you have tried to change from its present form, and why?

Chapter 3 Civil Liberties

REFLECTION: On any given day, how, specifically, does the way you live your life reflect the Constitutional Amendments?

Chapter 4 Public Opinion

REFLECTION: What is your opinion on the following issues? Which issues would you feel strongly enough about to try to influence lawmakers if you had the opportunity?

Chapter 5 Political Parties

REFLECTION: Where do you stand on the liberal-conservative continuum?

Questions for reflection features might also take specific forms of the following general patterns:

- If you were presented with the following situation what would you do?
- In the following situation what could you say to [e.g., reduce tension and redirect the conversation]?
- Rate the following statements on a five-point scale from "strongly agree" (1) to "strongly disagree" (5). Your ratings will help you clarify your philosophical stance on this issue.
- Record in your journal three reasons you think you would like to become a gerontologist.

Reflection questions often require critical thinking, and many college textbooks offer sets of critical thinking questions instead as part of the chapter pedagogy. Critical thinking questions also can be appended to other feature types to make them interactive, link them to chapter content, and guarantee reader response. Chapters 8-10 of this book contain many examples of this use of critical thinking questions.

Unlike discussion and review questions, critical thinking questions are not answerable directly from the chapter narrative and do not have one right answer or established parameters for an expected range of answers. Critical thinking questions are not merely rhetorical, however, nor are they simply statements of opinion. The questions involve the reader's experiences and expectations outside the course, and students support their opinions with reasoned judgments or argue from premises or data.

Some textbooks have reflection-based rating forms that invite readers to interact with text literally by writing in the book. Write-on lines are provided in the margins or in spaces designed to resemble note cards. At one time, if students wrote in your book, its sales would increase, because many college bookstores would not buy back "defaced" books for resale as used books. However, that standard, too, has fallen. Resale operators buy back books at the full used book price regardless of students' underlinings, marginal notes, or completed exercises.

In addition, blank spaces for student write-ins can take up a lot of expensive space in a textbook, leaving you with less room to accomplish your instructional goals. If your course requires many opportunities for on-page student practice, it might be best to plan a lower-cost student supplement to accompany your textbook, such as a manual, workbook, or study guide.

The best way to get students to keep your title on their shelves is to provide a work that is so full of valuable, relevant information that users see it as indispensable. Students tend to hold on to reference books, handbooks, bibliographies, directories, and professional resource guides. Many authors add appendices or reference sections to their books that serve student interests and encourage retention. The reality is, however, that by the end of your textbook's first semester of availability students will sell back as much as 60 percent of your print run, which will be sold as used books to the next semester's students.

Thematic Boxes

A selling point for a textbook is its currency, not only in source citations, but in the presence of themes that reflect the latest hot topics or professional concerns and trends in the field. For example, genome research may be a central concern in the life sciences, new medications and new assistive technologies may be issues in special education, crime scene investigation and crime mapping may be hot in criminal justice, and nonethnocentric reinterpretation may be a trend in U.S. history. Each of these examples could serve as a unifying theme for a feature strand in the form of thematic boxes.

Each chapter in a life sciences textbook, for example, could have an informational box on how genetics research relates to the chapter or on the implications of genetics research for the chapter's main subject. There could be boxes on food staple genomes in relation to world hunger, mutagenic environments, the preservation of natural pharmacopoeia, endangered species, gene therapies, square watermelons, pharaonic DNA, and so on, throughout. In the special education textbook, each chapter could have an informational box on medications or assistive technologies for students with different kinds of disability or for inclusive classrooms. Each chapter of the criminal justice textbook could feature a relevant technology, such as 911 emergency systems, crime mapping, electronic surveillance, DNA testing, sex crimes databasing, interrogation videotaping, cruiser-mounted cameras or computers, and the like. Finally, each chapter of the history text could have a cultural awareness box that calls attention to interesting or relevant ethnocentric views or interpretations of historical figures and events.

The content of thematic boxes reinforces points made in the narrative but does not attempt to substitute for narrative text, where all important exposition should appear. Reinforcement of information in a history textbook, for instance, might be provided through thematic chronologies or time lines or through descriptions of critical decisions, benchmarks, or turning points.

A theme adaptable to many disciplines is the investigative report, media application, or research brief. For example, you might have a box in each chapter describing recent important research in your field in the form of an abstract or a summary of the findings. Imaginative, well-written, and well-designed thematic boxes add contemporaneity, interest, pertinence, and visual appeal for your readers. In addition, thematic feature strands support one of the metacognitive aims of education: the integration of knowledge.

Examples of effective thematic boxes appear in the online sample Chapter 6 of D. Hales' textbook, *An Invitation to Health* (**www.wadsworthtours.com/ptours/**). The "Across the Lifespan" and "Savvy Consumer" features in every chapter support, respectively, the overall text theme and a "hot topic" in the field.

Supplement Tie-Ins

In integrated textbook packages, having pedagogical features that link supplements to the text can be an important selling point. If your textbook will come with a reader, magazine, videotape, software, CD-ROM, or companion web site, for example, you and your editor should think about embedding feature strands in the text that relate to them. Likewise, your instructor's manual should suggest ways that instructors can use the textbook features in conjunction with supplements to advance student learning.

Your ability to tie in supplements will depend on what your publisher plans or already has to put with your textbook. If your package will include a videotape, for example, you might have a feature that addresses the subject of a related video segment. If your textbook will appear as an interactive edition with web links and other media assets, you may want to plan an intext feature strand that relates to these capabilities. Decisions about supplements, a subject that is beyond the scope of this book, are made by managers and editors in consultation with authors. See *Writing and Developing Your College Textbook Supplements* by this author, forthcoming.

Your Pedagogy Plan

Survey the textbooks you have at hand to examine and analyze the use of pedagogical features. As a framework for this study, use your notes from the Chapter 8 Appendix, Developing Your Pedagogy Plan and the Chapter 9 Appendix, Planning Your Apparatus. Then use the planning grid in this chapter's appendix, Planning Your Feature Strands, to think of possibilities for features for your textbook. Here are some tips to consider as you plan:

Tips for Choosing Feature Strands

Choose feature types that
- address proven needs in your course.
- address new concerns in your field.
- fit your subject.
- match or top what your competitors offer.
- make visible a special strength or unique aspect of your textbook.
- express your mission or key themes.
- are relevant to the audience.
- engage student interest, curiosity, and desire.
- can be fulfilled realistically and efficiently.
- can be provided systematically throughout the textbook.

After choosing the feature types that have the most promising applications for your book, consult your working TOC to start brainstorming suitable topics for features of each type for each chapter. Also note sources of information for each feature or the names of possible contributors. Add these ideas to the ideas you developed for chapter apparatus, and then communicate these ideas to your sponsoring editor or development editor, who might also have some useful suggestions, samples, or models for you to consider. Then revise and submit the Pedagogy Plan you developed after reading Chapter 8 reflecting your and your editors' decisions.

In some cases your editors may submit a proposed pedagogy plan to you for your review. Either way, everyone eventually must buy in to the planned apparatus and pedagogy for your textbook, and once this happens you may not change it. You will be expected to carry out the approved plan or to arrange for it to be carried out, or the publisher might hire someone to carry out the pedagogy plan in your place. The reason that changes may not be made after a certain point is that changes cost time and money. Substantive changes to a book's approved design, for example, which includes complex coding for each element of your apparatus and pedagogy, often are too costly to bear.

Now you have a plan for chapter apparatus and pedagogy that will make your book competitive in the marketplace and that everyone likes. In the planning and development process—in an ideal world—you are ready to draft or revise your manuscript in earnest, and this is the subject of the next chapter. Your first chapters, with all apparatus and pedagogy in place, will be submitted for design.

Appendix: Planning Your Feature Strands

Feature Type	Possible Textbook Applications
Case studies	_____
Profiles	_____
Debates	_____
Primary sources	_____
Models	_____
How-tos	_____
Reflections	_____
Critical thinking	_____
Thematic boxes	_____
Supplement tie-ins	_____
Other	_____

Decisions about Feature Strands

Selected Type of Feature	Possible Name for Feature Strand	Possible Topical Applications by Chapter
Strand Type 1		Ch. 1
		2
		3
		4
		5
		6
		7
		8
		9
		10
		11
		12
		13
		14
Strand Type 2		Ch. 1
		2
		3
		4
		5
		6
		7
		8
		9
		10
		11
		12
		13
		14

Selected Type of Feature	Possible Name for Feature Strand	Possible Topical Applications by Chapter
Strand Type 3		Ch. 1
		2
		3
		4
		5
		6
		7
		8
		9
		10
		11
		12
		13
		14
Strand Type 4		Ch. 1
		2
		3
		4
		5
		6
		7
		8
		9
		10
		11
		12
		13
		14

Make Drafting and Revising Easier on You

You can make authoring easier on yourself in basic ways, beginning with:

- observing your publisher's requirements for manuscript preparation.
- submitting complete manuscript.
- making a commitment to consistency in style.
- developing checklists to manage the drafting process.
- doing your homework and systematically managing chapter resources.
- monitoring balance in topical development.
- completing references as you draft.

How can you accomplish these tasks efficiently?

Preparing Manuscript

Authors who follow manuscript preparation guidelines decrease the cost of producing their books in countless small ways. These costs affect their earnings as well as their publishers'. Thus, as mentioned previously, you should follow or question even seemingly trivial requests from publisher guidelines or editors, because there probably are practical or technical reasons for those requests.

Consider Author X. In undertaking a revision of his textbook, Author X combined new material with tearsheet (actual pages from the last edition), but neglected to secure tearsheet as requested (taped down on all sides). As a result, the 1,500-page manuscript had to be hand fed into a copier one page at a time. This was after a supplier was paid to type all the authors' unreadable handwritten corrections, which he had written sideways in the margins. In addition, because in pasting up tearsheet Author X used a type of tape that cannot be overwritten, a copyeditor had to key corrections on flags (self-stick notes) and separate sheets, which raised the cost of copyediting by 40 percent. Furthermore, Author X ran figures in with text, left in old figure and table numbers from the last edition, and ran together chapter manuscripts for captions and annotations instead of starting each chapter on a fresh page. As a result, an editor spent 11 hours cutting and pasting the manuscript at $30 per hour, which was charged to the book. Also, the caption manuscript had to be rekeyboarded to prevent confusion for the copyeditor and layout artist and to prevent both penalty charges and incorrect length estimates from the compositor.

In a way, Author X was lucky. The publisher took care of his lapses. More than in the past, many houses are unwilling to incur extra production costs such as the above, however, even when these costs are charged against your book and passed back to you. Your improperly prepared manuscript is simply rejected as "unacceptable" and is returned to you for correction. Depending on how long it takes you to fix it, your book can lose its place in the publishing queue. In some smaller houses, unfortunately, the publisher simply publishes whatever you send as camera-ready copy, acceptable or not. In camera-ready copy, your physical manuscript pages are mounted in a vacuum frame, photographed, and printed from the film.

The advantage of camera-ready copy is that the publisher does not have to invest in book design or page make-up. The advantage of using tearsheet for a revision is the savings in copyediting costs. Only new material has to be copyedited and not previously published material that already has gone through the copyediting process. Actually, however, the days of pasted-up tearsheet and camera-ready copy are pretty much over. New computer technologies are sufficiently cost effective to make up for redundant copyediting. Thus, your revision, like your first edition, probably will go to into production on a corrected disk and be copyedited from scratch.

Each publishing house has its own unique rules for how manuscript should be prepared, but all will request that the hardcopy and diskcopy that you submit as final manuscript match exactly. Following are some examples of generic manuscript preparation guidelines that contribute to controlling the cost of producing a book.

All-Purpose Guidelines for Manuscript Preparation

1. Double space all copy, without exception, regardless of its context or intended use.
2. Do not underline anything for any purpose unless the editor agrees. Use italics only for words as words, and use boldface sparingly and consistently, e.g., for key terms.
3. Do not use hard returns in text except after headings and to start new paragraphs.
4. Put each figure and table on a separate sheet (unless instructed otherwise), keyed to text for location.
5. Identify each photo, figure, and table and its caption by double-number and title.
6. Be consistent in heading styles, text formats, and fonts; use a single simple basic font, such as Times New Roman, Arial, or Courier New, and do not change type sizes for effect or use design features (unless you are submitting your book camera ready).

7. Unless otherwise instructed, number all pages consecutively with each chapter starting on page 1.
8. Completely fill manuscript pages, leaving standard or wider margins.
9. Complete all parenthetical source citations and notes or references.
10. Submit complete chapter manuscript all at once or in batches as the publisher allows.

Submitting Complete Manuscript

A chapter that lacks a summary, the figures, or the boxes is not complete. Furthermore, your manuscript technically is not complete when you submit all your chapters, as a textbook also may contain some or all of the following elements:

- preface and acknowledgments
- table of contents
- parts and chapters
- figures and tables
- apparatus and pedagogy
- appendices
- photos or photo specifications and captions
- source citations, notes, references, and credit lines
- annotations or glossary entries
- author index and subject index
- permissions log and grants to date

As noted previously, these elements may be your responsibility to provide, depending on your agreement with the publisher. Many houses treat frontmatter and endmatter separately, in which case these elements are permitted to trail the rest of the manuscript into production. An index, especially, is not complete until the manuscript has been put into type and paged. Nevertheless, a "complete" manuscript technically includes all the listed elements. Some houses put manuscripts into production in batches, while others will do absolutely nothing for your book until the manuscript is 100 percent complete, including all grants of permission. An incomplete manuscript can mean significant delay and unanticipated extra cost.

Preparing a Draft

If you are preparing a revision, you might be working with actual pages of your last edition (tearsheet), but more likely you will be working with disks onto which your last edition text has been scanned. Some houses will send a copy of the actual disks used in printing the last edition, or your publisher may authorize you to revise on copies of your original chapter files in your computer. Revising electronically is much easier and quicker for the author than cutting and pasting tearsheet.

Every house has its own guidelines for preparing a revision and varies in strictness in observing guidelines. Your publisher may require that you type any change or addition consisting of three words or more, for instance, rather than write it on tearsheet. Or, your publisher may require that you redline edited material as you alter the original files so that editors can track your changes. Following are some widely used rules of thumb for preparing a revision manuscript:

Guidelines for Revising

- Neatly write minor corrections legibly using a medium that photo-copies easily (for example, not hard pencil or nonreproducible blue). Take care to form numbers correctly.
- Write corrections above or beside text to be edited, using insertion carets to show where the changes go. Do not write at the top or bottom of the page and then key changes with long arrows. Also, do not write sideways up the margins.
- Type any change involving more than a few words. Key the correction or addition for location, and insert the new copy on a separate sheet as the next page. Number additional pages the same as the insertion page plus a, b, etc. Double-space all keyboarded corrections and additions.
- Avoid using numbered and circled paragraphs to indicate a change in the sequence of text, especially if the change affects more than one page. Rather, cut and paste these sections (physically or electronically) into the new order.
- Cut and paste (or print out) each tearsheet figure and table and place it on a separate page.
- Check changes in the wording of headings and feature strands and in the numbering of figures and tables.
- Pay special attention to updating statistics, parenthetical source citations, credit lines, and references.
- Use standard-size paper and fill each page with roughly the same number of lines. Both incomplete and overfilled pages make it difficult to estimate manuscript length accurately.
- Exclude last edition photos or any elements that are being dropped.
- Create separate annotation, reference, caption, and glossary manuscripts, as relevant, realphabetizing as needed.

Your publisher probably will have other specific requirements for manuscript preparation. For example, as mentioned previously, if you are revising on disk and providing a new hardcopy, your publisher will want the diskcopy and hardcopy to match exactly. The copyeditor probably will be working on the hardcopy, while at the same time your disk may go to the packager for other production procedures. You also must be vigilant to ensure that the correct, most current version of each chapter is the one that goes into production.

Manuscript preparation can be a real pain. The level of detail involved definitely is not for everyone. If this kind of attention to mechanical details proves a burden to you, take the initiative in advance to enlist the aid of a paid or volunteer helper who can do this for you. Authors are wise who optimize the time and attention they can give to content over form.

Make a Commitment to Consistency

In publishing, consistency is rarely foolish (and therefore is not a hobgoblin of little minds). Inconsistency, large or small, leads to structural weakness, imbalance in exposition, and loss of reader confidence. Consistency can be difficult to achieve, however—another authoring task that requires mindfulness and self-monitoring. Issues of consistency in the fulfillment of chapter apparatus and pedagogical feature strands have already been addressed in Chapters 8, 9, and 10. When editors or reviewers identify a pattern of inconsistency they might also be referring to discrepancies in voice, tone, reading level, writing style, editorial style, heading structure, or amounts of topical detail, discussed in Chapters 5, 6, and 7.

As noted in Chapter 5, if the editor does not send you Author Guidelines with information on house style, you should request them. Consistently follow house style first, then consistently follow the preferred style of your discipline (for textbooks, not for journal articles) on everything the house style does not cover.

In drafting, some authors get into a muddle over style and format. For instance, they arbitrarily switch verb tenses, subject pronouns, reference styles, or formats for headings and key terms. During the production process, professional copyeditors catch these things and rightfully insist on congruence, but this comes just at a time when you thought you were done with your book and perhaps have exhausted yourself. You can save yourself a lot of eleventh-hour hassles from copyeditors by attending to these matters as much as possible beforehand. You can also save yourself money (directly or indirectly depending on your contract) and embarrassment. Professional copyeditors make $20 to $30 an hour or as much as $3.00 per page. Whatever inconsistencies they miss end up in print.

Develop Drafting Checklists

The trick to achieving consistency is to decide at the outset how you will treat various mechanics and to draft a checklist of those decisions. Such a checklist saves you having to redecide repeatedly, risking inconsistency, or to lose time by flipping through manuscript to see how you did things previously, or by constantly consulting manuals of style. As you go along using a personalized checklist, you will establish time- and hassle-saving drafting habits. Eventually you will not need to refer to your checklists at all.

The following list identifies the decisions you should include on your Mechanics and Style Checklist.

Mechanics and Style Checklist

For your own use, use a checklist like this to record a sample of how you plan to treat each of the following elements or directions for how they should look.

ELEMENTS	RULE OR EXAMPLE OR STYLE
A-heads	
B-heads	
C-heads	
Lists	
Quotations	
Parenthetical citations	
Notes	
Credit lines	
References	
Figure captions	
Table captions	
Photo captions	
Key terms	
Glossary definitions	
Annotations	
Other:	

Inconsistency in even small things, such as embedded lists, can lead to error and confusion. If some of your lists are numbered, some bulleted, and some plain, there has to be a clear reason or rationale. If some of your key terms are boldfaced, some italicized, and some undistinguished, what should the reader conclude?

Your Mechanics and Style Checklist also can include miscellaneous reminders based on your particular needs, such as remembering to reference your figures and tables by number in the narrative, remembering to key the placement of figures and tables in your manuscript, or remembering to monitor length.

Keep your Mechanics and Style Checklist on hand along with an Apparatus and Pedagogy Checklist, which should contain reminders for what to include in every chapter and self-directions for how you will treat the mechanics of your pedagogy. Use the decisions you made in Chapters 8, 9, and 10 to develop your Apparatus and Pedagogy Checklist. For your own reference record the following decisions about apparatus and pedagogy to apply in every chapter: the title and subtitle style of each feature, the number of each type of feature per chapter, what has to be in each chapter opener and in what order, and what has to be in each chapter closer and in what order.

Apparatus and Pedagogy Checklist

ELEMENTS	DECISIONS	
Parts	Title/Subtitle Style Part Opener Contents Part Closer Contents	No. of Parts
Chapters	Number/Title Style	No. of Chapters
Ch. Openers 1 2 3 4 5	Contents 1 2 3 4 Introduction 5 1st A-head	
Ch. Closers 1 2 3 4 5	Contents 1 Conclusion 2 3 4 5	
Feature Strands 1 2 3 4 5	Title/Subtitle Style 1 2 3 4 5	No. per Ch.

In addition, some authors keep a separate Style Sheet that lists reminders about using the house style and the editorial style they have chosen. Some authors personalize their style sheets by noting errors of English composition, spelling, and grammar to which they are prone and specific usages they need to include or avoid, such as technical or politically sensitive terms.

Common usage errors in college texts include, for example, *may* and *might, can* and *could, if* and *whether, which* and *that, reason why* (redundant), etc. Finding these kinds of errors is the copyeditor's job, however. As author, once you have recorded your decisions in drafting checklists and have achieved consistency, your time and effort are better spent attending to the content of your book rather than to English composition, even if you are writing in English as a second language.

An important exception is if your first draft chapters are being sent out for peer review. In this case you should make every effort to provide error-free copy. Reviewers tend to be indignant, even harsh, over errors of spelling and grammar, which negatively skew their perceptions of your content. Your editor must then defend your book to the publisher against negative reviews. The appendix at the end of this chapter lists some resources on English composition and expository writing for academic authors.

Manage Resources

As you network, develop checklists, and gather materials for your textbook, arrange these resources in a way that will help you manage your project. Resource management can include setting up chapter-by-chapter folders with clipping files or computer files of items to include or reference in each chapter, such as current articles and events, references, notes, bibliographies, instructional strategies, student activities, applications, illustrations, or examples, as relevant. Include complete information as to sources and copyright holders, because these are a nightmare to search for after the fact.

Chapter folders will make life easier for you as you draft or revise. They have multiple uses, serving as reminders of what to beef up or add; models for pedagogical features; ideas for figures or special content; concrete examples to use in exposition; or items for your instructor's manual, margin notes, or test bank. Even if you are an experienced writer, cumulative resource folders can be a comfort as you begin each chapter on a blank screen.

Monitoring Balance in Topical Development

As a textbook author you naturally will have more to say about your favorite topics and those you know best. At the same time, you might be tempted to skimp or overgeneralize on topics at the fringes of your interest or expertise. You might even be tempted to omit some topics even though they are within the scope of your book and are expected by your customers. Overcoming these temptations is another authoring task requiring self-discipline. The overall balance of your book is at stake, not to mention perceived intellectual soundness.

Fortunately, you can check for topical development as you draft:

- Does Chapter 6 list three times as many key terms as Chapters 4 and 5? Perhaps you have gone into too much technical detail in

Chapter 6 and/or not enough detail in the other chapters. Maybe you need to redistribute your material.

- In each chapter do the most important topics use the most space and the least important the least space? The number of lines or pages devoted to a topic indicates its comparative importance, and the reader naturally uses comparative length and detail to make judgments about degree of importance. Maybe you need to drop paragraphs from some topics and add paragraphs to others.

- In each chapter do your topics of clearly equal importance have roughly equal space? For example, does your chapter on child development devote a similar number of pages to early, middle, and later childhood? Assuming you are not attempting to propagandize your Introduction to Economics readers, does your section on the pros and cons of regulating interest rates devote a similar number of paragraphs to both the pros and the cons? Research shows that the amount of exposure a reader has to a topic will affect what the reader both values and retains in memory.

A good way to prevent problems of balance in exposition is to map out topics in advance in terms of the numbers of paragraphs, pages, or chapters that you plan to devote to each one. Enter these counts on a copy of your drafting outline or table of contents and keep this information with your drafting checklists. Classroom instructors perform a similar content analysis when they decide how much class time to spend on each part of a lesson, unit, or course. This practice will also help you meet the length requirements for each chapter and for the book as a whole while still saying everything that really needs to be said in the space you have.

Managing Source Citations

Cite sources. It is expected in all academic disciplines. And it is expected at all levels. Some authors claim that first-year, "low-level," vocational, or community college students don't need source citations. Other authors actually claim that they are the source of all the ideas in their book or that all the facts cited are common knowledge. These authors are an embarrassment to themselves and their publishers. Sometimes—in lawsuits—they are liabilities as well. Another excuse for malfeasance is that source citations clutter up the text, interrupt reading, and anyway are lost on undergraduate readers, who don't know enough to use them. However, all students in postsecondary education are entitled to know the origins of ideas and information they read, whether or not they appreciate or use them.

Generally, undergraduate textbooks should contain either parenthetical source citations or superscript note numbers with chapter end notes. The latter often are preferred, especially if citing is extensive, because of the space that parentheticals can consume when embedded within basal text. Sometimes the chapter end notes are collected by chapter in the endmatter of the book rather than at the ends of chapters.

You would be wise not to insist on footnotes. If the information is not important enough to include in the narrative and cannot be treated as a source note, then it probably is a conceit—a costly conceit because it involves printing outside of the normal text block, which is always more expensive. Footnotes are more expensive to copyedit, set into type, and correct. In addition, in the trade footnotes immediately identify a text as graduate or postgraduate level. You also would be wise to complete source citations as you draft. Do not leave strings of parentheses enclosing only question marks, to be completed later, for you no doubt will regret it. Complete source citations also should accompany all figures and tables.

Completing Notes and References

Publishing a textbook is contingent on the completion of key authoring tasks other than writing the book manuscript. Chief among these are citing sources, completing notes and references, and acquiring permissions.

Consider Author X, who has not made time to survey the literature to update the sources for her revision. She feels that stopping to check references interferes with her creative flow. Getting to the library is inconvenient, and she's sure she remembers where she saw something or can scrounge what she needs from her bookcase. She plans to rectify everything in her final draft. As a result, her manuscript contains many passages like the following:

> At the turn of the twentieth century architects and architectural engineers shifted their focus from facades to infrastructures (DeVries ???). According to Eldridge, this shift was "a direct consequence of further technological developments in the manufacture of steel" (1993: ??).

Her draft references look like this:

> Davis, Arnold. 1952. *Twentieth Century Architecture*. Boston: Little, Brown.
> DeVries
> Eggan, Charles. 1987. *Facades Through the Ages*. New York: Macmillan.
> Eldridge. 1993. *Steel*.

Author X would have acted differently if she knew what agonies were in store for her. The copyeditor repeatedly flags or queries every incomplete source and reminds her that authors cited within the narrative rather than in parenthetical citations must be identified by both their first and last names. Just when she is working day and night to make deadline for page proof, Author X discovers she needs to hire someone to track down her sources and fill in the missing information in both the narrative and the references. She also discovers that no authoring task is more spirit-killing than trying to find page numbers after the fact. (Ask anyone who has suffered this lapse.) In addition, she worries that the graduate student she has shanghaied into doing it isn't really up to the task. Unbeknownst to her, the hired hand, frustrated, is not above fudging things when necessary. And the publisher won't help, insisting that sources and references are strictly the author's responsibility. So Author X is out of pocket as well.

Don't think like Author X. Source citations, notes, references, and credit lines can be a torture for everyone involved in the publishing process. Together with permissions they are among the most common reasons for a book being pulled from production, missing its publication date, missing its copyright year, or failing to see print. The best time to complete citations and references is in your first draft, even if some material is later dropped.

You can also make drafting easier on yourself by drafting to length and meeting authoring schedules, the subjects of Chapter 12, and by doing permissions right. Advice on how to do permissioning is the subject of Chapter 13.

Appendix: Selected Resources on Expository Writing

Survey sites on writing resources, including references and advice on academic writing, technical writing, and textbook writing. Also try support sites for writers and canvass for writing aids or other textbook writers with whom to discuss writing, e.g.,

Educational Writers Association (EWA): **www.ewa.org**
Text and Academic Authors Association (TAA): **www.TAAonline.net**
National Writers Union (NWU): **www.nwu.org/nwu/**
Indispensable Writing Resources: **www.quintcareers.com/writing/**
Purdue Online Writing Lab: **owl.englishpurdue.edu/**
Paradigm Online Writing Assistant: **www.powa.org/**

Cantor, Jeffrey A. *A Guide to Academic Writing*. Praeger, 1993.

Cheney, Theodore A. Rees. *Getting the Words Right: How to Revise, Edit and Rewrite*. Writer's Digest Books, 1990.

Cook, Claire Kehrwald. *Line by Line: How to Edit Your Own Writing*. Houghton Mifflin, 1985.

Einsohn, Amy. *The Copyeditor's Handbook: A Guide for Book Publishing and Corporate Communication*. University of California Press, 2000.

Grossman, John. *The Chicago Manual of Style*, 14th ed. University of Chicago Press, 1993.

Judd, Karen. *Copyediting: A Practical Guide*, 3rd ed. Crisp Publications, 2001.

Lanham, Richard. *Revising Prose*, 3rd ed. Allyn and Bacon, 1992.

Luey, B. *Handbook for Academic Authors*. Cambridge University Press, 1987.

Miller, Casey, and Kate Swift. *The Handbook of Nonsexist Writing: For Writers, Editors and Speakers*, 2nd ed. Lippincott, 1988.

Skillin, Marjorie E., and Robert Malcolm Gay. *Words into Type*, 3rd ed. Pearson, 1974.

Strunk, William, Jr., and E. B. White. *The Elelments of Style*, 4th ed. Allyn & Bacon, 2000.

Tarutz, Judith A. *Technical Editing: The Practical Guide for Editors and Writers*. Perseus, 1992.

Zinsser, W. *On Writing Well*, 5th ed. Harper & Row, 1994.

Control Length and Manage Schedule

As you now know, publishers have length requirements for books, based on what they know of their markets, what directly competing books do, and what they think they can sell. There are practical considerations as well. College courses typically run for 15 or 16 weeks, including a week or more for testing, but at some schools semesters run for only 10 to 12 weeks. Your book realistically might have 12 to 16 chapters to be read and studied at a rate of one chapter per week, or 20 or more brief ones that can be absorbed easily at a rate of two chapters a week.

An average of 50 pages of reading and study per week per course is the recommended maximum on a majority of campuses nationwide. In bookmaking for undergraduate markets, 40 pages or fewer per chapter is the general preferred standard, depending on the nature, scope, and level of the course. Using the preferred maximums, and depending on the trim size (the actual physical dimensions), your introductory textbook might be around 544 book pages, for example, with frontmatter and endmatter adding another 64 pages for a total of 608 pages.

Why Length Is Important

Book length is determined in advance. That is, in commercial textbook publishing you do not have the luxury of waiting to see what you come up with. The publisher will want to know how many pages you estimate your book will be or will tell you how many pages of manuscript or how many words to supply. This number probably will be in your contract, and you will be expected to meet it. If your manuscript is significantly under length, you will be asked to supply more copy, and if it is significantly overlength, you will be asked to cut. As you read in Chapter 3, contracts often give publishers the power to hire someone else to meet length requirements if you cannot or will not do so.

Why is length so important? As you may recall from Chapter 1, the publisher has book buyers who contract for the materials, such as paper, and the vendors who will manufacture your book. All decisions about your book as a physical object, such as the number of pages and grade of paper and type of cover and binding, and about the budget for your book, are made well before the book is ready for production, sometimes even before it exists in reality as a manuscript. No money can be dispensed on behalf of your book until the budget is approved, and, once approved, the budget tends to be regarded as bottom line.

The budget includes the cost of the paper, which is bought in bolts by weight and allocated to each title according to the number of signatures and half signatures in a book. A signature is 32 pages, and in traditional manufacturing the imposition (sequence) of pages at the printer typically is based on eighth-of-a-signature flats. A flat—a sheet of paper with four pages printed on it—might juxtapose pages 3, 35, 67, and 99, which, when merged with other flats, folded, cut, and bound, all come out in their right places for the correct numerical sequence of pages. Books are bound in signatures whether or not there is type on all the pages, which is why you sometimes see books with blank pages at the end.

The cost of paper is why you must take length seriously. If the company had to buy (or reallocate) an extra signature of paper for your book, possibly at a higher price because of the small quantity and the rush, and if your print run were 20,000 copies (although initial print runs usually are much lower), that comes to 8 flats and 640,000 pages that are not in the budget. Your book also would have more bulk, taking up more space, and more weight, which would raise the cost of storing, packaging, and shipping each copy. As you can imagine, the cost of those extra pages ultimately would add significantly to the overall cost of manufacturing your book and bringing it to customers. This example is moot, however. Publishers who often incur these kinds of costs do not stay in business for long.

Publishers attempt to cut costs by exporting manufacturing to developing countries and by taking advantage of new computer-based technologies, which are more efficient but by no means cheap. Nevertheless, extra length always translates into extra cost. And what costs your publisher costs you. It is worth your while, therefore, to estimate the length of your book accurately in advance in collaboration with your publisher. The market for your book dictates its optimal length for it to be competitive. Depending on the market, your introductory textbook might max out at 624 pages and your brief or concise edition might need to come in at 432 pages.

Calculating Length

Managing length is an author's responsibility, and along with managing schedule it is one of the most important responsibilities an author has. The best way to prevent a length problem is to draft to length in the first place and then to monitor for length creep from draft to draft.

1. Start by deciding how much space (number of pages, paragraphs, lines, or words) you would like to allot to each topic, and note these decisions on a copy of your chapter outline. These decisions relate to your previous decisions about topical coverage and topical balance, as reflected in your table of contents and heading structure (recall Chapters 7 and 11). Allot space on the basis of a maximum total of 40 book pages per chapter or on whatever maximum your publisher gives you.

2. Set a standard format for margins, number of lines per page, and

page numbering system, and draft continuously, filling each page. Avoid unnecessary blank space or page breaks, which make length estimation less accurate.

3. Calculate the average number of words per line you are getting as you draft, and multiply this number by the average number of lines per page. This gives you your average number of words per manuscript page (msp).

4. Find out the planned trim size of your book. If it will be an 8- by 10-inch book, for instance, you can expect to fit at least 500 words on a book page (bp). To convert msp to bp in this case, you would multiply the average number of words per msp by the number of pages in the chapter manuscript to find the total number of words in the chapter. You would then divide this figure by 500—the number of words you can expect to fit on an 8-by-10 page. Even easier, your word processing program will tell you the total number of words you have keyboarded, which you can then divide by the trim size figure.

5. The result is the number of book pages your chapter will occupy, not counting photos, figures, and tables. To add in these elements, tally the number of photos, figures, and tables and multiply by .33. If you have 3 photos, 2 figures, and 4 tables in Chapter 5, for instance, you would multiply 9 X .33 = 2.97 = 3 book pages. This calculation assumes that each of these elements will occupy an average of about one-third of a book page. If you have a very long figure or table, therefore, count it as two to get a more accurate page count.

6. As a final step in getting an accurate page count, multiply your subtotal for the number of book pages by .05 and add the result to the overall bp count. This result accounts for the white or blank spaces on each page before and after headings, around photos, and between figure captions and text. The following formula for estimating length summarizes these steps.

Formula for Estimating Length

Trim size	Estimated words per book page
under 7 X 9	350-400
7 X 9	450
8 X 10	500
above 8 X 10	550-600

To convert manuscript pages to book pages:

Words per line X number of lines per page = number of words per page, X number of pages = total number of words in the manuscript, divided by the number of words per book page (based on trim size from the above table) = number of book pages, + total number of photos, tables, and figures X .33, + subtotal X .05 white space = number of book pages. Suggested maximum working number of book pages per chapter = 40.

Your publisher may have different trim size counts and a different system for calculating length than the one shown above. If this information is not provided in the company's Author Guidelines, ask your editor, especially if you are working without editorial assistance.

If the total bp in any chapter exceeds 40, be prepared to make cuts before final draft or to move material to other locations in the book or its ancillaries. A topic might go just as well in another chapter, for instance. Your very long table might make a good handout master, your extra chapter closing activity might be a good addition to your Instructor's Manual, and your extra mini-case might make a good basis for items in your test bank, interactive edition, or companion web site.

Depending on your purposes and the needs of your subject, it is a good idea to plan chapters of roughly equal length, as a practical strategy and for consistency. Once you find out how many of your manuscript pages equals a book page you can easily monitor your progress to control length. You probably will get between one and one-third and two and one-third manuscript pages per book page. Once you reach your maximum bp for a chapter, simply delete a sentence or paragraph for every sentence or paragraph you add. This same rule applies for revisions in which overall book length must stay the same.

Disaster Control Guidelines for Length

Following Hippocrates, these solutions for correcting length problems are ordered in terms of the principle of least intervention. In addition, following the principle of the conservation of energy and matter, solutions aim to preserve content in some form while cutting length.

Scenario A: Your chapter is too long and there is simply no way you can cut it without destroying its brilliance and integrity.

> **Solution 1:** Scour for wordiness and tighten your prose (see Chapter 5). Especially look for strings of unnecessary prepositional phrases, unnecessary qualifying remarks and disclaimers, and any gratuitous-seeming or jargony elaborations. Change every sentence to active voice.

> **Solution 2:** Search for paragraphs you can drop. Especially drop a paragraph whose source citation is more than ten years out of

date, unless this source is an essential classic. Also, ruthlessly drop paragraphs that are in any way tangential or digressionary, however er amusing or clever. Then consider dropping extra examples and applications, shortening them, or substituting more economical ones.

Solution 3: Check that you have the prescribed number of peda-gogical features and chapter elements. Choose the best ones and then combine, condense, move, or drop any extras, however good they are. Consider repurposing the best of them for use in your ancillaries or supplements.

Solution 4: Where possible, condense and convert portions of nar-rative to a figure or table. For example, the formula for estimating length took only 12 lines of type but essentially replaces 54 lines of manuscript preceding it.

Solution 5: Where possible, depending on your evaluation of their importance for your purposes, drop long figures or tables and pre-serve the content in condensed or summarized narrative form. For example, "Research clearly shows that sleep deprivation has a neg-ative effect on productivity in the workplace (Smith, 2002)" might easily replace a graph occupying one-third of a book page.

Solution 6: Ask your editor for suggestions or assistance in reduc-ing the length of the chapter. It is important to identify and discuss any dropping of whole topics or headings and sections. Your editor might have reason to believe that some of your proposed cuts will compromise meeting customer needs. Avoid cutting any elements that are part of the publisher's book plan, because this is the plan for marketing, advertising, promoting, and selling your book, which are already underway.

A development editor or a professional copyeditor who is knowledgeable in your subject area also can help you cut. Especially if you are working with a devel-opment editor (who ideally has seen you through thick and thin over the course of a year or more), never deliver a surprise for final manuscript. If in taking mat-ters into your own hands you have exercised poor judgment, the development editor may not have time at that point to "save" your book. Editors are required to hand off your manuscript to the compositor or packager by a certain date regardless of its readiness. If your book is significantly not ready, it is likely to be cancelled or postponed at great loss to all.

Scenario B: You did not pay attention to length. Your book is now in production and you have been informed that the compositor's cast-off puts it at 100 book pages over length.

> **Solution:** Consult with your publisher. You may have to drop chapters, cut appendices, lose figures and tables, and make other painful radical changes. Dropping topics now will require resetting your chapter and table of contents into type and making up new pages, which would add greatly to the cost of production and also essentially makes the prepublication promotion a lie. Any forced changes to the book design (if changes to design specs are permitted at all) also could put your book as much over budget as adding signatures. The best solution to this scenario is to avoid it like the plague.

Avoiding Length Creep in Revisions

Development editors can help prevent length problems by performing length estimates on a chapter-by-chapter basis and warning you of any "length creep" between drafts. Without such help, you need to be able to monitor length yourself.

It is easy to get lazy about maintaining length, and length creep is the result. If you compare the 1st, 3rd, and 6th editions of a popular introductory textbook, you may see physical evidence of this phenomenon. An *Introduction to Psychology*, for instance, may become ever longer and more dense and bulkier on the bookshelf. Students have to pay a lot more for this book but have no hope of getting through it in a semester, and you must pick and choose which chapters to assign and which to discard from the course.

Length creep is caused by continually adding new material without deleting the old. Revisions, in their attempt to update sources and address reviewers' requests for more coverage of this and that, are especially prone. There is only one way to prevent length creep, and that is to drop before adding: word for word, sentence for sentence, paragraph for paragraph, figure for figure, box for box.

Production managers have a bag of tricks for handling length problems, but you should not count on combinations of the following as solutions to length problems:

- Running a line long: an extra line of type is added to each page, which gives your book a crowded appearance with very small margins at the top or bottom.

- Reducing leading around heads: space is removed above and below A- and B-heads, which also gives your book a packed look.

- Running photos in the margins: vertical photos are printed exceptionally small in the margins so they don't take up text space, which can detract from the visual presentation of your book.

- Reducing type size: elements of your book are produced in smaller type, which makes for a dense, less readable text.

- Double- and triple-columning: elements of your book are produced in two, three, or four columns to fit more on a page, which also can make for a dense, less readable book.

Some things cannot be done, however, and in the last analysis, there is only so much anyone can do with the absolute limit of a physical page. The only sensible thing to do is to plan for and control length from the beginning. For example, an average of 12 manuscript pages per chapter (with a range from 9 to 20) was the planned length for this book. As you can see, then, it is entirely within an author's power to deliver a manuscript of appropriate length.

Why Schedule Is Important

Just as the physical page has absolute limits, so has the time frame for publishing a textbook. Why is the time frame so important? For one thing, as you read in Chapter 1, if your book is not available in time for customers to see and order it well before the first term of its copyright year, it is dead at the gate. To be in the running, textbooks need to be in the warehouse by the preceding summer or fall, the earlier the better.

Also, your publisher is in competition to capture market share, and the early bird gets the worm. Sales representatives having to field a late book find that professors have already ordered current editions for their courses from competitors. Needless to say, the loss of investment is not just your publisher's; it is yours as well. Late books, even very good ones, do not have an opportunity to succeed.

Late first editions are not as vulnerable, because they lack market recognition and a track record. However, late revisions of established textbooks are at great risk. Field representatives attempt to "roll" their customers, that is, to get them to order, sight unseen, the new edition of a book customers are using presently in their courses. The loyalty factor often drives these roll-over sales, but if the new edition and its supplements are not ready in time, the trust factor kicks in, and you and the company lose business. Thus, schedules, along with budgets and book lengths, are bottom lines.

Types of Schedules in Publishing and Key Dates

In commercial textbook publishing, your project probably will have the following basic schedules.

Publishing Schedules

Drafting Schedule—dates by which chapters, revised drafts, and final complete manuscript are due

Reviewing Schedule—dates by which portions of manuscript are sent out for peer review and reviews are received and honoraria paid

Production Schedule—schedule for setting your book into type, including dates by which copyedited final manuscript and stages of proof are sent to you for corrections and dates by which proof must be returned

Marketing Schedule—schedule for presenting, advertising, promoting, and selling your book

Manufacturing Schedule—schedule for printing and binding your book

Supplements Schedule—dates by which samples and final manuscript for each supplement are due

Fulfillment Schedule—dates by which books and supplements are sold, ordered, in stock, inventoried, and shipped

As you might suspect, slippages in schedule can have a disastrous ripple effect on outcomes. The following dates, spanning a period of as much as two years or more, are the chief benchmarks in producing major market textbooks, although the precise order varies according to publishers' unique systems and procedures:

Scheduling Benchmarks for Your Textbook

- final book plan approval
- manuscript complete
- reviewing complete
- sample manuscript to design
- budget and production schedule approval
- marketing plan approval
- final manuscript and permissions complete
- release to production
- manufacturing initial pricing review
- design approval
- copyediting complete
- release to composition
- proofreading complete
- art and photo approval
- final page proof
- pages out complete
- indexing complete
- cover design approval

- finals to printer
- art and photo package to printer
- press okay
- bound book to warehouse

You need to meet schedules during the development, drafting, reviewing, and production stages. Your most important date is "final manuscript complete," because other than reviewing nothing will be done for your book until you deliver it. During the production stages, you need to meet schedules for checking or correcting and turning around copyedited manuscript and one or more stages of proof. Your last real chance to make minor changes to manuscript is in the copyediting phase. Any changes you make to proofs are called "author's alterations" (AAs), and they are charged against your book. Now that authors see computer-generated page proof rather than unpaged typeset galleys, if your changes are too great, computer page make-up artists have to redo the pages at significantly greater cost.

Scheduling problems often strain author-publisher relations and cause other difficulties. Consider Author Z, who no longer answers his phone to avoid talking to his editor. He is experiencing excruciating time pressure and feels guilty about putting a strain on relationships with loved ones and losing touch with the rhythms of family life. He also feels angry and frustrated about having to neglect or underperform various professional obligations. Yet he is working days, nights, and weekends and can't seem to let go of manuscript that seems less than perfect, regardless of due dates. He resents acidly the editor's constant reminders about deadlines. The editor, meanwhile, does not know what is going on and therefore cannot help. Author Z has not expressed his feelings and automatically interprets every contact with the editor as just another crack of the whip.

Author Z has a problem. Getting a college textbook published in time should not and need not cause personal and professional hardships and author-publisher misunderstandings. Author Z needs a better attitude, a stronger support network, and a more structured approach to managing time.

Developing Your Own Drafting Schedule

How can you avoid becoming like Author Z? To start, by far your best option is to develop and monitor your own drafting schedule, based on your own personal, professional, and family needs in relation to the due date for "manuscript complete." You can do this by using the following strategies:

1. Ask your publisher for the schedule of core due dates. Count the number of weeks from now until the "manuscript complete" due date and divide by the number of chapters. This tells you how many weeks or days you have to draft or revise each chapter. Everyone works at different rhythms and paces, but as a rule of thumb, regard a rate of a chapter a week as a bare minimum,

based on full-time drafting.

2. Consult your appointment schedule and subtract the weeks or days you will not be drafting, including professional obligations, conferences, office and classroom hours, exam grading, vacation travel, personal commitments, family obligations, and holidays. Adjust your estimate accordingly for how much time you will have realistically to draft or revise each chapter.

3. Enter your personal due dates chapter-by-chapter on a planning calendar, allowing one or two days for each mailing of batched chapters. Batching manuscript often helps the publisher with work flow as reviewing and any developmental editing can be done in installments. Adjust your calendar to allow more time for longer, less developed, or more difficult chapters.

4. Stop and reflect on your calendar. Can you really do it? Should you plan now to get someone to help you on specific chapter components, nondrafting tasks, or other authoring responsibilities? What can you do for back-up or a Plan B?

5. Send your drafting schedule to your editor, and note any concerns you have. The editor can help you address concerns or even arrange for help. If you do not provide a schedule, the editor should construct one, send it to you for your approval, and revise it according to your response. Notify the editor immediately if unforeseen conditions or events arise that will affect the schedule.

6. Make sure both you and your editor are clear and in agreement on scheduling. Some editors will want you to create interim draft chapters by revising as you go along, for instance, rather than waiting for completion of draft manuscript. Also, the editor needs a solid drafting schedule to create a reviewing schedule. Reviewers typically are lined up and contracted for in advance according to their availability. The editor tells them when they can expect to receive manuscript and when the reviews are due back. If your chapters are late, reviewers might have only a few days to respond. Worse, reviewers often drop out because they are no longer available, and the editor has to reduplicate time and effort to find replacements. Late reviews can delay final draft. In a worst case scenario, your book gets fielded without reflecting any of the expert and market feedback for which the publisher has paid.

7. With your schedule planning calendar in hand, consult the copy of

your drafting outline on which you have recorded your length planning. Then further subdivide drafting tasks in relation to the time you have set out for them. For peace of mind, standardize your personal commitment as much as possible. For instance, you might establish the goal of completing a working draft of one A-head section of your outline per working day. Keep your length planner and schedule calendar handy, along with your mechanics, pedagogy, and style checklists (see Chapter 11).

8. Set up economies and efficiencies for accomplishing authoring tasks. For example, you might schedule blocks of time for library research on a chapter-by-chapter basis, and you might set aside every other Tuesday for consulting with coauthors or updating your permissions log (see Chapter 13). Also preserve time for rest and recreation in your schedule, including self-rewarding activities for personal benchmarks achieved.

9. Formally prepare family members, friends, colleagues, students, and department chairpersons or deans for the personal and professional challenge you are undertaking in writing a textbook. As much as possible, find ways to enlist the support of these people and include them in your project. Be creative. The fruits of having a strong support network can lead to getting a semester sabbatical, having a chapter class-tested, or spending quality time with a spouse, offspring, or student who is assisting you in some meaningful, practical way. Even children might enjoy pasting up your figures from tearsheet, alphabetizing your glossary, or feeding you intelligence from the Internet.

10. When your schedule for drafting manuscript is complete, develop a new calendar for completing permissions, responding to reviewing suggestions; revising for final draft; following through with any remaining frontmatter, endmatter, and nondrafting authoring tasks; and meeting the production editor's schedule for turning around copyedits and proofs.

Thus, as with length, managing schedule is entirely within your control, barring the unforeseen. If the unforeseen happens, and if it promises to compromise your schedule by more than two weeks or to compromise it in some way that cannot be made up later, tell your editor right away. It may not be too late to postpone without incurring losses, and there may be some remedy or relief. Editors usually have access to a range of talent and services to help authors complete their projects in time.

Do Permissions Right

n college textbook publishing, requesting and tracking grants of permission for use of others' work is usually the author's task. The publisher might provide the service of paying the grant fees as part of the cost of production. Large houses maintain permissions departments and may agree to evaluate authors' permissions or to conduct permissions research.

Copyright Law

Copyright law is reasonably clear on the subject of what permissions you need, although there are gray areas and new issues often crop up. The latest issues relate to electronic publishing and intellectual property rights on the Internet. Ask your publisher for permissions guidelines. It is such a critical matter that even small houses have policies and guidelines. You might consult one or more of the following sources (see also the legal guides listed in Appendix B of Chapter 3, which are not repeated here).

Selected Sources on Copyright Law

U.S. Copyright Office: **www.loc.gov/copyright/search/**
Copyright Clearance Center: **www.authors.copyright.com**
Copy Law: **www.copylaw.com**
"10 Big Myths about Copyright Explained"
   www.templetons.com/brad/copymyths
Keyword Search ("copyright law"): Digital Millennium Copyright Act
   (Public Law 105-304, Oct. 28,1998)
Columbia Guide to Online Style:
   www.columbia.edu/cu/cup/cgos
Besenjak, C. *Copyright Plain and Simple*, 2nd ed. Career Press, 1997.
Munger, David, and Shireen Campbell. *Researching Online*.
   Addison Wesley Longman, 2001.
Stim, Richard. *Getting Permission: How to License and Clear Copyrighted Materials Online and Off*. Nolo Press, 1999.

As a rule of thumb, you can use and cite 300 words inclusively from any one book-length source without permission, and publishers increasingly risk up to 500 words. With citation you also can use up to 5 percent of journal articles or other works that are less than book length. You must have permission, however, for any part of a poem, song, speech, letter, email, unpublished thesis or dissertation, child's artwork, or student's writing. The authors of these works or their legal guardians own copyright by law.

You must have permission to use (reproduce), adapt, or abridge all figures and tables regardless of the number of words they contain, and for most photos, cartoons, and illustrations. To "adapt" any text is to change some words or parts of the piece or to add new information to it. To "abridge" is to leave words or parts out of the piece or to shorten (condense) it.

Whether textual material is permissionable or not, always use quotes or the indented excerpt format, and cite the source. Cite sources directly below figures and tables. If you have already received a grant to use a figure or table by the time you submit chapter manuscript, also include the credit line after the source. For instance, some grantors will request that you write "Used with permission of...." Otherwise, provide a credit line manuscript as soon as all permissions for a chapter are in. In some houses a production editor or packager performs this service for you.

Public Domain and Paraphrases

Public domain includes most (but not all) material published by the United States government; various classes of historical and documentary materials; expired copyrights; and matters of public record, such as vital statistics and news articles without bylines. There are murky areas. Government reports might contain copyrighted material, for example, requiring permission. See *The Complete Guide to Citing Government Information Resources: A Manual for Writers & Librarians* (Congressional Information Service, 1993) by Diane L. Garner and Diane H. Smith.

Some authors seek to avoid the necessity for permissioning sources by paraphrasing text—restating using other words or forms. Paraphrases, however, contrary to popular belief, are not safe from litigation for copyright infringement. For example, changing the order of words in a quotation, changing or dropping articles or pronouns, and adding or dropping items in a list do not constitute legal paraphrase. Quotations must be substantively rewritten in your own words to satisfy the rule for paraphrase. At the same time, creating derivative works (e.g., the same model using different labels or the same story using different names for characters and a different ending) without permission also is illegal (unless you are writing a parody).

Fair Use and Other Restrictions

Also keep the following facts in mind:

- As of April 1989, everything created in the United States is protected whether or not it carries a copyright notice.
- Nothing is in the public domain unless the owner explicitly puts it in the public domain in writing. This includes postings to computer networks.

- All email is automatically copyrighted and owned by the original creator.
- Fair use applies only if you are directly writing a commentary on, reporting on, or educating about a work itself, not if you are writing only about the subject of the work.
- Fair use involves short excerpts that are attributed and do not ruin the commercial value of the work they come from.
- You must get permission from your publisher to quote from your own previously published work.
- Raw data from any source are not copyrightable.
- Never assume that a colleague would appreciate free publicity by being quoted at length and cited in your textbook. Request permission.
- Written permission to use works of minors or photographs of minors must be obtained from a parent or guardian.
- In most circumstances, photos cannot be used without written model releases from anyone in the picture who can be identified, as well as the photographer, photo agency, or news syndicate.
- Most copyright infringements involve suits in civil court. However, commercial copyright violations involving more than 10 copies and/or value over $2,500 is a felony.

Permissioning Internet Sources

If you want to use something in your book that you find online, you must request permission, unless a grant of release is appended to the material. Otherwise, if a copyright statement is not on a web site or at the end of the web page, contact the webmaster and request information about the copyright holder. Then send a letter or email explaining how and where you wish to use the work and requesting information for a proper credit line. You may receive a form and fee request in response. In any case, keep a hardcopy file copy of any grants of permission.

The editorial style guidelines you are using for your textbook (see Chapter 5) will have information on how to cite online sources. As an alternative, consistently use the Columbia Online Style, which lists the author, the title of selected work (in quotes), the title of the larger work where the selected work resides (the name of the homepage), the publication date (or date as of access; that is, date last revised), the URL (universal resource locator, or electronic address), and the date you accessed the work.

Example: Citing an Online Source
Freelance Editorial Association, "Fee and Scheduling Guidelines," Freelance Editorial Association Resources, May 13, 2000, **www.tiac.net/users/freelanc/fees.html**, May 1, 2002.

Permissioning Photos and Art

Permission is necessary for any artwork (illustration) from another source, unless (1) the subject is common knowledge in your field and must be rendered in a certain way (such as a representation of the human brain) *and* (2) your publisher is planning to have it redrawn or rendered in a different style.

If art from a secondary source credits the primary source of the art, you need permission only from the primary source. However, if the secondary source adapted or redrew the art and you are using that, you will need permission from both the primary and the secondary sources.

Photographs also must be permissioned and credited, although a corpus of copyright-free images does exist online. Even snapshots you take yourself involve carefully obtaining signed releases from subjects, even family members. Specific images you choose for your textbook can be traced (by you or by the publisher's photo researcher) only if you provide complete information about the sources, including the names and addresses of copyright holders. Even then, specific images may not be traceable or may not be available (or affordable) when found. If your publisher is doing photo research for your book and you supply guide photos to aid the photo researcher, be sure to identify them as such or you will likely find them reproduced in your textbook. Photo researchers rely mainly on your photo specs and captions as guides, a subject of Chapter 14.

Cost of Permissions

Individual permissions can range from gratis to shockingly expensive, and overall costs can mount significantly. Scientific textbooks, textbooks with extensive illustration programs, and literature anthologies are especially dear. A one-time use of a single cartoon cel from a syndicate or movie can cost $300 or more. Permissions fees for an undergraduate textbook on human evolution might exceed $8,000, not counting the permissions researcher's fee. If the publisher is disbursing payment for fees, these costs typically are charged against your book.

Textbook authors who have relied heavily on others' works often become more creative when they have had a few surprises or see how permissions fees can add up. You might be asked to pay $1,500 for a page from a children's book whose copyright owner is its author. Materials regarded as essential to a course of study are not safe from high, some would say excessive, fees imposed by an individual author, a famous person's estate, or certain publishing conglomerates. More than one history, mass communication, and literature textbook has chosen to reduce usage of the texts of speeches of Martin Luther King Jr., for instance, to keep overall permissions costs in line.

If the copyright owner is a publisher or a professional organization, you generally will find reasonable standard fee scales. Many publishers, journals, and stock photo agencies have standard rates. An article from a professional journal might be permissioned for $35 per page, for example, and a photo for use as a 4-color full-page chapter opener might be permissioned for $500. Professional associations often request that you also obtain permission from the authors as well, as a courtesy. Some publishers have grant forms requiring payment prior to publication or setting a time limit for payment beyond which the permission will be void. Pay these requests promptly, or forward the forms to your publisher for prepayment.

Despite whatever language is used in requests to try to extend use rights, permissions typically are good only for one edition of a specified print run of a particular title. Because of the possible costs involved, if you are responsible for doing all your own permissions research, you would be wise to find out the fee policies of sources in advance and to choose only the best and most essential material to use in your textbook. Commercial textbook companies typically take responsibility for photo research and may assist the author in text permissions by helping to locate the names and addresses of copyright holders.

Sources of free and low-cost images are the Library of Congress, state and local historical societies and museums, labor and trade associations, NASA and other federal organizations, and archived image banks on the Internet. Internet photos and clip art require careful research and selectivity, however. Recently, for instance, Google produced a million and a half sites for a keyword search on "free stock photos," and those photos included a great many that one would not want to see in a textbook on any subject.

Developing a Permissions Log and Tracking Requests

However permissions are being handled for your textbook, you will need a permissions log for each chapter. This is the best way to make permissioning easier on yourself and others. For each chapter, identify permissionable material as you go along and record intended requests on a six-column table or log. The contents of such a log are shown below, but your publisher may have its own detailed record-keeping and tracking letters and forms for you to use.

Minimum Contents of a Permissions Log

Title: Chapter number, working chapter title, and date

Column 1: manuscript page number (msp) on which the material appears

Column 2: the complete source of that material (including page numbers)

Column 3: the name and address of the copyright holder (to be filled in when you find out; the actual copyright holder may not be the same as the source.)

Column 4: the date of request (to be filled in when you send your letter of request)

Column 5: the date of grant (to be filled in when you receive the grant of permission)

Column 6: the amount of the fee you or your publisher must pay in order to use the material. Sometimes the "fee" may be a complimentary copy ("comp") of your textbook when it is available.

If the publisher's Author Guidelines does not provide a form for logging and reporting permissions, ask your editor for one. Publishers' forms may have additional columns for identifying the specific rights granted.

As you develop your permissions log, take the time to make two photocopies of the permissionable material and the page on which it appears. One set goes out with your request (so the grantor can see what you are doing with it), and one set stays in your file to help you keep track. If you later decide to cut the material, or have to drop it because you cannot locate the copyright holder, or if the fee is too high, or if permission is denied, then you can conveniently forward this extra copy to your editor or production coordinator in time to keep it out of print in your book. All you need to do then is notify copyright holders that the material they gave you permission for is not being used after all. It is far better to cancel a permission than to be without.

So, when you complete your draft, you will have a permissions log for each chapter and two copies of each piece for which you are requesting permission. By that time you should have researched the sources, located copyright holders, and sent out your letters of request. In fact, it is better not to wait to apply for permissions, as they can take months to obtain. For addresses and phone numbers consult the most recent LMP (*Literary Market Place*) online or in the reference section of your campus or public library. Sort your pieces by publisher or copyright holder for efficiency. You can make multiple requests to the same grantor in one mailing.

Requesting and Handling Grants of Permission

If your publisher has not sent you a sample form letter for requesting permission, ask for one. Getting the wording right is important for legality, and every company has its own requirements. You need to know if you should request world rights, foreign language rights, reprint rights, rights to digitized versions, and so on. Also determine the planned publication date for your book, the estimated page count, whether it will be casebound or paperback or both, the number of copies your publisher plans to print, and the price for which the publisher plans to sell it. Grantor companies often request this information and sometimes base their fees on the size of print runs and price.

Your letter will go something like this.

Introduction: I (we) and (the publisher) would like permission to (use, reprint, abridge, adapt) the following material in (your name(s)), (title of your book), (publication date), (page count), (paperback or casebound), (size of print run), (initial pricing):

Insert complete source of material, including the page numbers and the number of words or lines you want to use

Body: Your publisher's legal statement about rights requested and various disclaimers, such as assuming that the signer is the legal copyright holder.

Conclusion: Your signature, the date, and various write-on lines for grantors to sign and date.

Enclosure: A copy of what you are requesting permission for and the context in which you are using it.

Make two copies of each letter, one for you and one for your publisher. Large grantors will respond to your letter by sending you their own special form to fill out. Your request for permission is not officially made until they receive this form. As grants come in, write the date received on your permissions log. Then, when you submit the final draft of your manuscript for production, include your completed permissions logs, copies of your requests, and the originals of the grants. Many grantors will state the precise wording they want you to use in the credit line. As much as possible, insert credit lines on your final manuscript.

Keep a copy of the grants for your files. Publishing houses without functioning permissions departments, large and small, have been known to lose such files in production, misplace them during housecleaning or staff turnovers, or lack the will to find them in dead storage. If your book goes into another edition two or three years later, your copy of the first-edition permissions grants could prove invaluable. As mentioned earlier, textbook permissions are almost always granted for one time use only. If you want to reuse material in a new edition, therefore, you likely will need to reapply.

Disaster Control Solutions for Permissions
Scenario A:
You procrastinated on permissions and now you don't have time to do it:

    Solution 1. Quickly go through a copy of each chapter with a marker and identify everything you think you need permission for. Give this manuscript to a full-time helper or hired hand along with your publisher's form letter for requests. Have the helper make the permissions logs, research the addresses and phone numbers, generate the request letters, do the mailings, and track the grants.

Solution 2. Immediately notify your publisher. Ask the publisher to hire a professional permissions researcher and, if necessary, to charge it against your royalties or plant costs.

Scenario B:

It's late and you are worried that you will not receive outstanding permissions in time.

Solution 1. Phone copyright holders and beg. Get a verbal agreement, a fee estimate, and the name and title of the person you speak to. Record and date this information in a phone log. Include the phone log with the permissions logs when you submit the final manuscript.

Solution 2. Immediately notify your editor and ask for reassurance.

Scenario C:

You did not get or could not afford all the permissions you wanted.

Solution 1. Convert selected tables to figures and vice versa. You do not need permission for an original table you create from someone's labels in a figure or for an original figure you create using someone's labels from a table. Just credit the source of the information.

Solution 2. Cut any unpermissioned quotes to 299 (or 499, depending on the standard being used) words or less per source (this includes words of one character).

Solution 3. Interweave paraphrases of material from two or more different sources, and list all the sources together in one parenthetical citation (separated by semicolons).

Solution 4. Substitute for or drop any remaining unpermissioned material, however painful it may be.

In all the above scenarios, it is crucially important to notify your editor or production coordinator immediately of any changes you are making to final manuscript. While you are dropping a figure, the publisher might be paying an artist to draw it. The best solution by far is to avoid permissioning problems by not procrastinating and by working within a budget. The more you can do for your book on your own the better. The next and last chapter guides you in developing your figures and tables, art and map specs, and photo program.

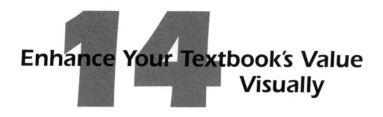

Enhance Your Textbook's Value Visually

Presentation refers to the tangible physical characteristics of your book—how it feels in the hand and how it looks as it pages. Your publisher's choice of a trim size, paper type, binding type, cover, book design, art style, and palette (if color is involved) all affect presentation.

The Importance of Presentation

The visual presentation of your book is important in marketing and selling it to customers. Depending on the budget, based on the sales projection, you may have opportunities to provide pedagogically valuable graphics and visual interest through a specified number of tables, figures or illustrations, and photographs. At signing, negotiate with your publisher the numbers of these elements that your book can have. The cost of acquiring and producing them will result in restrictions.

Textbook publishers have diverse ways of treating visual elements to which you must conform. For instance, you might need to include tables within your narrative if they will be typeset, or on separate sheets if they will be treated as art or appear in a 4-color design. You might be required to provide camera-ready or plate-ready figures on disk yourself, or your publisher might gather all your figures into an art manuscript and commission an artist to create them. Find out, therefore, what your contract requires exactly and what your publisher will need. If your editor does not provide you with guidelines for preparing figures, tables, and photos, ask for them.

If you are doing your own development, you continually will want to remain mindful of opportunities to present information visually. The following sections describe ways to visualize information that you can use in your textbook, beginning with the basic graphic organizer.

Using Graphic Organizers

A graphic organizer is a visual representation of a chapter, topic, sequence, or concept. In a chapter opener, a graphic organizer prepares students for what you intend they should learn. For example, a diagram or flowchart might convey the progression of ideas you develop in the chapter, while a concept map or web might trace relationships among the topics subsumed under the chapter's unifying concept. Thus, at the beginning of chapters or sections, graphics function as "advance organizers." Readers have a chance to recognize a basic relationship in advance of reading about it. Graphic organizers also can contribute to exposition within the body of chapters or at the end to summarize or connect up data.

Visualizing verbal information is an art, and some authors and editors are more talented in this art than others. Whatever your subject area and your talents, however, the possibilities are worth considering. Begin by determining the basic purpose or function of the information you want to convey visually, and then draw sketches to experiment with how this information might be visualized. There always is more than one way to do this. Evaluate the likely effectiveness of the visualizations as a piece of art, and choose one that seems to work.

See the following examples of graphic organizers in an online sample chapter of a child development textbook. In each case, what instructional purpose is being served?

www.ablongman.com/fabestour/pdf/Fabs_ch02.pdf:
Figure 2.4 Bronfenbrenner's Ecological Model, p. 40.
Figure 2.5 A Dynamic Systems Model of Walking, p. 42
Figure 2.7 Cross-Sectional Design, p. 50
Figure 2.8 Longitudinal Design, p. 52

The chapter appendix provides templates showing how information can be organized graphically in ways that are appropriate to particular instructional purposes.

Presenting Figures and Tables

Figures and tables are more commonly seen in college textbooks than graphic organizers. Technically, a table presents numerical information in tabular form, while a figure presents information graphically or through illustrations. There are four basic types of figures:

- charts and matrices with cells containing text
- line, bar, and pie graphs
- conceptual graphics (such as diagrams, flowcharts, concept maps, or graphic organizers)
- rendered art (representational drawings or paintings)

Some publishers refer to any figures that have to be drawn, rather than simply typeset or reproduced from film or digital media, as "art."

Common practice in commercial publishing requires you to provide each figure as a full-size printout, photocopy, sketch, or tearsheet on its own separate manuscript page. Recall that each figure and table is identified with a double-number (e.g., Figure 2.4 would be the fourth figure in Chapter 2), and appears with a title, complete source, credit line if needed, and preferably a caption. If captions are planned, every figure should have one. Figure captions go beyond the figure title to elaborate on the content, call attention to something in the figure, or partly interpret it for the reader.

Figures and any tables not embedded in the manuscript are keyed to text by using the assigned double-numbers. For example, Figure 2.4, above, would be keyed on the manuscript on a separate line to mark the best location for it, as a kind of placeholder, like this:

<Insert Figure 2.4>

This notation alerts the copyeditor and later the compositor or page make-up artist of the existence of numbered "art" and its desired location. The sidewise carets (or alternatively an enclosing circle) alert production people that the insertion note itself is not to be set into type as part of the book, this illustration aside.

The best location for each figure and table is at the end of the paragraph in which you call the reader's attention to it. It is good practice to refer to each figure by number within the chapter narrative as you discuss the content the figure serves. Your text reference can be parenthetical (e.g., see Figure 2.4), or you may refer to the figure in a sentence. In some subject areas, such as mathematics, a figure often immediately follows the referring sentence.

Use Figures and Tables Appropriately

Many authors treat figures and tables as ancillary to the text or purely decorative and neither refer to them nor relate the information they contain to the section in which they appear. This is not good practice. For figures and tables to have pedagogical value, their presence, relevance, and significance must be explained, however briefly.

Another common misconception is that figures and tables replace text. However, in good exposition the function of tables and figures is to elucidate text, not substitute for it. Figures and tables should not introduce new information without text support, therefore, nor contain any undefined terms.

Provide Narrative Context for Figures and Tables

Following are some examples of alternative ways to refer to your figures and tables within the narrative and to key them for location. Note the differences in style.

Example A:
Principles of Gestalt psychology rest on the observations of Max Wertheimer, Kurt Koffka, and Wolfgang Köhler that people perceive whole units rather than bits of sensation, that the whole of sensation is more than its parts. In Figure 6.3, for example, you readily see a circle even though bits of the circle are left out. This illustrates the principle of closure, which states that people organize their perceptions so that they are as simple and logical as possible, filling in gaps in perceptions as needed.

<Insert Figure 6.3>

Example B:
Principles of Gestalt psychology rest on the observations of Max Wertheimer, Kurt Koffka, and Wolfgang Köhler that people perceive whole units rather than bits of sensation, that the whole of sensation is more than its parts. Look at Figure 6.3, for example. What do you see?

<Insert Figure 6.3>

Your ability to see a circle even with parts of it missing illustrates the principle of closure. In closure, people organize their perceptions so that they are as simple and logical as possible, filling in perceptual gaps as needed.

Example C:
Principles of Gestalt psychology rest on the observations of Max Wertheimer, Kurt Koffka, and Wolfgang Köhler that people perceive whole units rather than bits of sensation, that the whole of sensation is more than its parts. The principle of closure, for example, states that people organize their perceptions in the simplest and most logical way, filling in perceptual gaps as needed. For instance, people can readily recognize and identify incomplete forms (see Figure 6.3).

<Insert Figure 6.3>

In this example, in the manuscript the illustration for Figure 6.3 would appear on its own separate sheet with the figure number, title, source, credit line, and possibly a caption, although some publishers prefer to have captions in a separate manuscript. According to the publisher's wishes, the sheet with the figure might be placed in context, following the page that refers to it, or in a separate art manuscript consisting of all the figures for the chapter, gathered at the back of the chapter manuscript.

If a figure comes from a published source, provide a good-quality photocopy or original tearsheet. To modify a figure, adapt or edit it on the page, as needed, writing clearly in soft pencil or pen if only a few words are involved. Otherwise, type the changes. Compositors do not like to set type or rekeyboard from handwriting and may refuse to do so or may charge the publisher a penalty fee. That fee gets charged against your book.

Preparing Art and Map Specs

If your figure is a computer graphic you created, provide both hardcopy and diskcopy. This is a good time to explore to the limit the graphical and art capabilities of your software, including the generation and placement of labels and symbols in a diagram. If an artist or cartographer is assigned to your book, on the other hand, you need only provide a sketch. Even if your sketching is skillful, however, you probably will need to provide a specification sheet to enable the artist-specialist to render what you want. Your spec might include the following information:

- figure or map double-number and title
- manuscript page number on which the figure or map is keyed to appear
- source (and credit line, if possible)
- permission status
- relative importance in the chapter (e.g., 1 = most important)
- suggested approximate size (e.g., 1/4-, 1/3-, 1/2-, 2/3-, 3/4-page)
- labels (e.g., showing A-, B-, and C-levels of heading)
- brief note to artist or cartographer explaining in words what is wanted

Note, however, that artists as a rule prefer to receive information visually. Many go by what they see rather than taking time to read descriptions or explanations. Make your note to the artist brief, therefore, and do not attempt to dictate the specific size, design, or colors to be used in the art. The artist must follow the publisher-approved book designer's plan, and actual sizing is done by people in production according to page make-up and design options for art treatments.

Following are some suggested criteria for determining the relative importance of a figure or map, based on a three-point scale with 1 as "most important:"

- Is it necessary to make sense of text? Give it a 1.
- Is it the chapter's visual showpiece? Give it a 1.
- Does it have other pedagogical value? Give it a 2.
- Does it augment or enrich exposition? Give it a 2.
- Is it fun but pedagogically optional? Give it a 3.
- Is it uninteresting but obligatory? Give it a 3.

Your rating will help determine how much time and, therefore, money to lavish on each piece. Such a rating also helps in deciding what to drop if that becomes necessary for any reason (e.g., for overlengthage or permissions problems). You may find, however, that your publisher has different standards or is not at all interested in your ratings of relative importance. Author input on production tasks is a traditional nicety that many twenty-first-century editors don't have time for, have forgotten, or ignore.

The size of a piece can be an indication of importance or merely of the amount of information a figure is attempting to convey. Readability and length are factors in determining the size of art objects, which normally is determined by the publisher's agents. As a rule of thumb, keep figures and tables to one book page or less, preferably less. Exceptions include chronologies (which might need a whole spread), comparative grids, and appendices (which might have several pages of tabular information). Sizing is an exact measurement in picas and, as noted above, relates to the book's design and budget.

The labels for each figure or map may be set from your art spec. In most cases you should type labels one to a line in the order they appear in the figure (left to right, top to bottom, or clockwise). Distinguish between umbrella labels and subordinate ones to show their relationship or relative importance. Otherwise all the labels might be set in the same size type, which might make interpretation difficult. Labels for maps and figures with insets should be organized by the differentiations within their keys. Here is an example of a labeled sketch and the typed labels sheet that would accompany it. Labels for a map spec would be done in a similar fashion.

Example: Art Sketch

Example: Typed Labels Sheet for Art Sketch

Figure 9.2 Types of White-Collar Crime

Forms of Theft
Embezzlement
Fraud
Forgery
Extortion

Crimes Against Government
Bribery
Obstruction of Justice
Official misconduct
Perjury

Areas of Corporate Crime
Administration
Environment
Labor
Manufacturing
Trade

Visualizing Information and Creating Original Figures

Authors often find it difficult to create pedagogical figures beyond simple bar graphs and matrices. With a little imagination, however, charts and graphs can be embellished for greater visual interest. A common method of embellishing graphs is to choose an appropriate metaphor for the information being conveyed and then visually represent the metaphor through objects or colors. Print news media do this all the time to attract attention. For example, rising and falling commodities markets might be represented through the metaphor of stairs, elevators, or escalators, or a commodity might be shown as a mountain climber achieving a summit or tumbling down.

Effective metaphors also can be simple, such as a pencil for school achievement in a bar graph comparing student achievement in different countries, in which pencil length stands for amount of achievement on the graph. Another familiar example is the dollar bill divided to represent percentages of expenditures or revenues.

What might be apt metaphors for data sets in your field? For example, for the rate of global warming? For voting behavior in relation to gender? For runaway depreciation of the baht? For imports of pepper and cloves to Spain in the 16th century? For the hardness of minerals? For the distance of stars? Sometimes the thing itself is all that is needed. Imagine how much more exciting the formula for fractal geometry might be, for instance, if framed within a form generated by that formula.

As noted before, delivering verbal information visually is an art, but you don't have to be an artist to do it, just able to think a bit divergently. You might find the following process helpful:

1. Identify the main components of an important conceptualization, analysis, process, or synthesis that you want your chapter to communicate. Discover this by asking: What is most important about this chapter (or section)? Why do readers need to know it? What is most critical for them to remember about it? What do I want them to come away with after reading it?

2. State the main idea that results from this line of questioning. For example, suppose you come up with the following statement for Chapter 2 of your macroeconomics textbook: Analysis of economic decisions is based on five fundamental principles: opportunity cost, marginalness, diminishing returns, spillover, and reality.

   Other types of statements might be in any of the following forms (see also the chapter appendix). How could you represent each statement visually if x stood for a concept, condition, situation, or object in your field?

   There is a certain number of different approaches to x.
   There is a certain number of degrees of x.
   There is a certain number of stages of x.
   There is a certain number of types of x.
   There are certain steps in the process of x.
   There are certain positive and negative aspects of x.
   There are certain causes and effects of x.
   There are certain factors to consider in solving x.
   There are certain changes in x over time.
   There are certain similarities and differences between x and y.

3. Now, determine and draw the relationships among the principles. For instance, the principles might be of equal importance, as in the example of principles of economic decision making, or else might be contingent on each other in some way, as in a causal or chronological relationship.

4. Then determine and draw the relationships between each principle

and economic decision. For instance, opportunity cost applies to decisions to sacrifice something for something else. The marginal principle applies to decisions to make small changes. The principle of diminishing returns applies to decisions to expand. Spillover applies to benefits external to one's own decisions; and the reality principle applies to decisions to use one's actual purchasing power.

5. Whatever relationships you state, experiment with different ways to represent them visually. Keep it simple, with as few short labels as possible to fully convey the point. Choose or create your own design elements to express the idea or metaphor, such as icons, arrows, geometric shapes, other symbols, or line drawings. Following is an attempt at a figure for the five economic principles. Does it work?

Principles of Economic Analysis: An Example

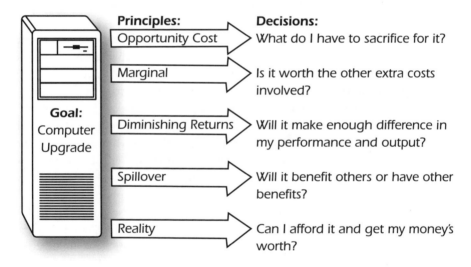

Principles:	Decisions:
Opportunity Cost	What do I have to sacrifice for it?
Marginal	Is it worth the other extra costs involved?
Diminishing Returns	Will it make enough difference in my performance and output?
Spillover	Will it benefit others or have other benefits?
Reality	Can I afford it and get my money's worth?

Goal: Computer Upgrade

Planning a Photo Program

Technically, photographs are any image on film or digitized, regardless of content. In other words, the content might be a document, a drawing, a cartoon, a famous painting, a page of a book, or a facsimile, in addition to the images one normally thinks of as photographs. In publishing, anything on film or digitized usually is treated as a photograph, and, as you have learned, photographs must be researched, permissioned, and credited.

Photos often are obtained from individual freelance photographers responding to a publisher's "needs list" and from stock agencies; film and video archives; museums; news agencies, television networks, and other media sources; chambers of commerce; other government sources, such as the Department of Labor, the Library of Congress, and state historical societies; business and industry sources; and professional and public service organizations. Larger commercial publishing houses might maintain inhouse stock shot specifically for their known list needs.

Many authors mistakenly regard photos as window dressing for their book. In textbooks, however, as much as any other pedagogical element, images teach. You can remain mindful of this fact by framing questions that readers could answer by looking at the picture or by relating chapter content to the image.

Evaluating and Choosing Images

If the publisher is obtaining the images or film for general photo requests, you will need to provide photo specs—a description of the desired image—and, if possible, a photocopy or tearsheet of an image like the one you want, as well as a likely source. The photo researcher and editor might solicit and select one to three images for each spec to view and then forward copies to you for your review. For major market books, the publisher's agents often pick the photos, do the permissions research, and pay the use fees, which normally are charged against your book.

Photographs, both black and white and color, can be very expensive to obtain and to reproduce. Different rates apply based on the size at which the image will be reproduced on the page. Because of the costs, high visibility, and market sensitivity of photographs, and because of technical matters concerning image quality in printing, most college houses retain control over final photo selection. The market, sales projection, and budget for your book will determine the number of photos you will be allowed, whether they will be four-color or black and white (duotone), and whether you or the publisher will be responsible for getting them. These decisions will be part of your contract negotiation. In undergraduate textbooks, chapters typically have a chapter opening photo and one or more internal photos.

If you are supplying images for your book personally, unless you are trained in photographic techniques, do everyone a favor and hire a professional photographer. Your snapshots very likely will not be good enough for reproduction and your digital images will not print large enough with any quality. If you have existing images that you must use, consider hiring an expert to scan them and improve them and enhance their reproducibility in the computer through PhotoShop or a similar image-manipulation program. Your publisher usually can arrange to have this done for you as needed also.

The visual and verbal content of photographs is a critical and complex concern in publishing. Customer complaints often involve images regarded as misleading, offensive in some way, or outdated. This is especially true in elementary and secondary school publishing, where more than one textbook has failed in adoptions because of the photo program alone. Also, untrue or injudicious photo captions can be seen as unethical and have been known to lead to slander or defamation suits. Following are some general rules of thumb for selecting and captioning photographs:

- Reject images that reflect stereotypes of any kind (racist, classist, sexist, ageist), unless stereotyping is the subject.

- Choose images that accurately represent people, places, and subjects, that fairly portray population diversity overall, and that show balance in your treatment of the subject.

- Reject images with salacious or suggestive content, especially involving children.

- Check that any foreign language print evident in images is not profane.

- Reject images containing commercial brands or trademark labels or slogans, unless advertising or popular culture is the subject.

- In captioning, do not ascribe characteristics to people or imply conditions, unless you can verify empirically and ethically that those characteristics or conditions are present. For example, you would not identify a recognizable child in a stock agency photo as hearing impaired, poor, pregnant, abused, or having AIDS. Also take care in making attributions about public figures.

- Reject images with dated hair and clothing styles, outdated technology (including car and computer models) and passe social contexts, unless your subject or purpose is historical.

Writing Photo Specs

Writing photo specs is an authoring task, although specs may be written by editors for managed books. Photo specs are double-numbered in the sequence in which the photos will appear in each chapter. Like figure specs, photo specs are keyed to text to show the optimal location. In placing images, consider the best way to achieve the right kind of visual impact and pedagogical payload for your book. You might space out images regularly throughout a chapter to suggest both richness and continuity, or you might pair or cluster images to achieve a particular aim. Note, however, that photo placement on a page is a technical matter, ultimately decided by the publisher's agents.

Submit photo specs (or photos) and a photo caption manuscript along with your text manuscript. Your publisher should supply guidelines for writing photo specs, which need to be worded briefly in a way that nonexperts in your field can understand. The best photo specs include a brief description of what has to be in the picture and the concept the picture serves, and the best captions provide comprehensive factual information or ask application questions.

Examples of Photo Specs and Captions:

Photo 11.1 Chapter opener: Japanese and American business-persons shaking hands in a corporate setting. Illustrates the chapter theme of International Business.

Photo 11.2 Msp. 17 Asian black market.
CAPTION: Unofficial, or "black," markets are free markets that operate outside the control of the government. Black markets arise wherever a currency is not fully convertible, but the term is also used to describe the buying and selling of goods that are officially or legally unavailable.

Photo 11.3 Msp. 31 Okavongo power plant in Botswana, Africa, with workers.
CAPTION: This power plant project in Botswana was funded by the World Bank through the International Monetary Fund. International development banks such as the World Bank give loans and assistance for government-guaranteed projects. Funding is designed to improve national economies and stimulate international trade and investment.

Be realistic in your photo specs. With all the pictures there are in the world, even professional photo researchers have great difficulty filling specs that are overspecific or overdetailed, as well as those that describe rare or improbable sights. "A smiling 8-year-old Eskimo playing wheelchair basketball in a traditional parka with white fur trim" just isn't going to happen. And if it did happen, you need to provide the specific name, date, and place so that the photo researcher can find out if an official photographer was present who might have taken such a picture. At the opposite extreme are photo specs that are not specific enough for the photo researcher to find, such as "a mug shot of that serial rapist they executed recently," or are too abstract, such as "an illustration of capitalism."

The Art of Writing Captions

As noted, many authors (and some editors) miss teaching opportunities by treating visual elements strictly as illustration. The elements are left captionless or are given a few uninspired lines of general information. Yet good descriptive captions can reinforce learning, and visuals offer opportunities for readers to interact with text through reflection, critical thinking, and application. Give some thought, therefore, to captioning your figures, tables, and photos in meaningful, pedagogically useful ways. Captions might briefly interpret graphs, draw conclusions from statistics, provide background information, or ask questions of the reader.

Compare the following treatments of photographs for textbooks on English composition, marine biology, and foundations of education, respectively. In each case, which caption, A. or B., probably would have greater value to the learner?

<Photo of Ichabod Crane>

A. In characterization a writer describes the qualities and peculiarities of a person.

B. In characterization a writer describes the qualities and peculiarities of a person. Using the guidelines on p. 87, write a characterization of this imaginary person.

<Photo of clownfish with anenome>

A. By "innoculating" themselves against the anenome's venom, these clownfish gain protection from predators.

B. By "innoculating" themselves against the anenome's venom, these clownfish gain protection from predators. In this example, how does the autoimmunity of one species contribute to the adaptation of another?

<Photo of parent helping child with homework>

A. Parental involvement is an important factor in academic achievement.

B. Parental involvement is an important factor in academic achievement. Which of Eisner's six functions of parental involvement are represented in this picture?

In every case, you probably chose caption B. These captions all share the following three characteristics:

1. The reader must "read" the image; that is, the reader must take time to look at "this imaginary person," "this example," and "this picture."

2. The reader must interpret the image in terms of main concepts presented in the textbook (i.e., the concepts of characterization, autoimmunity and adaptation, and parental involvement).

3. The reader must do something or answer a question that demon-

strates comprehension or application (i.e., use specific guidelines to write a characterization, explain an adaptive relationship in nature, apply a specific functional model to a case).

Try to develop your art program so that every chapter has tables, figures (including possible maps), and photos that will contribute to the pedagogical value, visual continuity, and appeal of your textbook. Education research supports the use of visual information in textbooks at all levels of academic attainment.

Putting It All Together

It's hard to end a book on writing and developing a college textbook. Textbook authors tend to have the same difficulty, with last chapters taking longer to arrive at the editor's desk. In actuality, for both the author and the editor, so long as a book is in print, work is never done.

This book has attempted to convey some of the complexities of providing sound print support for a course of study in higher education while also providing a product that can compete successfully in the marketplace and make money for both its author and publisher. In keeping with the theme of this chapter, this book closes with a graphic organizer summarizing those complexities. In writing and developing your college textbook, I wish you the best of luck. Yes, you can do it, and yes, it's worth it.

Writing and Developing Your College Textbook: The Essentials

Understand Your Market
Decide Your Mission
Find Your Audience
Know Your Competition

Get Signed
Choose a Publisher
Establish a Relationship
Negotiate a Contract

Develop Your Textbook
Write a Table of Contents
Plan Your Apparatus
Plan Your Pedagogical Features
Plan Your Presentation

Prepare Your Manuscript
Choose Your Style
Find Your Voice
Draft to Length
Draft to Schedule
Do Permissions

Appendix: Ways of Visualizing Information

Purpose: To illustrate a process

Purpose: To summarize steps in a procedure

Purpose: To trace a sequence of events

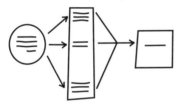

Purpose: To indicate cause and effect

Purpose: To show effects of or influences on a subject

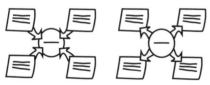

Purpose: To explain the relationship among topics

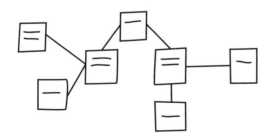

Purpose: To classify information

Purpose: To show the parts of a whole

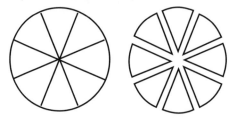

Purpose: To illustrate the relationship of parts to a whole

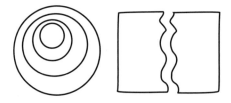

Purpose: To show the relationship of ideas to a concept

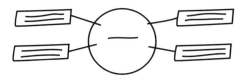

Purpose: To trace a logical extension of ideas

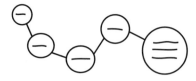

GLOSSARY

A-book (or AA, AAA) A high-investment, typically 4-color, title.

Abridge Change text by omitting words or paragraphs to shorten it.

Academic presses Smaller commercial presses that publish textbooks and scholarly works with minimum investment.

Active learning Self-directed learning through experience or through interaction with text or other information source.

Acquisitions Publishing phase that ends when you submit an acceptable manuscript for which you are under contract.

Acquisitions editor (AE) Publishing professional (also called sponsoring editor or series editor) responsible for getting you under contract to provide a work for publication and for presenting your project to the company and its agents.

Adapt Change text by altering words or adding material to make it fit your purpose.

Advances Payments in advance of earnings, which are deducted from future royalties.

Affective objectives Learning objectives that specify desired changes in feelings or values.

Agreement Legal contract for publishing your book ("the Work").

Ancillaries Student supplements without which your textbook would be incomplete, such as a web site in a text-web hybrid or a text-dedicated workbook.

Annotation (or anno) A brief identifying description, often used in marginalia in textbooks, especially in instructor's editions.

Apparatus Regular elements of your textbook structure, such as the way chapters or sections open and close.

Art manuscript A separate compilation of the figures for your textbook to be rendered by an artist or computer graphics specialist.

Art specs A descriptive list of requested content for the creation of original figures for your textbook.

Audience The people who will buy and read your textbook.

Author team Two or more coauthors who directly collaborate on a textbook manuscript.

Authorial voice Who you are as a person and as a teacher as revealed through your writing.

Authoring Writing and publishing a college textbook and in a timely manner attending to all the nonwriting tasks associated with that process.

B-book A medium-investment, typically 2-color, title.

Backlist Formerly published titles in a subject area the publisher serves.

Bibliography An alphabetized list of all the sources you consulted as you wrote your textbook, whether or not you had occasion to mention them or cite them in the body.

Binding Mechanical means by which pages of a book are permanently put together.

Book organization The division and sequencing of course content into the parts and chapters of a textbook.

Book outline 1. The preliminary drafting outline you send to the acquisitions editor with your prospectus. 2. The revised drafting outline that serves as a basis for your table of contents.

Book pages The number of pages in a manuscript based on printed pages.

Book plan The publisher's plan for publishing, marketing, and selling your book.

C-book A low-investment, typically 1-color, title.

Captions 1. The numbers and titles of figures, tables, and photos. 2. Brief descriptions, interpretations, or questions to readers about the content of figures, tables, and photos.

Case studies Pedagogical features for case-based instruction and analysis.

Cast-off The compositor's length estimate of a manuscript in terms of the calculated number of book pages.

Chapter outline The heading structure and titled features in terms of which a chapter is presented.

Clarity Clearness of expression and meaning.

Closers Pedagogical elements at the end of a chapter, as part of the chapter apparatus.

Cognitive objectives Learning objectives that match levels of cognitive functioning (knowledge acquisition, comprehension, application, analysis, synthesis, and evaluation).

Coherence The quality of writing that shows sequentiality, integrity, or togetherness.

College textbook publishers Larger commercial publishers of textbooks and supplements for undergraduate and graduate courses.

Comparative review Review of a revision compared to its last edition.

Competitive review Review of a book or manuscript compared to leading competing books by other publishers.

Complete manuscript Manuscript that contains all the planned elements, including frontmatter, apparatus, pedagogy, figures and tables, source notes, endmatter, and so on.

Composition (comp) A stage of production during which your book is set into type and other pre-manufacturing tasks are accomplished.

Compositor The professional responsible for putting your book into type and providing page proofs.

Conclusion As part of the chapter closer, a unifying thought, an interpretation, or a statement of significance of the chapter content.

Concrete examples Specific empirical or nonabstract examples, such as facts, observations, evidence, or cases.

Condense Change text by shortening it through abridgments.

Consistency The quality of regularity or conformity in the application of style and in the treatment of apparatus and pedagogy.

Contributing Writing original materials for a textbook or its package on the work-for-hire basis, such as a series of boxes, a chapter, or a study guide.

Copyeditor (CE) Specialist in publishing who corrects or queries errors, ambiguities, or inconsistencies in spelling, grammar, punctuation, usage, or meaning.

Copyright holder The person or entity that holds the rights to publication and use of a work and can tell you who and where the copyright owner is.

Copyright law A body of laws that defines and regulates the ownership and transfer of intellectual property.

Copyright owner The person or entity that owns the rights to publication and use of a work, whose permission you need.

Copyright year The year for which your publisher legally registers copyright for your book, which is not the same as the year your book is published and may be sold, which typically is in the year prior to your copyright year.

Credit line A line of type crediting the source of a photo, figure, table, or excerpt.

Critical thinking questions Questions to students in the chapter pedagogy or apparatus that require the use of critical thinking skills.

Critical thinking skills Skills that enable learners to define and clarify problems, judge information, draw conclusions, and problem solve.

Custom publishing An emerging publishing industry in which instructors author or customize books and materials, sold through the college bookstore for their own courses or departments.

Debates Pedagogical features that present opposing views on chapter content.

Developmental review Hands-on review of a book or manuscript compared to the publisher's development and market plan for it.

Development 1. Publishing phase during which you draft and revise your manuscript in response to editorial input, marketing plan, and peer reviews. 2. A complex recursive process through which your manuscript is brought to market level and prepared for production through a collaboration between editors and authors.

Development editor (DE) Publishing professional responsible minimally for seeing that the writing, organization, and content of your textbook are at market level and competitive.

Direct instruction Direct transmission of information that all students are expected to master.

Discussion questions Questions to students that are appropriate for verbal interaction in the actual or virtual classroom.

Drafting checklists Authoring tools in which you remind yourself of all your final decisions about writing mechanics and style and the form and content of your textbook.

Drafting schedule Dates by which your chapters, revised drafts, and final complete manuscript are due.

Elements of style Word choices and usages; sentence and paragraph construc-tions; writing rules, conventions, and formats; and your personal distinguishing communication values and expression of self.

Emphasis The quality in writing that shows focus, interest, and control.

Endmatter 1. All the elements that follow the last paragraph of narrative in a chapter (chapter closers). 2. All the elements the follow the last chapter of a book (backmatter), such as appendix, glossary, and index.

End notes Notes citing complete sources of material (referenced through either parenthetical source citations or superscript note numbers) that are gathered at the end of a chapter or by chapter at the end of a textbook.

Epigrams Brief quotations relating to chapter content, often used as an element in the chapter opener.

Expert review Specialized review of a portion of a book or manuscript by a sub-ject expert.

Expository writing Narrative prose in the service of explanation, description, or analysis.

Fair use Legally defined conditions in which another's work can be used without permission, especially uses that do not destroy the commercial value of the origi-nal work.

Feature strand A type of feature, distinguished through title and design, that appears regularly with different relevant content in the body of chapters through-out the textbook.

Figures Labeled illustrations and representations in a textbook, such as drawings, diagrams, charts, and graphs.

Flat Four discontinuous printed pages of a book, which—when folded, assembled with other flats, and cut—show the correct numerical sequence (imposition) of pages.

Focus questions As an element in chapter openers, a set of questions that fol-low or are embedded in the chapter outline, guiding student study.

Folios Typeset page numbers.

Fonts Styles of type, such as Arial or Times New Roman.

Footnotes Notes citing complete sources that appear at the bottom of the pages on which the referenced material appears, as designated by superscript note numbers.

Frontlist The current or coming year's titles in the company's publishing plan.

Frontmatter All the parts of your book that precede the opening page of the first chapter, especially the Table of Contents and the Preface.

Fulfillment Publishing phase during which your textbook is sampled, sold, and delivered to customers.

Fulfillment schedule Dates by which books and supplements are sold, ordered, in stock, inventoried, and shipped.

Galleys Unpaged typescript produced mechanically, seldom done in today's elec-tronic publishing, but sometimes used erroneously to refer to page proof.

Glossary An alphabetical listing of vocabulary items (key terms and concepts) with their definitions.

Grants Cash awards in advance of earnings that are not deducted from royalties and do not have to be returned.

Graphic organizers Visual representations of a chapter, topic, sequence, or concept, such as a flowchart, concept web, or diagram.

Heading structure The system of headings and subheadings in terms of which a chapter is organized.

Higher education publishing Industries that serve post-secondary educational, professional, and occupational markets.

House style Writing conventions that a publishing house adopts, to which your manuscript ultimately must conform.

Ideology Your personal political philosophy or other "isms" that are not the subject of discourse and therefore do not belong in your textbook.

Imposition The layout of pages in flats, resulting in the correct sequence of page numbers when the book is assembled.

Index An alphabetical listing of significant topics in your book and the pages on which information on those topics may be found.

Indexer Publishing professional responsible for writing indexes for books.

Institutional affiliation Your title and rank at the school, college, university, company, or corporation where you work, suggesting your qualifications for writing a textbook.

Intellectual property Original expressions of ideas in the form of writing, music, art, performances, brand names, and so on.

Intellectual property rights Area of law and specialty of lawyers dealing with copyright law.

Internal apparatus Pedagogical elements of a chapter that appear systematically between the chapter opener and the chapter closer, such as vocabulary glosses, marginalia, and interim reviews.

Introduction As an element in chapter openers, a brief description of the contents of a chapter, preparing readers for acquiring the information.

Leading Space on a page between lines of type and above and below other typographical elements, such as headings and captions.

Learning objectives As an element in chapter openers, statements specifying what students are expected to know or be able to do after studying the information.

Learning outcomes As an element in chapter openers, statements specifying the changes students can anticipate in their beliefs, attitudes, behavior, or skills as a consequence of reading the chapter.

Length estimate A calculation of the number of printed book pages that a typescript manuscript will fill.

Length creep The tendency for textbooks to increase in length from edition to edition.

Level of investment The publisher's designation of your book as an A-, B-, or C-book, indicating how much money will be spent on it.

Levels of heading A-, B-, C-, and D-heads, distinguished through type design and size, which range from the most inclusive to the most specific categories of information in terms of which a chapter is organized.

Literary Market Place (LMP) A significant, comprehensive source of information about all aspects of the publishing industry.

Mainstream text 1. A textbook that contains what is expected or usually taught in the course for which it was written. 2. A textbook with appropriate and nonidiosyncratic content.

Managing editor Editor responsible for channeling many titles through the drafting stage into production.

Manufacturing Publishing phase that ends with shipments of your printed and bound book to the warehouse.

Manufacturing schedule Dates on which your textbook is printed, covered, bound, and shipped to the warehouse.

Manuscript A work or portion of a work in double-spaced typescript form.

Manuscript pages The number of pages in a manuscript.

Manuscript preparation General term for the rules and conventions for submitting a complete, acceptable manuscript.

Map specs Instructions, labels, and models for the creation of original maps for your textbook.

Marginalia Internal pedagogical elements that are printed in the margins of pages in your textbook.

Market The field, course, departments, instructors, and students who will use your textbook.

Market research Investigations into what customers need, want, or will buy.

Marketing schedule Dates on which your textbook is announced, promoted and advertised, presented to the sales force, and sampled to customers.

Metavoice An overarching authorial voice that reconciles the voices of coauthors.

Mission Your compelling reason, purpose, or goal in writing your textbook.

Models Pedagogical features that apply or demonstrate practices, procedures, principles, theories, or laws.

Narrative context The textual environment in which readers make sense of the elements of apparatus, pedagogy, and art (figures, tables, photos).

Networking Communicating with colleagues and potential customers about your project and gathering information that will help you craft a successful product.

Niche market A small, technical, or nonmainstream market with a comparatively low sales projection.

Nondirect instruction Planned learning experiences by which it is intended that students will acquire information on their own or through interaction with peers or others.

Notes Information about your identified sources that enables readers to locate or access them, expressed in footnotes or endnotes.

Openers The pedagogical elements at the beginning of a chapter, as part of the chapter apparatus.

Overview As an element in the chapter opener, a brief explanation of the connections between the chapter at hand and previous chapters, units, or the course.

Packager A private company that your publisher subcontracts to produce your textbook.

Page count The actual number of pages in a book or manuscript.

Page proof Preliminary, designed layouts of typeset pages, showing how your book will actually look and read when corrected and printed.

Pagination The numbering of pages in the frontmatter and body of a text.

Palette In 4-color books, the array of colors chosen for the design.

Paraphrases Rewritings of another's written text using different words and phrases.

Parenthetical source citations Citations that identify sources by author's last name and the year of publication in parentheses at the end of the relevant sentence or paragraph.

Parts Sections of text that correspond to units of knowledge or units of instruction.

Passive voice Use of forms of the verb be, creating dull, wordy writing.

Pedagogical devices Regular internal elements in a chapter that serve a pedagogical purpose, such as glossary annotations, statements of main points, or interim reviews.

Pedagogy Regular written elements of your textbook other than narrative, such as features, which you intend will have educative value.

Pedagogy pitfalls Bad practices in using pedagogy and misuse of textbook features.

Pedagogy plan An editorial plan for the chapter apparatus and pedagogical features that will appear throughout your textbook.

Peer reviews Reviews of your manuscript by others who are experts in your field or have taught the course for which you are writing a textbook.

Permissioning The process of sending letters requesting permission to use others' material in your book, receiving the grants of permission, paying the use fees, and adding the credit lines.

Permissions General term in textbook publishing for complying with copyright law.

Permissions log A form for recording and tracking permissioning needs, including information about copyright owners, rights requested, restrictions, and fees.

Permissions researcher Publishing professional responsible for evaluating permissioning needs, contacting copyright owners, and keeping records of permissions grants and fees.

Photo specs List of requests for photos to be researched.

Plant costs Costs of manufacturing (printing, binding, and shipping) your textbook.

Political correctness In textbook publishing, writing that is not offensive or insulting to customers and readers.

Presentation A general term for the physical appearance of your book in all aspects (trim size, fonts, color, design, illustration, bulk, cover, etc.).

Print run Printing of a specified number of copies of your book.

Primary sources Pedagogical features based on passages from literature or excerpts from documents, first-person accounts, artifacts, or exhibits.

Production Publishing phase during which your final complete manuscript is set into type and sent out to be manufactured.

Production editor (PE) Publishing professional responsible for preparing your manuscript to be sent for manufacturing.

Production schedule Dates on which your manuscript is copyedited, set into type, proofread, corrected, indexed, and sent to the printer.

Professional book A book for practitioners in your field, which is by definition not a textbook.

Profiles Pedagogical features that offer descriptive accounts of particular examples or exemplars of chapter content.

Prospectus A comprehensive description of your textbook and analysis of its market to interest a company in publishing it.

Public domain Legally defined intellectual property that you can use without permission because it is published by the government, is a matter of public record, is sufficiently old or has an expired copyright, or consists of raw data.

Publishing cycle The movement of a manuscript through the five phases of book publishing (acquisition, development, production, manufacturing, fulfillment) over the course of two or more years.

Publishing schedules The dates by which benchmarks in each of the five phases of book publishing are achieved.

Readability tests Formulae for determining the grade level or intellectual level at which text is written.

Reading level (also called cognitive level, comprehension level, and difficulty level), largely subjective judgments about the appropriateness of writing for an audience based on vocabulary, sentence length, sentence construction, paragraph length, and level of conceptual abstraction.

References An alphabetized listing of all the works you actually refer to or cite in the body of your textbook.

Reflection questions Questions to students that require self-referential thinking and expression.

Reproduce Use text as is, without adaptation, abridgment, or condensation.

Resource management Developing a system for gathering and organizing information and sources for drafting a manuscript and carrying out other authoring tasks.

Returns Unsold books that bookstores return to the publisher, representing unrealized income.

Review questions Questions to students that guide their study and test preparation after they have read a chapter.

Reviewing 1. Your expert evaluation of another's manuscript, establishing a relationship with a publisher. 2. A stage of development in which your manuscript is sent out for professional peer review.

Reviewing schedule Dates on which reviewers are contacted and chapters of manuscript are sent out for review, reviews received, and honoraria paid.

Revision 1. A published new edition of your textbook representing an altered version of it. 2. The act of changing the form and content of your textbook.

Revision cycle The period of time that elapses between one edition of your textbook and the next.

Royalties Regular payments to you based on a percentage of net sales of your textbook.

Sample chapters 1. Chapters that you submit with your prospectus for consideration prior to signing. 2. Chapters that your editor submits for design prior to turning over your manuscript for production.

Sampling Sending of free advance copies of your book to potential customers for their inspection.

Scenarios Brief descriptions of simulated or real-life situations, usually involving named characters, usually set off from basal text.

Seeding adoptions Publisher practices that increase the likelihood of customers adopting your book, such as soliciting reviews or contributions from those with comparatively higher enrollments.

Signing Stage in the acquisitions process in which you and the publisher sign a legal contract to publish your book.

Self-publishing Becoming an independent publisher and writing, producing, marketing, selling, and shipping your own book by yourself.

Series editor Acquisitions or sponsoring editor responsible for managing a series of related titles.

Signature 32 book pages (half-signature is 16; quarter-signature is 8; an eighth is 4)

Source citations Identifications of your sources of information.

Sponsoring editor Editor responsible for recruiting authors, signing titles, and presenting them to the publisher.

Story Your book idea, stated succinctly in terms that can be used to market and sell your book.

Style 1. The way you use words to express yourself in writing. 2. The system of conventions you adopt to format your writing for your subject area, such as APA, MLA, etc.

Style sheet A list of important or expected writing conventions to be observed.

Subsidiary rights Other salable rights to your book, such as serial rights, electronic rights, foreign language rights, recording rights, and others.

Summary As part of the chapter apparatus, brief descriptions reviewing in full the content of a chapter or answering the focus questions.

Supplements Print and nonprint materials for students and instructors, offered as accompaniments to your textbook, such as a test item file, instructor's manual, videotape, or web site.

Supplements schedule Dates on which supplements authors are commissioned and samples and final manuscript for each supplement are due.

Supplement tie-ins Pedagogical devices that link content in the student text with content in the supplements that are part of the textbook package.

Tables Numerical information in tabular form, typeset but typically set off from basal text.

Table of contents (TOC) Also chapter outlines. A sequence of functional, pedagogical headings and subheadings that direct student learning of chapter content.

Tearsheet Pages cut or torn from a printed book and affixed to standard-sized paper, on which corrections are written for a revised edition.

Text sections Parts of a chapter that begin with an A-head.

Thematic boxes Pedagogical feature strands that express a theme in different contexts throughout a textbook.

Tone The quality of voice in your writing that reveals your affective response toward your subject, reader, and self.

Topical balance The relative weight or importance given to topics, expressed in the number of words or amount of space devoted to them.

Topical development The relationship among topics in a chapter, expressed in the amount and specificity of information given about them.

Tradebook publishers Publishers of adult nonfiction, fiction, and books in other genres for the mass market.

Trim size The actual physical dimensions of your textbook (e.g., 6x9, 8x10).

Turnover The first stage of production following the turning over of your manuscript to the production editor, typically involving production review, packager bidding, cover design request, budget analysis, and scheduling.

Undeclared bias Influential writing that is secretly slanted in a way that naive readers do not detect.

Unity The quality of writing that shows centrality, relevance, or belongingness.

University presses Scholarly publishers affiliated with, and often subsidized by, a college or university.

Unwarranted assumptions Untrue ideas you have about your readers or unmindfulness of who they are.

URL Universal Resource Locator, the Internet address of an information source.

User review Review of a textbook by an instructor who uses or has used it (versus a nonuser review).

Vignettes Brief descriptions of simulated or real-life situations, usually embedded in basal text.

Visualization The skill of imagining verbal or conceptual information in graphical form or as representational art.

Voice The way you speak to your audience, revealing who you are and your attitudes toward your subject and your reader.

Wordiness The habitual use of more words than are needed to adequately convey facts and ideas.

Working draft A nonfinal version of a chapter or manuscript, as a work in progress.

Writing outline Also drafting outline or book outline. A formal, hierarchical, logically exhaustive sequence of topics to be covered in a chapter.

REFERENCES AND BIBLIOGRAPHY

10 Big Myths about Copyright Explained:
  www.templetons.com/brad/copymyths

Acq Web: **www.acqweb.library.vanderbilt.edu/law/**

American Library Association: **www.ala.org/**

Applebaum, Judith. *How to Get Happily Published.* Harper and Row, 1992.

Association of American Publishers, *Author's Guide to College Textbook Publishing.*

Association of American Publishers: **www.publishers.org**

Association of American University Presses: **aaup.pupress.princeton.edu/**

Association of Authors' Reps: **www.aar-online.org**

Author's Guild: **www.authorsguild.org/**

Baker, John F., "University Presses: Hanging On in Tough Times," *Publishers Weekly*, June 2, 1997, 42-44.

Balkin, Richard, and Nick Bakalar. *A Writer's Guide to Book Publishing*, 2nd ed., Plume, 1994.

Barket, Malcolm E. *Book Design and Production for Small Publishers.* Londonborn Publications, 1990.

Beach, Mark, and Eric Kenly. *Getting It Printed: How to Work with Printers and Graphic Imaging*, 3rd ed. North Light Books, 1999.

Bell, Patricia J. *The Prepublishing Handbook: What You Should Know Before You Publish Your First Book.* Cat's paw Press, 1992.

Bennett, Christine I. *Comprehensive Multicultural Education.* Allyn and Bacon, 1990.

Berkowitz, Eric N., Roger A. Kerin, and William Rudelius. *Marketing.* Moseby, 1986.

Bernstein, Leonard. *Getting Published: The Writer in the Combat Zone.* Morrow, 1986.

Besenjak, C. *Copyright Plain and Simple*, 2nd ed. Career Press, 1997.

Bibliofind: **www.bibliofind.com**

Bloom, B. S., M. D. Engelhard, E. J. Frost, W. H. Hill, and D. R. Krathwohl. *Taxonomy of Educational Objectives.* David McKay, 1956.

Bodian, Nat G. *Direct Marketing Rules of Thumb.* McGraw-Hill, 1995.

Book Industry Study Group: **www.bisg.org**

Boswell, John. *The Awful Truth about Publishing.* Warner Books, 1986.

Branscomb, Anne W. *Who Owns Information? From Privacy to Public Access.* Basic Books, 1994.

Bronner, Ethan, "Textbooks Shifting from Printed Page to Screen," *The New York Times on the Web*, December 1, 1998,

www.nytimes.com/library/tech/98/12/biztech/articles/01school-etex.html.

Bunnin, Brad, and Peter Beren. *Writer's Legal Companion,* 3rd ed. Addison Wesley Longman, 1998.

Burgett, Gordon. *The Writer's Guide to Query Letters and Cover Letters.* St. Martin's Press, 1991.

Burgett, Gordon. *Publishing to Niche Markets.* Communications Unlimited, 1995.

Cantor, Jeffrey A. *A Guide to Academic Writing*, Praeger, 1993.

Cardoza, Avery. *Complete Guide to Successful Publishing.* Cardoza Pub., 1998.

Cheney, Theodore A. Rees. *Getting with Words Right: How to Revise, Edit and Rewrite.* Writer's Digest Books, 1990.

Chronicle of Higher Education: **www.che.com/**

Cleaver, Barry, et al. *Handbook Exploring the Legal Context for Information Policy in Canada.* Faxon, 1992.

Cole, David. *Complete Guide to Book Marketing.* Pushcart Press, 1987.

Columbia Guide to Online Style: **www.columbia.edu/cu/cup/cgos**

Cook, Claire Kehrwald. *Line by Line: How to Edit Your Own Writing.* Houghton Mifflin, 1985.

Copy Law: **www.copylaw.com**

Crawford, Tad. *Business and Legal Forms for Authors and Self-Publishers.* Allworth Press, 1999.

Daniels, John D., and Lee H. Radebaugh. *International Business*, 4th ed. Addison Wesley, 1986.

Driscoll, Marcy P., Mahnaz Moallem, Walter Dick, and Elizabeth Kirby. *How Do Textbooks Contribute to Learning?* Paper presented at the 1992 Annual Meeting of the American Educational Research Association, San Francisco, CA.

DuBoff, Leonard. *The Law in Plain English for Writers.* Wiley, 1992.

Dunne, Patrick, "The Selling of 'Complimentary' Textbooks: Boom or Bust for Marketing Education?" *Marketing Education Review* 3 (Summer 1993): 9-15.

Educational Marketer. Volume 26, Number 27, Simba Information Inc., August 21, 1995.

Educational Paperback Association: **www.edubook.com**

Educational Writers Association: **www.ewa.org**

Education Week: **www.edweek.com/**

Egan, Kieran. *The Educated Mind.* University of Chicago Press, 1997.

Einsohn, Amy. *The Copyeditor's Handbook: A Guide for Book Publishing and Corporate Communication.* University of California Press, 2000.

Engelhardt, T., "Gutenberg Unbound," *The Nation*, March 17, 1997, 18-29.

ERIC Clearinghouse for Higher Education: **ericsp.org**

Feeney, Mark, "Beyond the Voodoo Stick," *Boston Globe Magazine*, January 16, 1993: 10-18.

Fishman, Stephen. *The Copyright Handbook: How to Protect and Use Written Works,* 2nd ed. Nolo Press, 1994.

Frohbieter-Meuller, Jo. *Writing: Getting into Print: A Business Guide for Writers*. Glenbridge Pub. LTD., 1994.

Fry, Edward, "Fry's Readability Graph: Clarification, Validity, and Extension to Level 17," *Journal of Reading* 21, 1977: 242-252.

Gagne, R. M., and M. P. Driscoll, M. P. *Essentials of Learning for Instruction*, 4th ed. Prentice-Hall, 1988.

Gillen, Stephen E. "Ten Tips for Your Next Book Deal," *Academic Author*. Text and Academic Authors Online, 1997:1.

Gitlin, T. "The Dumb-Down," *The Nation*, March 17, 1997, 28.

Goldfarb, Ronald L. *The Writer's Lawyer: Essential Legal Advice for Writers and Editors in All Media*. Times Books, 1989.

Grossman, John. *The Chicago Manual of Style*, 14th ed. University of Chicago Press, 1993.

Harris, Lesley Ellen. *Canadian Copyright Law*. McGraw-Hill Ryerson, 1992.

Hed Up-Date: A Quarterly Publication of the Higher Education Division of the Association of American Publishers, New York, Winter 1993.

Hegde, M. N. *A Singular Manual of Textbook Preparation*, 2nd ed. Singular Publishing Group, 1996.

Henderson, Bill. *The Publish It Yourself Handbook*. Pushcart Press, 1987.

Indispensable Writing Resources: **www.quintcareers.com/writing/**

Judd, Karen. *Copyediting: A Practical Guide*, 3rd ed. Crisp Publications, 2001.

Kirsch, Jonathan. *Kirsch's Handbook of Publishing Law*. Acrobat Books, 1994.

Kneedler, P. "California Assesses Critical Thinking," *Educational Leadership*. Association for Supervision and Curriculum Development, 1985.

Kremer, John. *1001 Ways to Market Your Books*, 5th ed. Open Horizons, 2000.

Kremer, John. *Mail Order Selling Made Easier,* 3rd ed. Open Horizons, 1995.

Lanham, Richard. *Revising Prose*, 3rd ed. Allyn and Bacon, 1992.

The Learning Annex Guide to Getting Successfully Published. Carol Publishing Group, 1992.

Lee, Marshall. *Bookmaking: The Illustrated Guide to Design and Production*, 3rd ed. W. W. Norton & Company, 1997.

Levine, Mark. *Negotiating a Book Contract: A Guide for Authors, Agents, and Lawyers*. Moyer Bell, 1994.

Library of Congress: **www.loc.gov/**

Library Spot: **www.libraryspot.com**

Lichtenberg, James, "The New Paradox of the College Textbook," *Change* 12: 11-17 (September/October), 1992.

Literary Market Place: **lmp.bookwire.com/**

Luey, B. *Handbook for Academic Authors*, 4th ed. Cambridge University Press, 2002.

Madison, Charles Allan. *Irving to Irving: Author-Publisher Relations 1800 to 1974*. R. R. Bowker, 1974.

McHugh, John. *Managing Book Acquisitions: An Introduction*. McHugh Consulting,

1995.

McHugh, John. *Book Publishing Contracts: An Introduction*. McHugh Consulting, 1996.

Michener, James. *James A. Michener's Writer's Handbook*. Random House, 1992.

Miller, Casey, and Kate Swift. *The Handbook of Nonsexist Writing: For Writers, Editors and Speakers*, 2nd ed. Lippincott, 1988.

Miller, M. C., "The Crushing Power of Big Publishing," *The Nation*, March 17, 1997, 11-18.

Moxley, Joseph Michael. *Publish Don't Perish: The Scholar's Guide to Academic Writing and Publishing*. Praeger, 1992.

Munger, David, and Shireen Campbell. *Researching Online*. Addison Wesley Longman, 2001.

National Writers Union, *Guide to Freelance Rates and Standard Practice*, 1995.

National Writers Union: **www.nwu.org/nwu/**

Paradigm Online Writing Assistant: **www.powa.org/**

Parsons, Paul. *Getting Published: The Acquisitions Process in Scholarly Publishing*. University of Tennessee Press, 1989.

Pickert, Sarah H., "Preparing for a Global Community: Achieving an International Perspective in Higher Education," *Ashe-ERIC Higher Education Reports*. George Washington University, ERIC Clearinghouse on Higher Education, 992 (EDO-92-2).

Pinkerton, Linda F. *The Writer's Law Primer*. Lyons and Burford, 1990.

Powell, Walter W. *Getting into Print: The Decision Making Process in Scholarly Publishing*. University of Chicago Press, 1985.

Poynter, Dan. *The Self-Publishing Manual, How to Write, Print and Sell Your Own Book*, 8th ed. Para Publishing, 1995.

Publishers Marketing Association: **www.pma-online.org**

Publishers Weekly: **www.bookwire.com/pw**

Purdue Online Writing Lab: **owl.englishpurdue.edu/**

Rose, M. H., and Angela Adair-Hoy. *How to Publish and Promote Online*. Griffin Trade, 2001.

Ross, Tom, and Marilyn H. Ross. *The Complete Guide to Self-Publishing*, 4th ed. Writer's Digest Books, 2001.

Seidman, Michael. *From Printout to Published: A Guide to the Publishing Process*. CompuPress, 1988.

Shatzkin, Leonard. *In Cold Type: Overcoming the Book Crisis*. Houghton Mifflin, 1982.

Silverman, Franklin H. *Authoring a Textbook or Professional Books: A Guide to What Publishers Do and Don't Want Authors to Know*. CODI Publications, 1993.

Silverman, Franklin H. *Self-Publishing Books and Materials for Students, Academics, and Professionals*, 2nd ed. CODI Publications, 2000.

Skillin, Marjorie E., and Robert Malcolm Gay. *Words into Type*, 3rd ed., Pearson, 1974.

Slavin, Robert. *Educational Psychology*, 6th ed. Allyn and Bacon, 2002.

Small Publishers Association of North America: **www.spannet.org**

Stainton, Elsie Myers. *Author and Editor at Work: Making a Better Book*. University of Toronto Press, 1982.

Stim, Richard. *Getting Permission: How to License and Clear Copyrighted Materials Online and Off*. Nolo Press, 1999.

Strunk, William, Jr., and E. B. White. *The Elements of Style*, 4th ed., Allyn and Bacon, 2000.

Tarutz, Judith A. *Technical Editing: The Practical Guide for Editors and Writers*. Perseus, 1992.

Text and Academic Authors Association: **www.TAAonline.net**

Tufte, Edward R. *Envisioning Information*. Graphics Press, 1990.

Tyson-Bernstein. *A Conspiracy of Good Intentions: America's Textbook Fiasco*. Council for Basic Education, 1988.

Unwin, Stanley. *The Truth about Publishing*. Academy Chicago, 1982.

U.S. Copyright Office: **www.loc.gov/copyright/search/**

Van Til, W. *Writing for Professional Publication*, 2nd ed. Allyn and Bacon, 1986.

White, Jan V. *Editing by Design: Word and Picture Communication for Editors and Designers*. R. R. Bowker, n.d.

Woll, Thomas. *Publishing for Profit*, 2nd ed. Chicago Review Press, 2002.

Woll, Thomas. *Selling Subsidiary Rights: An Insider's Guide*. Fisher Books, 1999.

The Writer's Friendly Legal Guide. Writer's Digest Books, 1989.

Yudkin, Marcia. *Internet Marketing for Less than $500 a Year*, 2nd ed. Independent Publishing Group, 2001.

Zinsser, W. *Writing to Learn*. Harper & Row, 1988.

Zinsser, W. *On Writing Well*, 5th ed. Harper & Row, 1994.

INDEX

A-book, 5
A-head, 102-103
Abridge (text), 188
Academic presses, 2, 3
Acquisition phase of publishing, 1
Acquisitions, 3, 4
Acquisitions editor (AE), 4, 11, 26, 31, 37-38
Active learning, 115-116
Active voice, 79-80
Adapt (text), 188
Advances (on royalties), 41-42
Affective objectives, 131
Agreement (contractual), 41-45
Annotations, 138, 163
Apparatus (chapter), 29, 54, 117-118, 125, 143
Apparatus and pedagogy checklist, 167
Art manuscript, 190
Art specs, 198-201
Attitudes (toward subject), 87-89 (toward reader), 91-93, 97-98
Audience, 19, 53, 70-71
Author-editor relationship, 38-40, 56-58
Author team, 20-21, 95-96
Author's alterations (AAs), 183
Authorial voice, 87-96
Authoring (authorship), 65-66

B-book, 5
B-head, 102-103
Backlist, 4
Behavioral objectives, 129-130
Bias, 71-74
Bibliography, 170-171
Binding, 9, 43-44

Bloom's taxonomy, 130
Book content, 29, 53; see also *textbook*
    contract , 31-32, 41-45
    length, 175-176, 178-180
    list, 4
    manufacturing, 9-10
    outline, 28
        vs. table of contents, 101-102
    production, 7
Book pages (bp), 176-177
Book plan, 47, 179

C-book, 5
C-head, 102-103
Camera-ready copy, 162
Captions, 206-208
Case studies (as text feature), 146-149
Cast-off, 9
Chapter closers, 117, 138-142
    length, 178
    openers, 117, 125-126
    outline, 127-128
    sections, 103-105
Clarity, 78-79
Cognitive objectives, 129-130
Coherence, 80-81
College houses, 2, 3, 15-17, 33
College textbook industry, 2-3, 19, 47
Comparative review, 21
Competition analysis, 28, 59-60
Competitive review, 21
Composition stage of production, 8
Compositor, 8-9, 198
Conclusion (chapter), 138-140
Concrete examples, 109-111
Condense (text), 188

Consistency, 165
Contributing; contributed work, 3, 21
Copyediting stage of production, 8
Copyeditor (CE), 7, 43, 55
Copyright holder, 192
Copyright law, 187-189
Copyright owner, 192
Copyright year, 12
Cover letter (for manuscript proposal), 31
Credit line, 171, 188
Critical thinking questions, 120, 152-154
Critical thinking skills, 115-117
Custom publishing, 49
Curriculum vitae, 27

Debates (as text feature), 149-150
Development (editorial), 1, 6-7, 53-55, 58-59
  levels of, 55
Development editor (DE), 7, 55-58, 179
Developmental review, 22
D-heads, 102-103
Direct instruction, 113-114
Discussion questions, 154
Drafting, 11, 163-166
  checklists, 165-168
  schedule, 182-185

Ethical standards (in publishing), 42
Elements of Style, 81
Emphasis (in writing), 80-81
Endmatter, 163
End notes, 169-170
Epigrams, 136-138
Expert review, 22
Expository writing (exposition), 25, 169, 173-174
Fair use, 187-189
Feature strand, 145-155, 156
Figures (text), 196-198, 201-203
Flat (printing), 176

Focus questions, 127-128
Fonts, 162
Footnotes, 169-170
Frontlist, 4
Frontmatter, 163
Fulfillment phase of publishing, 1
Fulfillment schedule, 182

Galleys, 9
Glossary, 5-6
Graphic organizers, 195-196
Headings, levels of, 102-103
  meaning of, 105-107
  role in marketing, 111-112
  role in topical development, 107-108
Heading structure, 99-103
Higher Education Directory, 60
Higher education publishing, 2
House style, 81

Ideology, 73-74
Imposition, 9, 176
Imprint, 5
Index, 5-6, 43
Indexer, 7
Information, control of, 40
Institutional affiliation, 20
Instruction, models of, 116
Integrated pedagogical devices, 118
Integration of coauthors' voices, 95-96
  of pedagogy, 134-136
Intellectual property rights, 187-188
Interior feature strands, 118, 145-154
Internal apparatus, 138
Internet source citations, 189-190
Introduction (chapter or unit), 125-127
Investment, level of, 5, 45-46

Key terms, 138

Leading (in typography), 180, 181
Legal and business advice (for writers),

51
Learning objectives, 128-131
Learning outcomes, 128-131
Length creep, 180-181
Length estimate, 176-178
Length problems (solutions to), 178-180
Literary Market Place (LMP), 4, 25

Mainstream text, 19, 25, 71-72
Managing editor, 4
Manufacturing phase of publishing, 1
Manufacturing schedule, 182
Manuscript (complete), 7, 163
Manuscript pages (msp), 176-177
Manuscript preparation, 161-165
Manuscript proposal, 25, 27-29
Map specs, 198-201
Marginalia, 138
Market, 19, 23, 29, 53
Market research, 24-25, 33
Marketing schedule, 182
Marketing strategy, 8, 20, 23
Mechanics and style checklist, 166
Metavoice, 95-96
Mission (authorial), 69-70
Models (as text feature), 152
Monument Information Resource (MIR), 24

Narrative context, 133-136, 148-149, 197-198
Networking, 60-61
Niche market, 74
Nondirect instruction, 114-115
Nonuser review, 21
Notes, 163, 170-171

Overview (chapter or unit), 125-127

Packager, 7
Page count, 176-178
Page formatter, 7

Page proof, 9
Pagination, 176
Paraphrases, 188-189
Parenthetical source citations, 169-170
Parts (units), 5, 99-100
Passive voice, 79-80
Pedagogical devices, 118
Pedagogy, 29, 54, 113, 145
    functions of, 113
    forms of, 117-118
    role in marketing, 117
Pedagogy pitfalls, 119-120
Pedagogy plan, 120, 123, 143, 156-157, 159-160
Peer reviews (using), 21-23, 61-63
Permissions, 163, 187-188
    cost of, 190
    requests and grants, 192-193
Permissions log, 191-192
Permissions problems (solutions to), 193-194
Permissions research, 7, 42, 187
Personal pronouns, 92-93
Philosophical orientation, 89-91
Photo research, 7, 43, 190
Photo specs, 205-206
Photos, 190, 203-204
    evaluating and choosing, 204-205
Plant costs, 45-46
Political correctness, 40, 71-72
Political orientation, 89-91
Presentation (of textbook), 54, 195
Primary sources (as text features), 150-152
Print run, 10, 176
Production, stages of, 7-9
    costs of, 161, 190
Production phase of publishing, 1
Production editor (PE), 7-9
Production schedule, 182
Professional associations, 4
Professional book, 3
Profiles (as text features), 149

Proofreader, 7, 43
Prospectus, 27-29, 34-35
Public domain, 188-189
Publisher directories, 4
Publishing cycle, 11-13, 26
Publishing houses, 2, 3, 15-17, 19, 33
Publishing process, 1
Publishing schedules, 38, 181-183

Readability tests, 74-75
Reading comprehension, 75-78
Reading level, 74
References, 170-171
Reflection questions, 153-154
Reproduce (text), 188
Resource management, 168
Returns (of books), 12, 46-47
Reviews, 21-23, 61-63
    number of, 62
    analysis of, 62-63
    questions for, 61-62, 67-68
Reviewing schedule, 182
Revising, 164
Revision cycle, 24
Royalties, 41-42

Sample chapters, 7, 27, 31
Sampling, 12
Scenarios, 131-136
Scholarly presses, 2, 3
Seeding adoptions, 23
Self-publishing, 50
Series editor, 4
Signature (and half-signature), 176
Signing, 11, 37-39
Source citations, 169-170
Sponsoring editor, 4
Story, 27, 28-29
Style, 69, 81-82
    academic, 83-86
    authorial, 93-95
    editorial, 69, 81-82, 189
    house, 81-82

Style checklists, 165-168
Style sheet, 167-168
Subsidiary rights, 12, 43
Summary, 140-141
Supplements, 5, 6
Supplements schedule, 182
Supplement tie-ins (as text feature),
    155-156

Table of contents (TOC), 99-100, 101-
    102
Tables (text), 196-198
Tearsheet, 162-163
Textbook; textbook package, 5, 6
    design, 7, 141
    organization, 53, 99-100
    publishers (higher education; col-
    lege), 2, 3, 15-17, 19, 33
Text sections (of a chapter), 103-105
Thematic boxes (as text feature), 154-
    155
Titles, 100-101
Tone, 69, 91
Topical balance, 154-155
Topical development, 107-111, 168-169
Trade book publishers, 3
Trim size, 175
Turnover stage of production, 8

Unity (of writing), 80-81
University presses, 2, 3
User review, 21

Vignettes, 131-136
Visualization (of information), 201-
    203, 209-210
Voice, 69, 87, 93-94

Wordiness, 79-80
Writing outline, 101-102